Two Peas
& Their Pod

· COOKBOOK ·

Two Peas
& Their Pod

· COOKBOOK ·

Favorite Everyday Recipes from
Our Family Kitchen

Maria Lichty

with Rachel Holtzman

PHOTOGRAPHY BY COLIN PRICE

GRAND
CENTRAL
PUBLISHING
NEW YORK BOSTON

Grand Central Publishing
Hachette Book Group
1290 Avenue of the Americas, New York, NY 10104
grandcentralpublishing.com
twitter.com/grandcentralpub

First Edition: September 2019

Grand Central Publishing is a division of Hachette Book Group, Inc. The Grand Central Publishing name and logo is a trademark of Hachette Book Group, Inc.

The publisher is not responsible for websites (or their content) that are not owned by the publisher.

The Hachette Speakers Bureau provides a wide range of authors for speaking events. To find out more, go to www.hachettespeakersbureau.com or call (866) 376-6591.

Print book interior design by Laura Palese.

Library of Congress Cataloging-in-Publication Data has been applied for.
Names: Lichty, Maria, author. | Holtzman, Rachel, author.
Title: Two peas & their pod cookbook : favorite everyday recipes from our kitchen / Maria Lichty with Rachel Holtzman.
Other titles: Two peas and their pod cookbook
Description: First edition. | New York, NY : Hachette Book Group, 2019. | Includes index.
Identifiers: LCCN 2019004163| ISBN 9781538730133 (hardcover) | ISBN 9781538730157 (ebook)
Subjects: LCSH: Cooking. | LCGFT: Cookbooks.
Classification: LCC TX715 .L6918 2019 | DDC 641.5—dc23
LC record available at https://lccn.loc.gov/2019004163

ISBNs: 978-1-5387-3013-3 (hardcover), 978-1-5387-3015-7 (ebook)

Printed in the United States of America

LSC-C

10 9 8 7 6 5 4 3 2

To my favorite peas, Josh, Caleb, and Maxwell—
You are my forever happiness.
Thank you for making every day an adventure.

CONTENTS

••

Come on in, pick out
something tasty to
whip up, then roll up
your sleeves—our
kitchen is always open!

Cookies: *Make the World a Better Place*   237

Make Sure to Save Room Dessert   265

Feeding a Crowd Easy Entertaining   287

COME ON IN!

●●

From the moment I met (my now-husband) Josh, cooking together was a natural part of our relationship.

While we were dating—after a year of being best friends—instead of going out to eat in restaurants we would stay in to whip up a batch of something like pasta, tacos, or from-scratch pizza. It certainly helped us save what little money we had, but that was almost beside the point. We both just loved to get in the kitchen and dream up new, delicious takes on standby dishes that were simple to shop for and easy to prepare, and yet used whole, fresh ingredients. Not a small challenge! But we were both cut out for it. I grew up watching my dad turn our rural Illinois house into the go-to spot for a tasty meal and even tastier baked desserts. Josh learned to cook out of necessity, feeding his three younger brothers, but then continued feeding just about everyone—roommates, dorm mates, neighbors, *everyone*. We developed a great dynamic in the kitchen: Josh was the scientific one who loved to figure out the *why* behind how certain ingredients work together (coming a long way from Frito pie and from-a-can sloppy Joes), while I was usually standing over his shoulder going, *"Just make it already!"* (I guess you could say I'm more of a creative spirit!) So, you can see how we ended up catering our own wedding, complete with a giant Mediterranean spread of chicken and veggie kebabs with lemon rice, Greek salad, homemade hummus, and fresh pita bread; plus an over-the-top

dessert bar with some of my signature confections that coordinated with our black and white theme: classic chocolate chip cookies, chocolate crinkle cookies, chocolate-dipped Oreos, and hazelnut macaroons. Oh, and did I mention this was for *300 people?*

Being in the kitchen was our happy place; it's where we felt the most calm—even when we were feeding hundreds of people. (Which we've continued to do and we will give you our secrets for pulling off—but more on that in a bit!) But most importantly, our food was a success, so much so that many of our wedding guests asked for the recipes. At the time, Josh had a Blogspot account (it was just the beginning of the blogging craze!) that he used to keep in touch with family and post updates about things like hiking and skiing trips. So I posted some recipes there, along with pretty terrible photographs of the food (who knew you shouldn't use the flash?!). Lo and behold, people loved it—and demanded (okay, asked nicely for) more recipes. Since we were already cooking at home all the time, I was able to share new recipes every week. And because friends and family were following along, I could pepper in all kinds of stories that related to why we made the food we did—feeding our community, including our neighbors, our congregation, and our families; feeding friends whenever the mood to entertain struck (which, as you'll see, is often!), and eventually, feeding our two little boys, Caleb and Maxwell. At one point, we noticed that complete strangers had started checking out the site—and a steadily increasing number of them. At that point, we both worked full-time jobs and had no idea where this blogging business could possibly go. But we were intrigued, so we started going to conferences, meeting other bloggers, and getting tips on how to build a site, fill it with accessible recipes and tantalizing photographs, and most importantly, give it a name. *Two Peas & Their Pod* was born, and about two years later, we both quit our jobs to make what was once our favorite hobby our very favorite career.

●●

I've spent a good amount of time trying to wrap my head around what makes people love our blog so much because, at the end of the day, we're a couple of folks from Salt Lake City who are usually just trying to get dinner on the table or racing to pack up something to eat on the way to soccer practice. Maybe it's because there aren't many husband-and-wife teams who can say that they truly and honestly love to cook together. We really do believe that four hands are better than two! If we're making pizza, Josh is kneading the dough while I'm simmering the sauce and chopping the

Being in the kitchen was (and still is!) our happy place.

toppings. Sometimes one of us will say, "Go ahead, you just relax or get some work done while I make dinner," but nine times out of ten, we can't resist jumping in to help out. We've also honed a really great dynamic—I'm the vegetarian while Josh is the vegetable-loving meat-eater. Josh is the methodical one who is great with doughs and breads, while I love fresh new flavor combinations and coming up with twists on the classics like Roasted Butternut Squash and Pear Soup (page 128) or Pesto-Havarti Mac and Cheese (page 185). Josh is great at tackling the grocery shopping (except when he's bringing home *way* too much fresh fruit; see Peach Cobbler with Buttermilk Biscuit Topping, page 266), while I'm the writer of the family (though he'll be popping his head in throughout the book to offer his two cents!).

But mostly I think what makes our recipes special is that the food is real and fresh, though it doesn't take hours of prep. It's not from a box or a can, though it's not crazy gourmet. You get gourmet-type flavors, though nothing that's too trendy or out-there or that requires having to buy intimidating or expensive ingredients. These are recipes that every family can make and enjoy, no matter the cooking skill, no matter the budget, and no matter the time restrictions. And there's always something for everyone to eat, whether it's a loaded-up veggie dish like Spiced Cauliflower and Chickpea Tacos (page 182) that will satisfy even the meatiest of eaters (I've got the e-mails from our readers to prove it!), or gluten-free or vegan options, if those are your dietary preferences or your guests'.

This isn't a gimmick for us—this is *life*. We have two small boys, so there's no getting away with fussy and complicated. At 5 p.m., these guys want dinner and they want it *now*, so good and fast are the name of the game. The same goes for breakfast, lunch, and snacks—and ev-

erything in between that can be packed up and parceled out. It's why we've developed recipes such as Maple-Roasted Berry Yogurt Parfaits (page 38), Slow Cooker Meatballs (page 226), and Enchilada-Stuffed Sweet Potatoes (page 163): so there's always something to feed our kids, whether we're sitting around our dining room table, jetting around in the car between after-school activities, or joining friends for an impromptu neighborhood picnic. And it's not just food to put in their bellies, but also food that will *nourish* them. All the while, we're saving money, saving calories, and teaching our boys the importance of getting the family together in the kitchen.

●●

When it came to figuring out what our book would be, I didn't have to think too hard: It's real recipes—with real ingredients—that *work*. If it's in this book—just as if it's on our site—you better bet that the recipe is going to turn out...and will most likely become part of your family's rotation. You're certainly welcome to keep this book on your shelf or nightstand, but I'd rather it get battered, splattered, coated in flour, and dog-eared within an inch of its life. My other hope is that you'll start to see cooking as not just something you *have* to do, but rather something you *want* to do. We have a saying, both in real life and on our blog: "Our kitchen is always open." And we mean it. If we happen to make a few too many of Our Favorite Chocolate Chip

Cookies (page 241), Josh'll be out on the porch yelling, "Hey kids, we've got extra treats!" Our neighbors, friends, and family will stop over unannounced because they know that either we have way too much food going on the stove, or we're only about 30 minutes away from a great meal. And we love that! The kids on the block will come hang out and watch a movie while we make some Baked Chicken Taquitos (page 198); we'll throw on a pot of Tomato Basil Soup with our favorite Cheesy Garlic Dunkers (page 131) while everyone packs in to watch the Golden State Warriors, University of Utah Utes, or the Patriots play; or if Josh's Steak Tacos with Chimichurri (page 210) are coming off the grill, we'll definitely have a few more settings at the table that night. And yes, for Fourth of July last year, we threw a Weekend Waffle Bar (page 291) breakfast for 200 people! It's because we've always wanted to be *that house*, the one with the open-door policy where kids and adults feel comfortable to make themselves at home. It's what I grew up having and what Josh always dreamt of, and we both really wanted that for our kids.

So in addition to our favorite simple and quick recipes, you'll find entertaining-friendly dishes and tips to capture that kind of giving-and-gathering spirit, from how to set up an Ice Cream Sandwich Party (page 306), Loaded Nachos Bar (page 294), or DIY Pasta Party (page 305), to creating the perfect party cheese board (page 301). I've also included a special section devoted to Cooking It Forward (page 136), so you'll always have just the thing for packing up and sending to kids in college or friends and family abroad, contributing to church and school events or neighborhood get-togethers, or bringing to new moms or anyone else in need of a home-cooked meal.

And of course there will be desserts, from Peanut Butter–Fudge Ice Cream Pie (page 270) to Lemon–Poppy Seed Bundt Cake (page 269), plus an entire chapter devoted to cookies (my pride and joy—see all 200 of my recipes on the blog as evidence!), because nothing says being neighborly like a batch of freshly baked cookies, and there's nothing easier than having a batch of dough in the freezer that you can bake off at a moment's notice.

This isn't a gimmick for us—this is life.

●●

Ultimately, I want to share all the incredible bounty that we've been so blessed with. I can honestly say that so much of our happiness started with great meals, no matter how simple or humble. Cooking good, nourishing food is what brightens our day every morning, brings our family together every evening, and connects us with our friends, family, and neighbors. There might not be time to sit around the table every day, and home cooking might mean defrosting a frozen batch of Chipotle–Sweet Potato Chili (page 123) or using leftovers for Chicken Pot Pie (page 219), but we always do our best to spend mealtime together. It's at the foundation of what brings us joy, and it's creating traditions that our kids will get to carry with them. I can't wait to pass this on to our readers and say: *Come on in, pick out something tasty to whip up, then roll up your sleeves—your kitchen is always open!*

TOOLS

FOR BECOMING A

CONFIDENT

HOME COOK

●●

Cooking at home is super easy when you have a few things in place:

- Useful kitchen tools

- A well-organized kitchen, including a fridge and pantry stocked with versatile staples

- Great meal-planning skills

- An efficient system for buying groceries

- Delicious recipes

I included this section so that you too can gain the confidence in order to become a great home cook. Imagine a kitchen that's a comfortable, happy place and full of ingredients that you love. You can have that! It takes a little planning, and it might require you to clean out a drawer or two that are full of past-their-prime condiments, but I promise that the tools in this chapter will help you create a home-cooking culture that your family will be so thankful for. Feel free to refer to this section again and again until you get into a rhythm that feels best for you and your family.

Kitchen Gear and Gadgets

When it came time to make a list of my "essential" kitchen tools, I had a hard time narrowing it down! The truth is, the items below get used in my kitchen almost every week. And because I have a tool for every job, cooking and baking are a whole lot easier. I'm not recommending that you go out and buy every single item on this list. Collect items over time, don't buy the best and the fanciest, and do the best you can with what you have.

SMALL APPLIANCES

- Blender
- Food processor
- Stand mixer
- Immersion blender
- Kitchen scale
- Slow cooker
- Toaster

POTS AND PANS

- Baking sheets
- Cake pans (round, rectangular, and square)
- Bundt pan
- Muffin pans
- Casserole/baking dishes (small, medium, and large)
- Roasting pan
- Dutch oven
- Skillets (small, medium, and large)
- Cast-iron skillet
- Saucepans (small, medium, and large)
- Large stockpot

TOOLS AND UTENSILS

- Mixing bowls
- Dry measuring cups
- Liquid measuring cups
- Measuring spoons
- Good knives (chef, paring, serrated—different sizes)
- Ladles
- Wooden spoons
- Spatulas
- Potato masher
- Slotted spoon
- Tongs
- Metal turner
- Vegetable peeler
- Whisks
- Microplane
- Instant-read thermometer
- Box grater
- Colander
- Mesh strainer
- Can opener
- Garlic press
- Kitchen scissors
- Citrus juicer
- Pastry brush
- Pizza cutter
- Salad spinner
- Cooling racks
- Bench scraper
- Pastry blender
- Rolling pin
- Silpat baking mats
- Parchment paper
- Ice cream scoop
- Pepper mill
- Salt cellar

Kitchen Gadgets We Couldn't Live Without

While it's helpful to be prepared with a variety of tools you might need, these are the ones we find ourselves reaching for every day.

HIS

Food processor: For chopping, pureeing, and mixing. I especially like using ours for making galette dough (page 278) and pesto (page 186).

Sharp knife: Every kitchen should have a good, sharp chef's knife.

Immersion blender: Pretty much the best thing ever for pureeing sauces and soups right in the pot.

Tongs: You gotta have a good pair of tongs for cooking, flipping, tossing, and chasing kids around the kitchen. Our boys call our tongs alligators, so we make a game to see who can escape getting chomped!

HERS

Stand mixer: My stand mixer is my BFF in the kitchen. (Please don't tell Josh—he might get jealous!) I love all of the different attachments—the paddle for creaming and mixing, the whisk for whipping egg whites and cream, and the dough hook for kneading bread and pizza doughs. I also love using a different color mixer for every season, but that's another story!

Microplane: Great for zesting lemons and limes, grating garlic, and shredding Parmesan cheese over pizza, pasta, soups, salads—just about anything.

Spatulas: I have a colorful collection of spatulas—you can never have too many! They're the secret weapon for clean, precise baking and essential for scooping the last drop out of cans and jars. And who doesn't like to lick it after making brownies, cookies, and cakes?

Blender: For making smoothies with the boys. I love being able to hide things like spinach, kale, chia seeds, flaxseeds, and nut butters in their breakfast. They think they are drinking milkshakes, so it's a win-win!

Organizing Your Ingredients

I'm going to let you in on a little secret: The key to becoming a great home cook isn't all about the actual cooking. A lot of it has to do with being *organized*. I've found that by keeping my kitchen orderly—including my pantry, fridge, and freezer—I have an easier time planning meals, coming up with last-minute meal and snack solutions, and cooking. That's because it's easy to see exactly which ingredients I have on hand, and I always know where to find them. (And if you don't have a pantry, all of these suggestions work for a kitchen cart!)

Here are some tips for keeping your kitchen in good order, no matter how much or how little space you have.

- **Divide your pantry items into categories.** For example, Canned Goods, Baking Items, Grains, Kids' Snacks. Use what you already have in there as your guide, and then group like items together.

- **Use baskets, bins, and containers.** Organizational tools like baskets and bins will help you keep the items from each category grouped together, while glass or plastic containers make it easy to see items you use frequently, such as flour, cereal, grains, or nuts (and look so much nicer than plastic bags or boxes!). Clearly label each basket and container. While you primarily want these items to be functional, if you choose coordinating bins, it also happens to look really nice!

- **First in, first out.** Arrange things in each bin so that older items are on top/in front.

- **Make it kid-friendly, or not.** If you want your kids to be able to help themselves to cereal in the morning or snacks in the afternoon, make sure those items are on a lower shelf where they can be reached. On the flip side, if there are treats that you don't want the kids getting into, make sure they're on a higher shelf.

- **Only buy what you need and have room for.** It can be really tempting to stock up on items that are on sale, but if you see that your assigned bin for soup ingredients is full, maybe hold off until you've put a dent in what you have. If you don't have room for an item or won't be able to use it before it expires, pass.

- **Use what you have before going to the store.** Challenge yourself to use what you have in the pantry to make meals and snacks—turn it into a game! And definitely use my un-recipes on pages 234 to 235 for inspiration. It will save you time and money.

◦◦
Spices

I keep my spices in a drawer, laid flat, in alphabetical order so I can easily find them. If you don't have a drawer large enough for this, you could store spices in a cabinet on risers or a turntable. There are tons of great organizational products out there, and I highly recommend using one.

Another thing to keep in mind is that spices do actually expire! Here's an easy reference guide for how long you should keep spices before tossing:

- **Seasoning blends:** 1 to 2 years
- **Dried herbs** (basil, oregano, parsley): 1 to 3 years
- **Ground spices** (nutmeg, cinnamon, turmeric): 2 to 3 years
- **Seeds:** 4 years (except for poppy and sesame seeds, which should be discarded after 2 years)
- **Whole spices** (cloves, peppercorns, cinnamon sticks): 4 years
- **Extracts:** 4 years (except for vanilla, which will last forever)

Staple Ingredients

Keeping your kitchen stocked with multi-purpose, mix-and-match-friendly ingredients is essential for making meal prep convenient, easy, and, most importantly, tasty! You'll be much more likely to reach for that new recipe if you know that most of the ingredients are already in your home, and that ultimately saves you time *and* money. It also makes on-the-fly meals and snacks so much easier to whip up when you're short on time.

Pantry

Grains and Breads

- **Bread:** Keep your favorite on hand for avocado toast or a quick sandwich. (And remember that bread freezes really well!)

- **Tortillas:** We like to have both flour and corn tortillas for tacos, wraps, homemade chips, and nachos.

- **Dried pasta** (whole-wheat and regular)

- **Rice and grains:** Keep a stash of your favorite short- or long-grain rice plus other options like quinoa, couscous, and farro.

Packaged Goods, Canned Goods, and Condiments

- **Roasted red peppers:** Perfect to toss into salads and pastas.

- **Canned tomatoes** (diced, crushed, whole, and fire-roasted): Great for slow cooker meals, soups, and sauces.

- **Tomato paste:** For great depth of flavor in stews and sauces. Try to find one that comes in a tube so you can save what you don't use.

- **Chicken and/or veggie broth or stock**

- **Mayonnaise:** For sandwiches, salads, dips, and dressings.

- **Ketchup:** For the dippers!

- **Mustards** (yellow, Dijon, and whole-grain): For sandwiches or to add to sauces, vinaigrettes, and marinades.

- **Hot sauce**

- **Soy sauce** (or tamari soy sauce if you want a gluten-free option)

- **Worcestershire sauce**

- **Coconut milk:** A great nondairy option for adding instant creaminess.

- **Canned beans** (black, chickpeas, pinto, and cannellini): For dips, salads, soups, and homemade veggie burgers.

- **Canned or jarred artichoke hearts**

- **Olives** (green, black, and Kalamata): Sprinkle them into salads, chop them into tapenade, or just set out a dish for snacking.

- **Jam:** Choose your favorite for sandwiches or roll-ups, or to top ice cream!

- **Nut butters** (almond, peanut, sunflower, and tahini): For sweet *or* savory toast, sandwiches, baked goods, granola, dressings, and sauces.

Oils, Vinegars, Spices, and Dried Herbs

- **Salt** (kosher and coarse sea salt)

- **Extra-virgin olive oil**

- **Coconut oil:** Great for baking and cooking.

- **Nonstick cooking spray** (olive oil, coconut oil, or vegetable oil): Essential for greasing pans.

- **Vinegars** (balsamic, golden balsamic [slightly less caramel-y than dark balsamic], red wine, apple cider, and rice wine): For dressings, sauces, and marinades.

- **Dried herbs and spices:** Use flavors that you love to dress up simple cooking preparations. Save money by buying these in bulk—just don't forget to refresh your stock every so often. See page 23 for when dried herbs and spices typically expire. And remember that you can usually swap out fresh herbs in a recipe and use one-third of the amount of dried herbs instead.

Baking Supplies

- **Unbleached all-purpose flour:** Good ol' AP flour can generally be used in any recipe and give you great results.

- **Whole-wheat flour and white whole-wheat flour:** Full of vitamins and fiber, these hearty flours give great nutty flavor to anything you use them in. The main difference between them is that white whole-wheat flour is made from a different variation of wheat, which gives it a lighter color. Feel free to substitute whole-wheat flour for up to 50 percent of all-purpose flour called for in a recipe!

- **Old-fashioned rolled oats:** For homemade oatmeal, overnight oats, oatmeal cookies, or to add extra body and creaminess to smoothies.

- **Granulated sugar**

- **Light brown sugar**

- **Honey**

- **Pure maple syrup**

- **Pure vanilla extract**

- **Baking soda**

- **Baking powder**

- **Cream of tartar**

- **Chocolate chips** (semisweet, milk, dark, or white chocolate; butterscotch; peanut butter): For cookies, tossing into trail mix or granola, or eating right out of the bag.

- **Unsweetened cocoa powder**

- **Dutch-process cocoa:** Produces a richer, deeper chocolate flavor than regular cocoa powder.

- **Chocolate chunks or chocolate bars:** Great for making homemade candies, ganache, chocolate chunk cookies, or even the occasional s'more…

- **Shredded coconut** (sweetened and unsweetened)

- **Nuts** (almonds, peanuts, cashews, pistachios, pecans, or walnuts): For snacking, baking, and cooking.

- **Dried fruit** (raisins, cranberries, apricots, blueberries, currants, mango, strawberries, or cherries): For stirring into cookies or quick bread, tossing into a salad, mixing into granola or trail mix, or as a snack on their own.

- **Flaked sea salt**

Snacks

- **Tortilla chips:** It doesn't get better than sheet-pan nachos or Friday afternoon chips and salsa!

- **Pita chips:** For dipping and scooping, or crumbling over salads.

- Pretzels

- Crackers

- Rice cakes

Fridge

- **Produce:** Opt for fruits and veggies that you know you'll eat! An assortment of greens, veggies for roasting, and fruits for throwing into lunch bags is a great place to start. Think about what's in season and what looks fresh at the market. Add things like garlic and onions and lemons and limes to the mix for extra flavor.

- **Fresh herbs and spices:** Buy what you love to eat and toss them into soups, braises, dressings, and roasts. Save money by planting your own herb garden or buying potted herbs.

- **Meat and seafood:** We buy in bulk and freeze things for later—it saves money and means we have a bigger selection to choose from, whether it's a whole chicken or breasts and thighs, ground meats, sausages, or various cuts of pork or beef.

Dairy and Eggs

- Butter

- Eggs

- Milk (cow's, almond, and coconut)

- **Plain Greek yogurt:** For dips, sauces, dressings, and smoothies.

- **Cheese:** Have a variety on hand for shredding, grating, melting, and snacking—cheddar, Havarti, mozzarella, feta, goat, pecorino, Parmesan—whatever you love most.

Freezer

- **Frozen fruits and vegetables:** A great shortcut! They're budget-friendly and full of flavor since they are usually picked and frozen at peak ripeness.

- **Chia seeds:** For baking, smoothies, and breakfast chia puddings.

- **Flaxseed meal:** Perfect for adding fiber to smoothies and another great staple for baking since it can be used to substitute for eggs.

- **Ice cream and sorbet—obviously!**

Meal Planning Tips

Meal planning is *essential*. I highly recommend taking an hour once a week to get yourself in great shape for the week ahead. It saves you time, money, and stress; and you will always have the answer to the question, "What's for dinner?" When 5 p.m. hits, you'll have everything you need to make one of your favorite recipes or pull together a quick un-recipe (see page 234). Pick a day that works well for you (I like Sunday) and see what you already have in your fridge and pantry (a great reason to keep things well organized!), then think about what you and your family love to eat (flip through this book for inspiration!) and check the week's schedule to see which nights might need to be meals on the go. Give breakfasts, lunches, and snacks some thought too. A little planning goes a really long way—you'll reduce the number of meals you eat out, the amount of food you throw away, and the amount of time it takes to pull something together on the fly. And the food you make will be so much more delicious. Everyone wins!

Here are tricks and tips I use every single week:

1. **Brainstorm.** When choosing recipes for the week, I think about these things:

- *What's the weather like?* Hot summer nights call for no-cook salads or simple grilled meals, versus chilly winter evenings that beg for something warm and cozy.

- *Do I have items I need to use up?* Check the fridge, freezer, and pantry for items that are either about to reach their expiration date or have just been sitting around for a while. It's a great challenge!

- *What's the theme?* So I'm not starting from scratch every week in terms of figuring out what to make, we designate theme nights—think Meatless Monday, Taco Tuesday, Breakfast for Dinner, Pizza Friday, etc. And don't forget about Clean Out the Fridge Night!

- *What do the kids want?* The best way to get your kids to eat new foods and recipes is to get them involved in picking them out. I always take requests when figuring out what's on the week's menu, or I let them pick dinner one night a week. Even if they pick pizza every time, you can get creative with how you're serving it up.

- *How can I use leftovers?* Take into account that many recipes will make enough to leave you with leftovers that can be repurposed for another meal. Either you can freeze them and serve as-is another night (maybe a couple weeks later so no one gets sick of it!), or you can use the components in different ways, like turning roast chicken into quesadilla stuffing or a soup topping. I love a two-for-one!

2. **Read the recipes.** If you're using a new recipe, be sure to read the recipe all the way through so you aren't surprised by how long it takes, or whether it calls for any special equipment.

3. **Set the menu.** After you've figured out what you're going to cook for which meal, write it down. Use a planner, calendar, or notebook. Or a really fun option so the whole family can get excited is to put a big dry-erase or chalkboard in the kitchen.

4. Don't forget about breakfasts, snacks, and lunches! Factor in these meals when either looking for recipes or thinking about what you can prep ahead of time.

5. Make a master shopping list. Aim to go to the store once a week. Of course, there will be exceptions when you might have to pop in for fresh produce or if your plans change, but by going once a week and getting everything you need you'll save time and keep yourself from making in-store impulse buys. See page 30 for more grocery shopping tips.

6. Get prepped. Look at what you'll be cooking that week and make ahead anything that will save yourself time down the road. Some of our favorite things to do on Sunday to get a good start for the week are: hard-boil eggs, bake a batch of granola, cut up veggies, wash salad, roast a chicken or shred a store-bought rotisserie chicken, cook rice (or quinoa or other whole grains), roast vegetables, and make any sauces that can be done in advance.

7. Have the right containers. Invest in storage containers that can hold prepped food and leftovers. These can do double-duty as portable meal and snack containers.

8. Save your recipes. Do this so you don't have to go digging for your favorites every time you want to make them. Use a binder or recipe box, download an app, store them in a spreadsheet, or create a board on Pinterest. Then any time you try something new that's a big hit, add it to the collection. And be sure to make notes as you go: Did you make any changes? What did you serve it with? Did you have a great way to repurpose leftovers? I promise that future you will thank present you for the tips!

9. Mix it up. Don't get stuck in a recipe rut! Make sure to try one or two new recipes every week so you don't get bored with the same old meals. You can of course stay in your comfort zone, and definitely don't give up on standbys that your family loves, but challenge yourself to take something new for a test drive. You might find the new family favorite!

Grocery Shopping Tips

Even though cooking more at home means more trips to the grocery store, that doesn't mean it has to be a major pain. With a little bit of planning—which will soon become second nature—and a few smart tips, your shopping excursions will be quicker, less expensive, and much more enjoyable.

- **Shop once a week.** Making several trips to the grocery store a week will cost you time and money. You may need to go back later in the week to freshen up your produce inventory, but aim for one big shop a week.

- **Make a plan.** Figure out what exactly you'll be preparing for the week, whether it's recipes or un-recipes (page 234). To help narrow down your choices, consider what's currently in season and also check out your store's weekly flyer to see what's on sale.

- **Take inventory.** Before going to the store, take a peek in your pantry, fridge, and freezer to see what you already have so you don't buy double. (This will take no time at all once you have things nice and organized—see page 22 for more tips about that!) Also take note of any items that are running low. Check out page 24 for a list of ingredients I usually have on hand because they lend themselves to recipes and to whipping things up at a moment's notice.

- **Keep a list.** This is a super helpful way to keep track of all kinds of kitchen business, from the weekly menu to a running grocery list. You could also do this with a dry-erase board, a notepad on the counter or fridge, or a clipboard.

- **Organize your list.** Once you've written down all the items you need, sort them by sections of the grocery store, such as produce, bulk, fish, meat, frozen, etc. Knowing the layout of your store is a great way to make your shopping more efficient. Also, write down the specific quantities you need and make any notes that will be helpful when choosing a product. For example: If you note that you won't be using your avocados until the end of the week, you'll know to get firm avocados instead of super ripe ones.

- **Buy in bulk.** When on sale or offered by a wholesale club, buying multiples of items that you use frequently will save you time and money. Designate a spot in your home to stock these items (a pantry, hall closet, garage), which will keep your kitchen from feeling too cluttered.

- **But don't buy things just because they're on sale.** Don't be tempted by the "Buy 5, Get 1 Free" promise, or any other, if you weren't going to buy that item anyway.

- **Stick to your list.** You made it for a reason! Impulse buys are what lead to more expensive grocery bills and more wasted food.

- **Don't go to the store hungry.** If you do, you'll only end up with a cart full of items you wouldn't normally purchase and definitely don't need. I'm looking at you, pint of ice cream!

- **Leave your kids at home (if you can).** You'll be able to shop more efficiently and won't have to deal with them begging for treats.

- **Compare prices by ounce, not just the sticker price.** Consider the size of a package when figuring out which is the better deal. A carton of chicken stock might seem less expensive than its neighbor, until you see that it's actually 8 ounces smaller.

- **Try store brands.** They're less expensive, and you might find you like them just as much as name-brand items.

- **If a sale item is out of stock, get a rain check.** This is one of my favorite tricks! Most stores will honor the sale price of the item at a later date if they're currently out of it.

- **Bring your own reusable bags.** This doesn't necessarily make shopping more efficient, but it is nice for the environment and, in the places where they charge for paper or plastic bags, can save you a few cents. Plus, if you invest in a few reusable bags with nice shoulder straps, it makes carrying the groceries into the house much easier.

- **Skip the trip.** Another great option for the time-challenged is to see if your grocery store offers an order-ahead or delivery service. Some stores will allow you to order your groceries online then pick them up without even having to go in the store, or will deliver them right to your home.

BREAKFAST

D rop in on any family at 7 a.m. on a weekday and you're sure to see the same mad dash—everyone racing to get dressed, gathering up backpacks and lunch bags, and running out the door in time to get to work or school. Our house is no exception! Which is why I've come up with this steady rotation of dependable breakfasts that can be made in advance, yet send everyone off feeling full and nourished. They say that breakfast is the most important meal of the day, and that goes doubly for us. No matter how busy we get, we try to make a point of getting everyone around the breakfast table. Sure, it helps that our boys wake up super early, but when they get up, they're *hungry*. That's when we reach for the Artichoke, Sun-Dried Tomato, and Feta Egg Casserole that just needs to be warmed in the oven or big bowls of our Best-Ever Granola.

Then when the weekend rolls around, we all look forward to a more leisurely morning meal. We still like to keep things simple—because let's be honest: life!—but we have a little more time to break out classics like Perfect Buttermilk Pancakes, Huevos Rancheros, and my Dad's world-famous cinnamon rolls, aka Parry Rolls. And we love opening our house to morning guests. We turn on cartoons for the kids, make a platter of fruit salad and scones, and call it a party—all without changing out of our slippers and pj's! Breakfast or brunch gatherings are a fun, less hectic alternative to a dinner event, especially when it comes to kids because there are no sitters or bedtimes to consider. Plus everyone has to eat breakfast—you might as well do it in good company!

artichoke, sun-dried tomato, and feta egg casserole

prep: **15 MINUTES** | cook: **40 MINUTES** | total: **55 MINUTES** | serves **12**

Nonstick cooking spray

1 tablespoon extra-virgin olive oil

½ yellow onion, chopped

1 (14-ounce) can artichoke hearts (see Notes), drained and chopped

1 (7-ounce) jar sun-dried tomatoes, drained and chopped

3 cups packed stemmed, chopped kale (see Notes)

3 garlic cloves, minced

Kosher salt and freshly ground black pepper

½ cup crumbled feta cheese

2 tablespoons chopped fresh basil

18 large eggs

½ cup milk

Thanks to the flock of chickens that we keep in the backyard, we always have a *ton* of eggs, so we're constantly thinking of ways to put them to good use. This recipe is pretty much the perfect solution because it not only calls for a whole bunch of eggs—18 of 'em!—but it also makes for a seriously versatile dish. We love whipping up this easy, cheesy casserole for breakfasts or brunches (it's a staple on our Christmas morning table!) because we can either cook it the night before and heat it up right after rolling out of bed, or we can easily throw it together just before guests arrive.

1 Preheat the oven to 350°F. Grease a 9 × 13-inch baking dish with nonstick cooking spray and set aside.

2 Heat the olive oil in a large skillet over high heat. Add the onion and cook until tender, about 3 minutes. Stir in the artichoke hearts, sun-dried tomatoes, kale, and garlic. Cook for 3 to 4 minutes, until the kale is wilted. Season to taste with salt and black pepper.

3 Pour the vegetable mixture into the prepared dish and spread it out evenly over the bottom of the dish. Sprinkle ¼ cup of the feta and the basil over the vegetables.

4 In a large bowl, whisk together the eggs and milk. Season with ½ teaspoon salt and ¼ teaspoon pepper. Pour the egg mixture over the veggies and cheese. Top with the remaining ¼ cup feta cheese.

5 Bake for 30 to 35 minutes, until the eggs are set and slightly golden around the edges. A knife inserted into the center should come out clean. Let the casserole cool for 10 minutes before slicing into squares and serving.

NOTES: *Feel free to use spinach instead of kale. And while I use canned artichoke hearts, you could use jarred marinated artichoke hearts instead. Just rinse and drain before using them. You can also feel free to use any type of milk here.*

chewy no-bake granola bars

prep: **15 MINUTES** | chill: **1 HOUR** | total: **1 HOUR 15 MINUTES** | serves **10 TO 12**

2 cups quick oats (see Note)

1 cup crispy rice cereal

½ cup sweetened coconut flakes

½ cup chopped almonds

⅓ cup pepitas

2 tablespoons flaxseed meal

2 tablespoons chia seeds

1 teaspoon ground cinnamon

½ teaspoon sea salt or kosher salt

¾ cup creamy unsweetened
   almond butter

⅓ cup coconut oil

⅓ cup honey

1 teaspoon pure vanilla extract

⅓ cup dried cranberries (optional)

NOTE: *I like using quick-cooking oats here because they hold together better. If you only have rolled oats, just pulse them a few times in a food processor.*

Granola bars are an essential for us—they're the ultimate breakfast/after-school snack/pre- or post-workout power-up/midnight treat (okay, maybe not midnight, considering I can never stay up past 10 p.m.!). That's why this recipe is one of my favorites, and also because these bars are beyond easy to put together (hello, no-bake!) and are so much better than store-bought because you can control what goes in them. I always keep the ingredients stocked in our pantry, which is really easy considering you can put in just about anything.

1   Line an 8-inch square baking pan with parchment paper and set aside.

2   In a large bowl, combine the oats, rice cereal, coconut, almonds, pepitas, flaxseed, chia seeds, cinnamon, and salt. Set aside.

3   In a medium microwave-safe bowl, combine the almond butter, coconut oil, and honey. Microwave for 30 seconds, or until the coconut oil is melted. You could also do this in a medium pot over low heat. Stir until the mixture is smooth and add the vanilla.

4   Pour the liquid ingredients over the oat mixture and use a large spoon or spatula to incorporate the ingredients. Fold in the dried cranberries (if using) and stir until all of the ingredients are moistened and combined.

5   Transfer the mixture to the prepared pan. Press down with your hands and then use the bottom of a glass or jar to make sure the mixture is packed firmly in the pan, as this will help the bars hold together. Cover the bars with plastic wrap and refrigerate for at least 1 hour or overnight.

6   When ready to cut the bars, use the edges of the parchment paper to help lift the bars out of the pan. Use a sharp knife to cut the bars into your preferred shape and size. (I like mine in rectangles that are about the size of a traditional granola bar.) Store them wrapped individually in plastic wrap or in an airtight container in the fridge for up to 10 days. Or you can wrap them individually, place in a freezer bag or freezer container, and freeze for up to 1 month.

maple-roasted berry yogurt parfaits

prep: **10 MINUTES** | cook: **20 MINUTES** | total: **30 MINUTES** | makes **8 PARFAITS**

• •

1 cup raspberries

1 cup blueberries

1 cup blackberries

1 cup chopped strawberries

2 tablespoons pure maple syrup

4 cups plain Greek yogurt

Best-Ever Granola (page 41, optional)

Our boys *love* yogurt and are always begging me to buy the fruit-on-the-bottom yogurts from the store, but I never do because they have too much sugar. Instead, I make them these parfaits at home, and they do the trick! Roasting the berries gives them a deeply sweet flavor, almost like jam but without having to babysit a pot. I like to use a blend of strawberries, blueberries, blackberries, and raspberries (though you could stick with whichever are your favorites) and give them a drizzle of maple syrup before roasting, which sends them over the top of fruity deliciousness—not unlike the store-bought version. Then I spoon over some tangy Greek yogurt, add a sprinkle of our Best-Ever Granola, and breakfast is served. I prep a bunch of parfaits in jars and store them in the fridge, which makes this a great meal or snack for grabbing on the way out the door.

1 Preheat the oven to 400°F.

2 Line a large baking sheet with parchment paper or aluminum foil. Arrange the raspberries, blueberries, blackberries, and strawberries on the baking sheet and drizzle the maple syrup over the top. Give the berries a gentle toss to coat. Roast for 20 minutes, until the berries are soft and juicy, then let the berries cool completely.

3 To assemble a parfait, spoon 2 tablespoons roasted berries in the bottom of an 8-ounce jar and top with a ½ cup yogurt. Repeat with the remaining ingredients to make 8 parfaits. Seal the jars with their lids and store them in the fridge for up to 1 week. When ready to eat, top the parfaits with a handful of granola, if desired.

best-ever granola

prep: **15 MINUTES** | cook: **40 MINUTES** | total: **55 MINUTES** | makes **ABOUT 6 CUPS**

• •

3 cups old-fashioned rolled oats

½ cup roughly chopped almonds

½ cup roughly chopped pecans

½ cup pepitas

½ cup unsweetened coconut flakes or chips

1 teaspoon ground cinnamon

¾ teaspoon fine sea salt

½ cup melted coconut oil

½ cup pure maple syrup

1 teaspoon pure vanilla extract

1 large egg white

1 cup dried cranberries

This granola is our ultimate pantry staple. We have a canister ready to scoop from pretty much at all times, and the granola is always getting put to good use, whether it's layered in yogurt parfaits, grabbed by the handful as a snack, sprinkled over ice cream sundaes, or packed up in a sweet jar to bring someone as a gift. And we never get bored of it because we're always mixing and matching ingredients—trying different nuts like walnuts and cashews, dried fruit like blueberries and cherries, or adding in other goodies like mini chocolate chips. I also get the boys involved so they can customize the granola however they like it. To make a vegan version, omit the egg white.

1   Preheat the oven to 325°F. Line a large baking sheet with a silicone baking mat or parchment paper. Set aside.

2   In a large bowl, combine the oats, almonds, pecans, pepitas, coconut, cinnamon, and salt. Stir to combine. Add the coconut oil, maple syrup, and vanilla and mix until evenly distributed.

3   In a small bowl, whisk the egg white until frothy. Gently stir the egg white into the granola mixture.

4   Pour the granola onto the prepared baking sheet, using a spatula to spread it into an even layer. Bake for 40 minutes, until the granola is golden brown, stirring halfway through.

5   Let the granola cool completely on the baking sheet without stirring. When cool, break it up into crumbles and mix in the dried cranberries. Store in an airtight container for up to 3 weeks.

cinnamon streusel french toast

prep: **15 MINUTES** | cook: **15 MINUTES** | total: **30 MINUTES** | serves **8**

●●

CINNAMON STREUSEL TOPPING

½ cup sugar

4 teaspoons ground cinnamon

2 teaspoons unsalted butter

FRENCH TOAST

5 large eggs

⅓ cup whole milk

2 teaspoons pure vanilla extract

½ teaspoon ground cinnamon

1 tablespoon unsalted butter, plus
more for serving

8 slices brioche bread, challah, or
Texas toast (see Note)

Maple syrup, for serving

NOTE: *I strongly encourage you to
try to find brioche for this recipe; it
really does make French toast that
much more special. I love the brioche
from Trader Joe's.*

This recipe is inspired by the Griddle Cafe in Los Angeles, our favorite breakfast spot when we're in the city. Their specialty is super-sized, slightly over-the-top breakfast classics, and I knew from my first bite of this turned-up toast that I'd be heading straight back to my kitchen to figure out how to re-create it. The key is using a thick, sweet bread like brioche (though Texas toast can also do the trick), coating it with a cinnamon-sugar streusel that gets griddled right into the toast, then finishing off the whole stack with a slab of butter, a drizzle of maple syrup, and an extra sprinkling of streusel to melt over the top. One slice will just about send you into the happiest sugar coma ever! I like breaking out this recipe for special occasions when I want to serve something extra indulgent for breakfast, especially around the holidays.

1   Preheat a griddle pan or large skillet over medium-high heat, or an electric griddle to 350°F.

2   Make the streusel topping: In a medium bowl, combine the sugar, cinnamon, and butter. Rub the mixture between your pointer finger and thumb until the butter forms pea-sized pieces. Set aside.

3   Make the French toast: In a shallow dish, use a fork or whisk to beat together the eggs, milk, vanilla, and cinnamon.

4   Melt the butter on the heated griddle or skillet. Dip the bread in the egg mixture, turning to coat both sides evenly. Let some of the excess drain off, then place the bread slices on the hot griddle pan or in the hot skillet. You may need to work in batches, depending on the size of your griddle or pan. Top each slice of bread with about 1 tablespoon cinnamon streusel. Cook until browned on the first side, 2 to 3 minutes. Flip and cook until the second side is golden brown, 2 to 3 minutes.

5   Transfer the French toast slices to a plate with the streusel side facing up. Sprinkle with an extra pinch of streusel while the French toast is still hot so it can melt. Repeat with the remaining batches, adding more butter to the griddle or pan if needed.

6   Serve with butter and maple syrup.

pumpkin–chocolate chip streusel muffins

prep: **15 MINUTES** | bake: **24 TO 28 MINUTES** | total: **45 MINUTES** | makes **12 MUFFINS**

● ●

MUFFINS

Nonstick cooking spray (optional)

1½ cups all-purpose flour

½ teaspoon baking soda

1½ teaspoons ground cinnamon

½ teaspoon ground ginger

¼ teaspoon ground nutmeg

⅛ teaspoon ground cloves

½ teaspoon kosher salt

1 cup canned pumpkin puree (not pumpkin pie filling)

½ cup granulated sugar

¼ cup packed light brown sugar

½ cup canola or vegetable oil

¼ cup buttermilk, at room temperature

2 large eggs, at room temperature

1 teaspoon pure vanilla extract

1 cup (6 ounces) semisweet chocolate chips

STREUSEL TOPPING

⅓ cup granulated sugar

3 tablespoons all-purpose flour

2 tablespoons unsalted butter, melted

I love pumpkin-flavored baked goods in the fall months, especially these bakery-style pumpkin muffins. They might be my favorite of all because they remind me of the pumpkin bread I grew up eating, and everybody knows that pumpkin bread is a perfectly acceptable breakfast—chocolate chips and sweet streusel topping included! And no, you don't have to wait for the fall to enjoy them. I sure don't!

1 Make the muffins: Preheat the oven to 350°F. Line the cups of a standard 12-cup muffin pan with paper liners or grease with nonstick cooking spray. Set aside.

2 In a medium bowl, whisk together the flour, baking soda, cinnamon, ginger, nutmeg, cloves, and salt.

3 In a large bowl, combine the pumpkin, granulated sugar, brown sugar, oil, buttermilk, eggs, and vanilla. Stir with a spatula until smooth.

4 Gradually add the dry ingredients to the pumpkin mixture and stir until just combined. Gently fold in ¾ cup of the chocolate chips. Don't overmix.

5 Divide the batter among the muffin cups, filling each three-quarters full.

6 Make the streusel: In a medium bowl, combine the granulated sugar, flour, and melted butter. Stir until the mixture is moistened.

7 Generously sprinkle the muffins with the remaining ¼ cup chocolate chips and streusel topping. Bake for 24 to 28 minutes, until the muffins are set and a toothpick inserted in the middle comes out clean. Allow the muffins to cool to room temperature. Enjoy immediately or store in a lidded container on the counter for up to 3 days. You could also freeze the muffins for up to 1 month.

perfect buttermilk pancakes

prep: 20 MINUTES | cook: 15 TO 20 MINUTES | total: 40 MINUTES | serves 6 TO 8

2½ cups all-purpose flour

2 tablespoons sugar

4 teaspoons baking powder

1 teaspoon baking soda

¾ teaspoon fine sea salt

3 cups buttermilk, at room temperature

4 tablespoons unsalted butter, melted and cooled to room temperature, plus more for cooking

2 large eggs, slightly beaten, at room temperature

1 teaspoon pure vanilla extract

Maple syrup, for serving

I believe that every family should have the ultimate recipe for the perfect stack of pancakes—and here it is! Whether you're serving these on a lazy Saturday or Sunday morning or for a surprise breakfast-for-dinner weeknight supper (a major favorite in our house), there's nothing more comforting and delicious than fluffy, slightly tangy buttermilk pancakes piled high and slathered with butter and syrup. This recipe is also a great blank canvas for just about anything you'd want to stir into the batter, whether it's fresh or frozen fruit, chocolate chips, or spices like cinnamon or nutmeg. Get creative! And they freeze really nicely, so we keep a stash for hectic mornings. If your family is as in love with pancakes as mine, I highly recommend investing in a stovetop or electric griddle, so you can whip up large batches in much less time.

1 In a large bowl, whisk together the flour, sugar, baking powder, baking soda, and salt.

2 In a medium bowl, whisk together the buttermilk, melted butter, eggs, and vanilla.

3 Pour the wet ingredients over the dry and whisk until just combined— the batter will be lumpy, but that's okay. Let the batter sit at room temperature for 10 minutes.

4 Preheat a griddle pan or large skillet over medium-high heat, or an electric griddle to 350°F.

5 Grease the griddle with a generous pat of butter. Pour the batter in ½-cup dollops on the hot griddle—as many as will comfortably fit with room to flip the pancakes. Cook the pancakes until bubbles form on the top and the edges are set, about 3 minutes. Use a spatula to flip and cook for another 2 to 3 minutes, until golden brown. Transfer the pancakes to a plate and continue making pancakes until the batter is gone. If desired, arrange the pancakes in a single layer on a large baking sheet and keep warm in a 200°F oven until ready to serve. Serve them stacked high with plenty of maple syrup. If making ahead, let the pancakes cool completely before storing them wrapped in plastic in the fridge for up to 5 days, or wrapped in plastic inside a freezer bag in the freezer for up to 1 month.

huevos rancheros

prep: **15 MINUTES** | cook: **15 MINUTES** | total: **30 MINUTES** | serves **4**

• •

1 tablespoon extra-virgin olive oil

½ yellow onion, chopped

1 garlic clove, minced

2 (14.5-ounce) cans fire-roasted diced tomatoes with green chilies, with juices

½ teaspoon chili powder

½ teaspoon ground cumin

¼ teaspoon smoked paprika

¼ teaspoon kosher salt, plus more to taste

Canola or vegetable oil, for frying

8 corn tortillas

8 large eggs

2 (15-ounce) cans black beans, drained and rinsed

2 ripe avocados, pitted, peeled, and sliced

1 cup shredded cheddar cheese

½ cup crumbled queso fresco

½ cup chopped fresh cilantro

2 scallions (white and green parts), thinly sliced

Josh always orders this traditional Mexican dish when we go out to break-fast, and it's a good thing because that means I get to steal a few bites! It's pretty much the perfect meal, with fried eggs served over crispy tortillas and smothered in a warmed salsa with lots of queso fresco. We don't exactly have many leisurely mornings to go out and order it in a restaurant, so Josh decided to create our own recipe that we could enjoy at home—and let me tell you, this version is better than any I've ever had out. We're always sure to save any leftover ranchero sauce in the freezer so we can easily make huevos whenever the mood strikes (including for dinner).

1   In a large saucepan, heat the olive oil over medium-high heat. Add the onion and sauté for 3 minutes. Add the garlic and cook, stirring occasion-ally so the onion softens but does not brown. Add the diced tomatoes, chili powder, cumin, smoked paprika, and salt. Stir and reduce the heat to low. Let the ranchero sauce gently simmer while you prepare the tortillas and cook the eggs.

2   Pour about ¼ inch canola oil into a large skillet and heat over medium heat until shimmering. Carefully lay a tortilla in the pan and fry, turning, until the edges are just crispy, about 20 seconds per side. Transfer the tortilla to a paper towel–lined plate to drain. Pat dry and sprinkle lightly with salt. Repeat with the remaining tortillas. You could also do this in a 400°F oven, lightly brushing them first with oil or spraying them with nonstick cooking spray and baking for 5 to 10 minutes, until crispy.

3   Carefully discard all but about 2 tablespoons oil from the skillet and place the pan over medium heat. Crack the eggs into the skillet, being care-ful not to break the yolks. Cook until the whites are set and the yolks have begun to thicken but are not hard, 3 to 4 minutes for slightly runny yolks, about a minute more if you want firmer yolks.

4   To assemble, place the crispy tor-tillas on a large plate and top with the ranchero sauce, eggs, beans, avo-cado, cheddar, queso fresco, cilantro, and scallions. You could also make single servings by putting two tortil-las and two eggs on each plate. Serve immediately.

cinnamon rolls, aka parry rolls

prep: **30 MINUTES** | bake: **28 TO 32 MINUTES**
total: **2½ TO 3 HOURS, INCLUDING 1½ TO 2 HOURS RISING** | makes **30 CINNAMON ROLLS**

● ●

CINNAMON ROLLS

4½ teaspoons (two ¼-ounce packages) active dry yeast

1 cup granulated sugar, plus a pinch

1 cup lukewarm water

¼ cup plus 2 tablespoons shortening (I prefer Crisco) or unsalted butter

1 tablespoon kosher salt

2 cups hot water

9 cups unbleached all-purpose flour, plus more for dusting

2 large eggs, beaten

Nonstick cooking spray

½ cup (8 tablespoons) unsalted butter, at room temperature

1½ cups packed light brown sugar

1 cup raisins (optional)

2 tablespoons ground cinnamon

FROSTING

4 tablespoons unsalted butter, at room temperature

4 cups confectioners' sugar

4 to 6 tablespoons whole milk

1 teaspoon pure vanilla extract

These are my dad's world-famous cinnamon rolls! He got the recipe from his mom, who passed before I was born, but these warm, gooey rolls give me the feeling that I would have really loved her. My dad has been making the rolls for as long as I can remember, and they're not only a family favorite, but they've also since been named after him, Parry. There's not a holiday where there isn't a batch of these on the table, and my dad is always happy to make them on-demand—which happens pretty much any time we all get together. So even though I'm always itching to put my personal spin on a recipe, this is one I will never, ever change.

One thing I will point out is that my dad loves raisins and insists on including them (he always tells people, "If you don't like 'em, pick 'em out!"), but if you're not a fan, feel free to leave them out.

1 Make the cinnamon rolls: In a small bowl, combine the yeast and a pinch of the granulated sugar with the lukewarm water and set aside for 5 minutes.

2 In the bowl of a stand mixer fitted with the paddle attachment, combine the 1 cup granulated sugar, the shortening, and salt plus the hot water and beat for 30 seconds. Let the mixture cool to lukewarm temperature. Add 2 cups of the flour and mix until smooth. Add the yeast mixture and mix until well combined. Add the beaten eggs and mix once again.

3 Fit the mixer with the dough hook. Continue mixing, gradually adding the remaining 7 cups flour. Mix for about 2 minutes. Turn out the dough on a lightly floured surface. Knead by hand, adding a light dusting of flour if the dough is still sticky, until the dough is satiny and smooth, about 1 minute. Return the dough to the mixing bowl and cover with a clean kitchen towel. Let the dough rise for 30 minutes, until doubled in size.

recipe continues

4 Grease two 9 × 13-inch baking pans with nonstick cooking spray and set aside. Divide the dough in half. With a rolling pin, roll one portion into a rectangle, about 22 × 13 inches. Spread evenly with 4 tablespoons of the butter. Sprinkle with ¾ cup of the brown sugar, ½ cup of the raisins (if using), and 1 tablespoon of the cinnamon.

5 Starting from one of the long sides of the rectangle, roll the dough into a log. Using a piece of unflavored dental floss (my dad's signature) or a thin piece of thread, cut the log into 1½-inch-thick rolls. Do this by first sliding the floss underneath the dough so you have at least a few inches on either side of the rolls. Pull up the ends of the floss and loop them together as though you were going to tie a knot. Tightly pull the floss until it slices through the dough. Arrange the rolls in one baking pan, swirl side up and about ½ inch apart. Repeat with the remaining portion of dough and the butter, brown sugar, raisins, and cinnamon.

6 Allow the rolls to sit at room temperature until they've doubled in size, 1 to 1½ hours.

7 Preheat the oven to 350°F.

8 Bake the rolls for 28 to 32 minutes, until golden brown and baked through. Let the rolls cool to room temperature.

9 Make the frosting: In a medium bowl, whisk together the butter, confectioners' sugar, milk, and vanilla. Generously spread over the cooled cinnamon rolls and serve.

NOTE: *You can refrigerate the unrisen, unbaked rolls overnight and bake them in the morning. After you cut the dough into rolls and place in the pans, cover with plastic wrap and refrigerate. In the morning, let the rolls come to room temperature so they can rise a little, then bake and enjoy!*

raspberry-lemon scones

prep: **10 MINUTES** | bake: **15 TO 20 MINUTES** | total: **30 MINUTES** | makes **8 SCONES**

● ●

SCONES

2 cups all-purpose flour, plus more for dusting

1 tablespoon baking powder

½ teaspoon kosher salt

3 tablespoons granulated sugar

Grated zest of 1 large lemon

6 tablespoons unsalted butter, cold, cut into ¼-inch cubes

1 cup heavy cream, plus 1 tablespoon for brushing the scones

½ teaspoon pure vanilla extract

½ teaspoon fresh lemon juice

1 cup fresh or frozen raspberries (see Note)

LEMON GLAZE

1 cup confectioners' sugar, sifted

2 to 3 tablespoons fresh lemon juice (2 large lemons)

NOTE: *I prefer frozen raspberries to fresh because they hold their shape better. Fresh berries will get a little smashed, but you will get a pretty pink color in your scones. Also feel free to use blueberries instead.*

A good scone is my favorite breakfast pastry—I'll take one over a muffin or doughnut any day. I say "good" because scones are often dry and tasteless—but not mine!

1 Make the scones: Preheat the oven to 400°F. Line a large baking sheet with a silicone baking mat or parchment paper.

2 In a large bowl, whisk together the flour, baking powder, and salt.

3 In a small bowl, combine the granulated sugar and lemon zest and rub with your fingers until fragrant. Add the sugar mixture to the dry ingredients and whisk until combined.

4 Using a pastry blender or by rubbing the mixture between your pointer finger and thumb, cut the cold butter into the flour mixture. Mix until the mixture resembles a coarse meal with a few pea-sized butter lumps. Try to work quickly so the butter stays cold.

5 In a small bowl, whisk together the 1 cup cream, vanilla, and lemon juice. Pour the liquid ingredients over the flour mixture and stir with a spatula until the dough begins to form. Don't overmix. Gently fold in the raspberries.

6 Transfer the dough to a floured work surface and gently knead by hand just until it forms a ball, about 1 minute. Don't overwork the dough. Pat the dough into a 1-inch-thick disc and use a sharp knife to cut the disc into 8 even triangular scones.

7 Arrange the scones on the prepared baking sheet. Using a pastry brush, brush the scones lightly with the 1 tablespoon cream. Chill the scones in the freezer for 20 minutes before baking. Bake for 15 to 20 minutes, until the scones are golden brown on the bottom and around the edges. Let the scones cool on the baking sheet for 5 minutes before transferring to a wire cooling rack to cool completely.

8 Make the lemon glaze while the scones cool: In a small bowl, whisk together the confectioners' sugar and 2 tablespoons of the lemon juice until smooth. Add up to another tablespoon lemon juice if the glaze is too thick.

9 Drizzle the glaze over the cooled scones. You can store the glazed scones in an airtight container at room temperature for up to 2 days, but these are best the day they're made.

sweet potato and kale hash

prep: **10 MINUTES** | cook: **30 MINUTES** | total: **40 MINUTES** | serves **4**

• •

1 large sweet potato, peeled and diced (about 2 cups)

2 tablespoons extra-virgin olive oil

½ large red onion, diced

1 red bell pepper, cored, seeded, and diced

1 yellow bell pepper, cored, seeded, and diced

2 garlic cloves, minced

2 cups packed stemmed, chopped kale

Kosher salt and freshly ground black pepper

4 large eggs

1 large ripe avocado, pitted, peeled, and sliced

There's a divide that usually happens at the breakfast table—team sweet and team savory. This dish is perfect for both because it calls for mixing together caramelized onions and peppers with roasted sweet potatoes for a hearty hash, then topping it off with sautéed greens, eggs, and sliced avocado. It's a great way to get in your veggies first thing, and for fueling a busy morning when you might not have time to stop to enjoy a proper lunch. I also love serving the hash for dinner. Either way, make sure to offer plenty of hot sauce or salsa for an extra kick.

1 Preheat the oven to 425°F.

2 Bring a large pot of salted water to a boil. Add the sweet potatoes and cook until fork-tender, 5 to 7 minutes. Drain well and pat dry with a paper towel.

3 In a large oven-safe skillet, heat the olive oil over medium-high heat. Add the sweet potatoes, spreading them out in an even layer. Reduce the heat to medium and cook for 5 to 7 minutes, stirring occasionally, until evenly browned. Add the onion and peppers and cook for 5 minutes longer, until softened. Stir in the garlic and chopped kale and cook for 2 minutes. Season with salt and pepper to taste.

4 Turn off the heat and make four indentations in the hash to make room for the eggs. Crack an egg into each indentation. Transfer the skillet to the oven and bake for 10 to 15 minutes, until the eggs are set.

5 Top the hash with the avocado slices, sprinkle with salt and pepper, and serve immediately.

bacon and cheddar quiche

prep: **15 MINUTES** | cook: **1 HOUR 15 MINUTES** | total: **1½ HOURS** | serves **8**

• •

6 slices bacon

1 tablespoon unsalted butter

2 small yellow onions, cut into ¼-inch slices

¾ teaspoon kosher salt

4 large eggs, beaten

1 cup heavy cream

½ cup grated Parmesan cheese

1¼ cups shredded cheddar cheese (see Note)

2 tablespoons Dijon mustard

¼ teaspoon freshly ground black pepper

Tabasco sauce (optional)

1 sheet (half 17-ounce package) frozen puff pastry, thawed according to package instructions

2 scallions (white and green parts), thinly sliced

NOTE: *You can substitute different cheeses for the cheddar: Gruyère and smoked Gouda are two of Josh's favorites.*

I give Josh full credit for coming up with this tasty savory pie, which is pretty much my boys' dream breakfast. The smartest thing about it is that it calls for ready-made puff pastry, which you can find in the freezer aisle of just about any grocery store. All you have to do is line a pie pan with the crust, whisk together the filling, and let it bake until set. It's a shoo-in as a brunch dish, is great for dinner, and, because it freezes so well, makes for a great Cooking It Forward dish (see page 136). We often make two at a time and either save one for later or take to friends.

1   Set a large skillet over low heat. Lay the strips of bacon in the skillet and cook until the bacon starts to buckle and curl. Use tongs to loosen the strips from the pan and flip to the other side. Continue flipping the slices every couple minutes as they cook until they are slightly crispy, 7 to 10 minutes. Keep in mind that the bacon will continue to cook as it cools. Transfer the bacon to a paper towel–lined plate to drain and cool to room temperature. Chop into small pieces.

2   Carefully discard all but 2 tablespoons of the bacon fat from the pan and place the pan over medium-low heat. Add the butter and onions and cook, stirring occasionally, until the onions are caramelized, 25 to 30 minutes. They should be soft, golden brown, and sweet. Season with ¼ teaspoon salt and set aside.

3   Preheat the oven to 350°F. Set aside a 9-inch pie plate.

4   In a large bowl, whisk together the eggs, cream, Parmesan, 1 cup of the cheddar, the Dijon mustard, remaining ½ teaspoon salt, the pepper, and a few shakes of Tabasco (if using). Stir in the caramelized onions and chopped bacon. Set aside.

5   Carefully line the pie pan with the puff pastry. Trim any overhang and use your fingers to gently crimp the edges. Pour the egg mixture into the pastry shell and sprinkle with the remaining ¼ cup cheddar.

6   Bake for 30 to 40 minutes, until the puff pastry is golden and the quiche is set. Check the quiche after 20 minutes; if the crust is browning too quickly, loosely cover it with aluminum foil. Let the quiche rest for 10 minutes, then slice into wedges and serve with the sliced scallions on top. If freezing, let the quiche cool completely, then store wrapped in plastic and foil for up to 1 month.

chocolate banana bread

prep: **10 MINUTES** | bake: **55 TO 65 MINUTES** | total: **1 HOUR 15 MINUTES, PLUS COOLING**
makes **1 LOAF (ABOUT 12 SERVINGS)**

● ●

Nonstick cooking spray

1 cup all-purpose flour

½ cup Dutch-process or unsweetened cocoa powder

1 teaspoon baking soda

½ teaspoon sea salt

3 large brown bananas, mashed (about 1½ cups)

4 tablespoons unsalted butter, melted and slightly cooled

¼ cup canola, vegetable, or melted coconut oil

¾ cup packed light brown sugar

1 large egg, at room temperature

1 teaspoon pure vanilla extract

1 cup (6 ounces) semisweet chocolate chips

If your kids are anything like mine, it sometimes seems like you're buying enough bananas for an entire house of monkeys—and none of them lasts long enough to turn brown. Well, after *weeks* of testing—mainly because I kept running out of bananas!—I came up with a banana bread so rich, so dense, and so chocolate-stuffed that we now buy extra bananas just so we can wait for them to get to that perfect banana bread–making over-ripeness.

It is completely acceptable to eat a slice of this for breakfast, at 3 p.m. for a chocolaty pick-me-up, or after dinner for dessert. Or even topped with ice cream at midnight. I won't judge!

1   Preheat the oven to 350°F. Grease a 9 × 5-inch loaf pan with nonstick cooking spray and set aside.

2   In a medium bowl, whisk together the flour, cocoa powder, baking soda, and sea salt.

3   In a large bowl, stir together the mashed bananas and melted butter. Add the oil, brown sugar, egg, and vanilla and stir until smooth.

4   Stir the dry ingredients into the wet ingredients until just incorporated; don't overmix. Gently fold in ¾ cup of the chocolate chips.

5   Pour the batter into the prepared loaf pan. Sprinkle the remaining ¼ cup chocolate chips over the top of the batter. Bake for 55 to 65 minutes, until a toothpick inserted into the center of the bread comes out mostly

clean. You may see melted chocolate on your toothpick from the chocolate chips. Don't let it fool you into over-baking the bread! Test the loaf in a few spots—you just don't want a lot of gooey batter.

6   Let the bread cool in the pan set on a wire cooling rack for 15 minutes. Run a knife around the edges of the bread and carefully remove it from the pan. Let the bread cool on the wire cooling rack until slightly warm. Slice and serve.

7   Store leftover bread wrapped in plastic wrap at room temperature for up to 4 days. Or, if you'd like to freeze the bread, let the loaf cool completely, wrap it in plastic wrap and aluminum foil, and store it in the freezer for up to 1 month. Defrost before slicing.

peanut butter–chocolate chip energy bites

prep: 10 MINUTES | total: 10 MINUTES | makes 12 TO 14 ENERGY BITES

● ●

1 cup old-fashioned rolled oats (use gluten-free oats, if you prefer)

⅓ cup shredded coconut

2 tablespoons flaxseed meal

1 tablespoon chia seeds

Pinch of sea salt

½ cup all-natural peanut butter (see Notes)

¼ cup honey

½ teaspoon pure vanilla extract

¼ cup mini chocolate chips (see Notes)

We always have energy bites in our fridge because they're perfect for on-the-go snacking. An energy bite is essentially the cookie's more nutritious no-bake cousin that needs fewer than ten ingredients—most (if not all) of which you probably have in your pantry at this very moment! That means you're never more than 10 minutes away from satisfying a major cookie craving—or from giving your kids the kind of treat that makes them think they're getting away with something. They're also perfect before or after a workout, or when you just need a little something sweet before bed.

1   In a large bowl, combine the oats, coconut flaxseed meal, chia seeds, and salt. Add the peanut butter, honey, and vanilla. Stir until the mixture is combined and moist. Gently fold in the chocolate chips.

2   Roll the mixture into small balls, 1 to 2 tablespoons each. Place in an airtight container and chill for 1 hour before serving. The bites will keep refrigerated for 1 week or frozen for up to 2 months.

NOTES: *Feel free to swap out the peanut butter for almond butter. You could also use raisins or dried cranberries in place of—or in addition to—the chocolate chips…but I'm not exactly sure why you'd want to do that.*

green "hulk" smoothies

prep: **5 MINUTES** | total: **5 MINUTES** | serves **1**

1 cup unsweetened vanilla almond milk (or your favorite milk)

2 handfuls spinach leaves (see Notes)

1 medium banana (see Notes)

Heaping ½ cup frozen mango chunks

Heaping ½ cup frozen pineapple chunks

1 scoop vanilla protein powder (optional)

1 teaspoon chia seeds

2 teaspoons flaxseed meal

Every family should have a smoothie in their rotation—they're beyond easy to make (toss in a blender and blend), and they are hands-down the best way to get some greens into *everyone*. This recipe got its name because Caleb and Maxwell think it's hilarious to pretend that they're turning into the Hulk while they sip, complete with flexing their muscles and flying around like super-heroes. I pack them each a thermos to take in the car, and I never forget to make myself a serving, whether it's for breakfast or a post-workout snack. Feel free to add a scoop of your favorite vanilla protein powder, if you like.

In a blender, combine the milk, spinach, banana, mango, pineapple, protein powder (if using), chia seeds, and flaxseed meal. Make sure the lid is on tight and blend until smooth.

NOTES: *I like to keep a bunch of peeled bananas in a freezer bag in the freezer just for this recipe because they give the smoothie extra creamy body. If you only have room-temperature bananas, throw a small handful of ice cubes in with the rest of the ingredients. You can also substitute other greens besides spinach if you prefer—kale is great. And if your kids are afraid of the green color, you could add ½ cup frozen blueberries for camouflage. They'll never know they are drinking their greens!*

Feeling Toasty

Sometimes breakfast doesn't have to be much more than delicious ingredients piled on your favorite toast. The same goes for lunch, dinner, and snacks too! Here are some of my favorite toast-topping combinations:

Savory

- Mashed avocado with sea salt or Everything-Bagel Seasoning (page 87) (a classic and pretty much a daily stand-by in our house). Add eggs to make it even more filling: hard, soft, or scrambled.

- Mashed avocado, grape tomatoes, chopped bacon, arugula

- Hummus, cucumber slices, grape tomatoes, Kalamata olives, crumbled feta

- Fresh mozzarella, tomatoes, fresh basil, a drizzle of balsamic glaze

- Basil pesto, fresh mozzarella, sun-dried tomatoes

- Cottage cheese, sliced tomato, sliced avocado, salt, pepper

- Cream cheese, smoked salmon, red onion, dill, capers

- Goat cheese, pear, prosciutto

- Goat cheese, roasted red peppers, fresh basil

Sweet

- Peanut butter, apple slices, honey

- Peanut butter, banana, chopped dark chocolate or mini chocolate chips

- Vanilla almond butter, peach slices, sliced almonds

- Plain Greek yogurt, berries, a sprinkle of granola

- Ricotta cheese, pear slices, chopped hazelnuts, honey

- Brie, cranberry sauce or berry jam, grated orange zest

- Cream cheese, sliced strawberries, chopped pistachios

- Cream cheese, fresh pineapple, toasted coconut

- Nutella, raspberries

- Nutella, clementine or thin orange slices

- Nutella, banana slices, chopped peanuts

- Applesauce, sliced apples, cinnamon

APPETIZERS

When Josh and I decide to have people over (which in Josh's case can be about 15 minutes before the actual party!), one of the first things we think about—besides what we're going to serve as our meal—is what we're going to put out as appetizers. This isn't to be fussy or over-the-top; appetizers are pretty much the perfect party tool: They set a nice, relaxing tone when guests have a bite after coming in and taking off their coats; they're the icebreaker of the party since everyone tends to gather around the food; they buy you time if you're still putting the finishing touches on the meal; and they're delicious! And the best part? They don't need to take a long time to prepare but can still hit all the right flavor notes—crunchy, spicy, salty, sweet.

The recipes in this chapter are updated versions of some of our most popular favorites. We reach for these just about every time we have people over, whether it's one or two for a smaller dinner or 10 or 12 for the big game-day crowd. Sometimes we skip the meal itself and just do a spread of appetizers—which no one ever complains about!

baked brie with apples
and salted caramel sauce

prep: **5 MINUTES** | bake: **10 TO 12 MINUTES** | total: **20 MINUTES** | serves **8 TO 10**

• •

1 (8-ounce) wheel Brie

1 tablespoon unsalted butter

1 large apple, cored and chopped (we like Honeycrisp, but Gala or Fuji would also work)

2 tablespoons packed brown sugar

⅓ cup Salted Caramel Sauce (recipe follows) or store-bought

Crostini, pita chips, or crackers, for serving

As its name suggests, this is the kind of ooey, gooey, savory-sweet goodness you want on a holiday spread. All it takes is sautéing apples in brown butter and brown sugar, pouring it over a warmed wheel of Brie, and drizzling the whole mess with a homemade salted caramel sauce—which you can make in advance, though you could absolutely buy the sauce and your guests would be none the wiser! The only downside is that people will demand you make it the next year…and the next. But they never have to know that it took only 20 minutes to put together.

1 Preheat the oven to 350°F. Line a large baking sheet with parchment paper.

2 Place the wheel of Brie on the prepared baking sheet and bake until it's warm, soft, and starting to ooze, 10 to 12 minutes.

3 While the Brie is baking, melt the butter in a small saucepan over medium heat. Add the chopped apples and brown sugar and cook until the apples are soft, about 5 minutes.

4 Carefully transfer the Brie to a serving platter. Spoon the sautéed apples over the Brie and drizzle with the salted caramel sauce. Serve while warm with crostini, pita chips, or crackers.

Salted Caramel Sauce

prep: **5 MINUTES**
cook: **15 MINUTES**
total: **20 MINUTES**, plus cooling
makes **2 CUPS**

Use this easy sauce in Peanut Butter Caramelitas (page 277), spooned over warm Deep-Dish Brownie Cookies (page 252), drizzled over ice cream, or as a dip for apple slices.

2 cups granulated sugar

¾ cup (12 tablespoons) unsalted butter, at room temperature, sliced into tablespoons

1 cup heavy cream, at room temperature

1 tablespoon fleur de sel or Maldon sea salt flakes

1 Be sure to have all of the ingredients ready, because once you start the sauce, you're going to want to pay close attention or it will burn.

2 In the bottom of a 2- to 3-quart saucepan, heat the sugar over medium-high heat. When it starts to melt, begin whisking. It will clump up, but keep whisking until the sugar is completely melted, 4 to 10 minutes, depending on your stove. Did I mention you have to watch it?

3 Continue cooking, stirring occasionally, until the sugar reaches a deep amber color, 8 to 12 minutes. Make sure you watch the pan very closely—this is where it's easy to burn the caramel! As soon as the sugar caramelizes, carefully add the butter and use a wooden spoon to stir until the butter is melted.

4 Remove the pan from the heat and slowly pour in the cream. Whisk until the cream is incorporated and the caramel is smooth. Whisk in the fleur de sel. Let the caramel sauce cool for about 10 minutes in the pan before using. Or, if not serving the sauce right away, transfer to a large glass jar and cool completely before storing in the refrigerator for up to 1 month.

peach caprese bruschetta

prep: **15 MINUTES** | bake: **5 TO 7 MINUTES** | total: **25 MINUTES** | serves **8 TO 10**

- 1 baguette, cut into ½-inch slices
- 1 tablespoon extra-virgin olive oil, plus more for brushing the bread
- 2 garlic cloves, peeled and halved
- 2 peaches, pitted and chopped (about 2 cups)
- 2 cups halved grape or cherry tomatoes
- 8 ounces fresh mozzarella, chopped
- ¼ cup finely chopped fresh basil
- Kosher salt and freshly ground black pepper
- Balsamic glaze, store-bought (see note on page 74), for drizzling

This easy appetizer tastes like *summer*. With the addition of ripe peaches to a traditional tomato-packed bruschetta, you're not only making something that your guests will request every time they come over, but you're also getting to use all the amazing sun-kissed produce that's in the market. I enrich the bruschetta topping with fresh mozzarella and top it all off with a drizzle of balsamic glaze (which you can find at almost any grocery store and is a pantry staple for us), which rounds out the sweetness of the fruit with a salty kick. It's sort of like a bruschetta and caprese salad are teaming up to make one amazing appetizer.

1   Preheat the oven to 425°F.

2   Arrange the baguette slices in one layer on a large baking sheet, or two if necessary. Lightly brush the tops of the slices with olive oil and bake until the bread is toasted and golden brown, 5 to 7 minutes. Rub the garlic over the toasted bread while it is still warm, pressing gently into the bread. Set the toasts aside.

3   In a medium bowl, combine the peaches, tomatoes, mozzarella, basil, and the 1 tablespoon olive oil. Gently toss everything together and season to taste with salt and pepper.

4   Spoon the bruschetta topping over the toasted bread slices. Drizzle with balsamic glaze and serve immediately.

puffed piglets

prep: **25 MINUTES** | bake: **18 TO 20 MINUTES** | total: **45 MINUTES** | makes **ABOUT 45 PUFFED PIGLETS**

● ●

FRY SAUCE

¼ cup mayonnaise

¼ cup ketchup

1 tablespoon of your favorite barbecue sauce

PIGLETS

2 sheets (one 17-ounce package) frozen puff pastry, thawed according to package instructions

All-purpose flour, for dusting

½ cup finely shredded aged cheddar cheese

1 (14-ounce) package Lit'l Smokies smoked sausages

1 large egg

¼ cup grated Parmesan cheese

Classic pigs in a blanket are the ultimate party food, but they're a little… old-fashioned. So I came up with a Two Peas version that still reminds you of your favorite bite, but with a more polished (and delicious) twist. First, I use puff pastry, which makes the piglets elegant enough to serve at a dressed-up event, but still perfectly suited for a backyard barbecue or kid's birthday party. But the super-special touch is tucking aged cheddar into the piggies, then topping them with Parmesan so they have a cheesy, buttery blanket with an extra melty surprise inside. I always serve ours with fry sauce, a Utah specialty that's traditionally a mixture of mayo and ketchup, but I add a little barbecue sauce for a tangy pop of flavor. (Though classic ketchup and mustard are also perfect condiments!)

1 Make the fry sauce: In a small bowl, whisk together the mayonnaise, ketchup, and barbecue sauce until thoroughly combined. Set aside.

2 Make the piglets: Preheat the oven to 400°F. Line a large baking sheet with a silicone baking mat or parchment paper. Set aside.

3 Unfold both sheets of puff pastry on a lightly floured surface. Use a pizza cutter or a sharp knife to cut each piece in half along the folds of the pastry. Cut each section of dough into 1-inch strips.

4 Sprinkle ½ teaspoon cheddar over each strip. Place a sausage on one end of one strip and roll up. Dip your index finger in water and pinch the seam where the end meets the roll. Place the assembled piglet seam side down on the prepared baking sheet. Repeat with the remaining sausages and pastry strips.

5 In a small bowl or ramekin, beat the egg with 1 tablespoon water. Using a pastry brush, lightly brush the piglets with the egg wash. Discard any unused egg wash.

6 Sprinkle the piglets evenly with Parmesan. Bake for 18 to 20 minutes, until the piglets are golden brown and the puff pastry is nice and puffed. Let the piglets cool on the baking sheet for 5 minutes. Serve warm with the fry sauce.

caprese garlic bread

prep: **5 MINUTES** | bake: **12 TO 15 MINUTES** | total: **20 MINUTES** | serves 8

• •

1 loaf ciabatta or French bread, cut in half horizontally

4 tablespoons salted butter, at room temperature

3 garlic cloves, minced

12 ounces fresh mozzarella cheese, sliced

2 medium tomatoes, sliced

Kosher salt and freshly ground black pepper

⅓ cup chopped fresh basil

½ cup store-bought balsamic glaze (see Note)

Garlic bread has always been a staple in our home. Growing up, it was on the table any time my dad made something Italian. Lasagna, spaghetti, ravioli—without fail, there was the garlic bread on the side. Carb overload? Sure. But who could complain about toasty, crusty bread slathered in garlic and butter? Now it ends up on our table just as often, but with an updated twist inspired by summertime, when our garden is bursting with tomatoes and basil. I layer ciabatta with a butter-garlic mix and then sliced mozzarella that gets melty in the oven. Then I add slices of fresh tomatoes, basil confetti, and a drizzle of a syrupy balsamic glaze. It's perfect as a quick hot-weather appetizer or side, especially for dinner parties when you want to make something super simple that looks impressively sophisticated.

1 Preheat the oven to 400°F.

2 Place both halves of the ciabatta on a large baking sheet with the cut side up.

3 In a small bowl, combine the butter and garlic and spread it evenly over the bread. Lay the mozzarella cheese slices on top, making sure the cheese covers the bread completely. Bake the bread for 12 to 15 minutes, until the cheese has melted.

4 Top the cheesy bread with tomato slices and season with salt and pepper to taste. Sprinkle with the fresh basil and lightly drizzle with the balsamic glaze. Cut into slices and serve while hot.

NOTE: *I call for using store-bought balsamic glaze here, but feel free to make your own! Simply simmer ½ cup balsamic vinegar in a small pot over low heat until the vinegar is thick and syrupy, 5 to 7 minutes. Store in the refrigerator for up to 3 weeks.*

rainbow vegetable summer rolls
with peanut dipping sauce

prep: **30 MINUTES** | total: **30 MINUTES** | makes **12 SUMMER ROLLS**

• •

PEANUT DIPPING SAUCE

½ cup creamy peanut butter

2 tablespoons hoisin sauce

2 tablespoons rice wine vinegar

1 tablespoon reduced-sodium soy
  sauce or tamari soy sauce

2 teaspoons Sriracha

1 garlic clove, minced

½ teaspoon grated fresh ginger

⅓ cup hot water

2 tablespoons chopped peanuts,
  for garnish

SUMMER ROLLS

12 (8-inch) rice paper wrappers
  (see Notes)

1 head butter lettuce, washed and
  leaves separated

6 ounces dry vermicelli rice
  noodles, cooked according to
  package instructions

1 red bell pepper, cored, seeded,
  and thinly sliced

1 yellow bell pepper, cored,
  seeded, and thinly sliced

1 large carrot, thinly sliced

1 cup thinly sliced purple cabbage

2 Persian cucumbers *or* 1 small
  English cucumber, thinly sliced

1 ripe avocado, pitted, peeled, and
  thinly sliced

Handful of fresh mint, basil
  (regular or Thai), and cilantro
  leaves

Summer rolls are probably my favorite appetizer of all time. I don't know if it's because of their super-fresh flavor, the dreamy peanut sauce that they get dunked in, or how pretty they look on a platter with their beautiful, bright colors. That's why they're almost always on our party menus. Sometimes they're ready and waiting for our guests, and sometimes I arrange all the ingredients in pretty dishes and bowls so that when people arrive, they can assemble their own. (One less thing for me to do while finishing getting the meal ready!)

1 Make the dipping sauce: In a medium bowl, stir together the peanut butter, hoisin, vinegar, soy sauce, Sriracha, garlic, and ginger. Whisk in the hot water until the sauce is smooth. If the sauce is too thick, you can add a little more water until you reach your desired consistency—it should be thick enough for good dipping but not gloppy. Pour the sauce into a serving bowl and garnish with the chopped peanuts. Set aside until ready to serve.

2 Assemble the summer rolls: Fill a wide, shallow bowl with warm water. Dip one rice paper wrapper in the water and let it soften for 10 to 15 seconds, until it's just barely pliable. If the wrapper gets too soggy it will rip. It will continue to soften as you add the other ingredients. Carefully remove the paper from the water and lay it flat on a damp, lint-free dishtowel.

3 Lay one piece of lettuce over the bottom third of the rice paper. Top with about 2 tablespoons rice noodles and equal amounts of peppers, carrot, cabbage, cucumber, and avocado. Finish with a sprinkling of fresh herbs.

4 Pick up the end of the rice paper closest to the filling and tightly fold it over the veggies. Fold in the sides, like you are making a burrito, then roll tightly. The paper will stick to itself, holding everything inside. Repeat with the remaining ingredients to make 12 summer rolls.

5 Arrange the summer rolls seam side down on a platter and serve with the peanut dipping sauce.

NOTES: *These would also be delicious with tofu or shrimp. You can find rice paper wrappers and rice noodles in the Asian section of most grocery stores, or at Asian markets.*

vegetable platter
with avocado green goddess dip
and greek yogurt ranch dip

•• •

As much as I love a good cheese board (and I *love* a good cheese board), my heart also belongs to a beautiful veggie platter. Not only are the colorful vegetables instant decoration, but they also give me an opportunity to showcase my two favorite dips: The homemade ranch is so much tastier than store-bought, and the green goddess is pretty much the most delicious, versatile spread that is just as good slathered on sandwiches or even grilled meats or fish as it is dolloped on veggies. They both feature my favorite secret weapon for getting in super-creamy tanginess without a lot of added fat—Greek yogurt—and pretty much have a permanent spot in our fridge for healthy snacking. They're the ultimate secret weapon in getting the boys to eat their veggies!

The really good news about making a great vegetable platter is that the vegetables do a lot of the hard work. When you buy nice, fresh veggies the day before or day of a party, they'll look just as vibrant as they taste. All you need is an assortment of colors to make the platter really pop. Some of my favorite veg to include are carrots, cucumbers, celery, grape or cherry tomatoes, broccoli, cauliflower, green beans, mini bell peppers, purple cauliflower, radishes, endive (leaves separated), and jicama. I usually plan on ½ to 1 cup vegetables per person. And while some people prefer to blanch some of the vegetables first (usually broccoli, cauliflower, snow peas, and zucchini), raw veggies don't bother me!

Use a large platter or board to display the vegetables. You want it to look full and bountiful, even if that means putting out more than you know people will eat. If you have leftovers, that's just more veggies and dip for you to snack on during the week (or repurpose in other dishes)! For the dips, choose small bowls that can be placed on your platter or board amongst the vegetables. I usually like to include at least two or three bowls of dip—including the green goddess and ranch dips below, along with Creamy Hummus (page 90)—so people aren't fighting over the dips.

recipe continues

Avocado Green Goddess Dip

prep: **10 MINUTES**
total: **10 MINUTES**
makes **ABOUT 2 CUPS**

1 cup mashed avocado (1 large
   avocado or 2 small)

1 cup plain Greek yogurt

¼ cup chopped fresh basil

¼ cup chopped fresh parsley

2 tablespoons fresh lemon juice
   (1 large lemon)

1 tablespoon chopped fresh chives

½ teaspoon kosher salt

¼ teaspoon freshly ground black
   pepper

1 teaspoon Sriracha (optional)

In a blender, combine all of the ingredients and blend for 30 seconds on high. Turn off the blender and scrape down the sides with a spatula. Blend again until the dip is smooth. If you want a thinner dip, add 1 to 2 tablespoons water. Transfer to a serving bowl and serve with assorted vegetables, or store in the fridge for up to 2 days.

Greek Yogurt Ranch Dip

prep: **10 MINUTES**
total: **10 MINUTES**
makes **ABOUT 1 CUP**

1 cup plain Greek yogurt

1 teaspoon fresh lemon juice

2 teaspoons chopped fresh chives,
   plus more for garnish

¾ teaspoon dried dill

¾ teaspoon garlic powder

½ teaspoon onion powder

¼ teaspoon dried parsley

Kosher salt and freshly ground black
   pepper

In a medium bowl, stir together the yogurt, lemon juice, chives, dill, garlic powder, onion powder, and parsley. Season with salt and pepper to taste. Garnish with additional chives, if desired. Serve with assorted vegetables, or store in the fridge for up to 5 days.

four-cheese spinach and artichoke dip

prep: **15 MINUTES** | bake: **20 TO 25 MINUTES** | total: **40 MINUTES** | serves **8 TO 10**

● ●

Nonstick cooking spray

1 (8-ounce) package cream cheese, at room temperature

½ cup plain Greek yogurt

1 (10-ounce) package frozen spinach, thawed and drained well

1 (14-ounce) can quartered artichoke hearts, drained and chopped

1 cup shredded fontina cheese

1 cup shredded mozzarella cheese

1 cup grated Parmesan cheese

¼ cup chopped fresh basil

Pinch of crushed red pepper flakes

Kosher salt and freshly ground black pepper

1 baguette, sliced and toasted, for serving

Spinach artichoke dip is a classic, and always the most popular dip at any party, but I'm normally not the biggest fan because I don't like mayo. I was tired of feeling left out (who doesn't want to scoop into a big bowl of dip?!), so I came up with this version which is delightfully mayo-free but no less creamy or decadent. Instead, I use four, that's right *four*, cheeses: cream cheese, fontina, mozzarella, and Parmesan. Sure enough, whenever there's a bowl of this dip set out, that's the spot at the party to be. I usually put out toasted baguette slices, but you could also offer crackers, pita chips, tortilla chips, or sliced veggies.

1 Preheat the oven to 375°F. Grease a 10-inch skillet or 8-inch square baking dish with nonstick cooking spray and set aside.

2 In the bowl of a stand mixer fitted with the paddle attachment, beat the cream cheese until smooth. Add the yogurt and once again beat until smooth. Add the spinach, artichoke hearts, ¾ cup of the fontina, ¾ cup of the mozzarella, and ½ cup of the Parmesan, along with the basil and pepper flakes. Mix until combined and season with a sprinkle of salt and pepper to taste.

3 Pour the mixture into the prepared pan and spread into an even layer. Top with the remaining fontina, mozzarella, and Parmesan. Bake for 20 to 25 minutes, until the cheese is melted, bubbly, and golden brown. Serve warm with the toasted baguette slices.

pear, brie, and rosemary flatbreads

prep: **5 MINUTES** | bake: **7 TO 10 MINUTES** | total: **15 MINUTES** |
serves **8 AS AN APPETIZER OR 2 AS A MEAL**

● ●

2 naan flatbreads

2 teaspoons extra-virgin olive oil

8 ounces Brie cheese, rind
removed and thinly sliced

2 medium pears (any type will
work), cored and thinly sliced

1 teaspoon chopped fresh
rosemary

Honey

Kosher salt and freshly ground
black pepper

Oh man, you guys are going to *love* this appetizer. It's beyond easy but feels super gourmet. When I'm feeling lazy but still want to impress our guests, this is the recipe I reach for. The biggest time-saver is using store-bought flatbread called *naan,* which is a pillowy, doughy Indian bread that you can find fresh in just about any grocery store (my favorite brand is Stonefire). They get layered with Brie, pears, and rosemary and baked until the Brie is melted and gooey and the pears are soft and slightly caramelized. The finishing touch is a drizzle of honey, which really puts this app over the top. This also doubles as a great meal for one or two. If I'm ever home alone, it's my go-to with a side of chick flicks. No boys allowed!

1   Preheat the oven to 400°F.

2   Place the flatbreads in a single layer on a large baking sheet, or two if they don't fit. Brush lightly with the olive oil and top evenly with the Brie, pears, and rosemary.

3   Bake for 7 to 10 minutes, until the pears have softened and the cheese has melted. Drizzle the flatbreads with 1 tablespoon honey (or more, if desired) and season with a pinch of salt and a couple grinds of pepper. Cut the flatbreads into pieces and serve warm.

everything-bagel cheese straws

prep: **20 MINUTES** | cook: **20 MINUTES** | total: **40 MINUTES** | makes **18 TO 20 CHEESE STRAWS**

⬤⬤

EVERYTHING-BAGEL SEASONING

2 tablespoons poppy seeds

1 tablespoon white sesame seeds

1 tablespoon black sesame seeds

1 tablespoon plus 1 teaspoon dried minced garlic

1 tablespoon plus 1 teaspoon dried minced onion

1 teaspoon kosher salt

CHEESE STRAWS

All-purpose flour, for dusting

2 sheets (one 17-ounce package) frozen puff pastry, thawed according to package instructions

1 large egg

1 cup finely grated Asiago cheese

One of my favorite indulgences is an everything bagel. Since I don't want to eat a bagel every day (well, I want to, but I probably shouldn't!), I've figured out how to make my own everything-bagel seasoning and then add it to just about anything for a little extra kick, whether it's avocado toast, eggs, vegetables, popcorn, or chicken. However, if you're in a pinch, store-bought seasoning works too.

For a special treat, I sprinkle it over these Asiago cheese straws, which are the perfect party food. You can make them in advance and store them in the fridge until they're ready to bake (since they're best enjoyed the day they're made). The layers puff up in the oven so you end up with a flaky, buttery, crispy treat with great cheesy flavor—like an Asiago bagel, Josh's favorite.

1 Make the everything seasoning: In a small bowl, combine all the seasoning ingredients. Stir until combined and set aside.

2 Make the cheese straws: Preheat the oven to 375°F. Line two large baking sheets with parchment paper or silicone baking mats and set aside.

3 Lightly flour a clean counter or table. Roll out each sheet of puff pastry to a 10 × 12-inch rectangle.

4 In a small bowl, beat the egg with 1 tablespoon water. Using a pastry brush, gently brush the surface of the pastry with the egg mixture. Sprinkle each sheet evenly with the cheese, about ½ cup per sheet, and everything-bagel seasoning, about 1 tablespoon per sheet.

5 With a rolling pin, lightly press the cheese and seasonings into the puff pastry. Using a sharp knife, pastry cutter, or pizza cutter, cut each sheet into about 10 long, 1-inch-wide strips.

6 Transfer each strip to the prepared baking sheets, placing them 1 inch apart and twisting the ends in opposite directions to give the straws a spiraled look. If the dough gets too warm and sticky, you can put one tray in the refrigerator while you are twisting.

7 Bake the straws for 15 minutes, until lightly browned and puffed. Turn each straw over and bake for an additional 5 minutes, until puffed, crispy, and dry to the touch. Remove from the oven and cool for 5 minutes. Serve the day they're made.

cauliflower-quinoa fritters with romesco sauce

prep: **20 MINUTES** | cook: **20 MINUTES** | total: **40 MINUTES** | serves **6 TO 8**

ROMESCO SAUCE

½ cup whole unsalted almonds

1 (12-ounce) jar roasted red peppers, drained

1 slice whole-wheat bread, or your favorite bread

¼ cup fresh parsley leaves

3 garlic cloves, minced

1 tablespoon tomato paste

1 tablespoon red wine vinegar

½ teaspoon smoked paprika

½ teaspoon kosher salt, plus more to taste

¼ teaspoon crushed red pepper flakes

½ cup extra-virgin olive oil

FRITTERS

1 medium head cauliflower, cored and cut into large pieces

2 cups cooked quinoa

1 cup bread crumbs

½ cup crumbled feta cheese

2 large eggs, beaten

3 scallions (white and green parts), sliced

Grated zest of 1 lemon

3 garlic cloves, minced

1 teaspoon kosher salt

1 teaspoon freshly ground black pepper

¼ cup extra-virgin olive oil, plus more if needed, for shallow frying

I decided to give this bar-and-grill staple a healthy-ish makeover by using cauliflower and quinoa in the fritters and quickly crisping them up in olive oil instead of deep-frying them. They're just as salty, creamy, and crispy as your favorite restaurant appetizer, and yet better for you. And the Romesco—a Spanish-inspired roasted red pepper sauce—is smoky and creamy. (And would also be delicious served with pita bread, chips, or veggies, and even fish, chicken, or steak.)

These fritters are perfect as a starter for a gathering, or even served for lunch on top of a simple green salad. I keep a bag in the freezer for any time a party pops up at our house, and also for easy dinners, especially because the boys can't get enough of them.

1   Make the Romesco sauce: In a food processor or blender, combine the almonds, red peppers, bread, parsley, garlic, tomato paste, vinegar, paprika, salt, and pepper flakes. Blend until smooth, about 1 minute. With the machine running, slowly stream in the olive oil until the sauce is smooth. You may need to stop and scrape down the sides of the bowl with a spatula and blend again. Taste and season with additional salt, if necessary. Set aside.

2   Make the fritters: In a food processor, pulse the cauliflower until it is the size of couscous.

3   In a large bowl, combine the cauliflower, quinoa, bread crumbs, feta, eggs, scallions, lemon zest, garlic, salt, and pepper. Stir until the mixture is well combined and moistened.

4   Form the mixture into ½-inch-thick patties, about 2 inches wide. Heat the olive oil in a large skillet over medium-high heat. Add the fritters in batches and fry, turning once, for 10 minutes, until crispy, adding more olive oil to the pan if necessary. Transfer the fritters to a large paper towel-lined plate and cover with aluminum foil while you finish cooking all of the fritters.

5   Serve the warm fritters with the Romesco sauce, either as a dip or dolloped over the top.

6   You could also let the fritters cool to room temperature and store in the fridge for up to 3 days, or in the freezer for up to 1 month. Reheat in the microwave, in a skillet with a little olive oil, or in an air fryer before serving.

creamy hummus with baked pita chips

prep: **15 MINUTES** | bake: **12 TO 15 MINUTES** | total: **30 MINUTES** | serves **6 TO 8**

HUMMUS

2 (15-ounce) cans chickpeas, drained and rinsed

½ cup tahini

¼ cup plus 1 tablespoon fresh lemon juice (3 large lemons)

2 tablespoons extra-virgin olive oil, plus more for serving

4 garlic cloves, minced

1¼ teaspoons kosher salt

Sprinkle of paprika, for serving

PITA CHIPS

½ teaspoon kosher salt

¼ teaspoon paprika

¼ teaspoon garlic powder

3 (5-inch) pitas

1 tablespoon extra-virgin olive oil

Listen, I know how easy it is to buy a tub of hummus at the store and have an instant appetizer for company. But you just can't beat homemade! This hummus is *so* much creamier and smoother than store-bought, and I promise (pinky swear!) that it takes no time to make. And that's a good thing because I like to always have a batch in the fridge for putting out as a dip with sliced veggies, or to spread on crackers, or to slather on sandwiches for lunch. Or I put it to work on Greek Salad Pita Pizzas (page 158). My favorite way to serve it up for company is with homemade pita chips. You don't have to make the pita bread from scratch, but by toasting up wedges yourself with a sprinkle of paprika and garlic powder, you end up with the most delicious, flavorful crisps.

1 Make the hummus: Roll the chickpeas on a clean towel to remove the outer skins. (This helps make the hummus extra-smooth.)

2 In a food processor, combine the chickpeas, tahini, lemon juice, olive oil, garlic, and salt. Puree until smooth. With the food processor running, slowly drizzle in ¼ cup water. Continue processing until the hummus is thick and creamy. Makes about 3 cups. You can store the hummus in the fridge for up to 5 days.

3 Make the pita chips: Preheat the oven to 400°F.

4 In a small bowl, combine the salt, paprika, and garlic powder.

5 Using a pastry brush, brush the pita bread with olive oil on both sides. Stack the pitas and cut them into triangles, creating 8 triangles per pita.

6 Arrange the pita wedges in a single layer on a large baking sheet. Sprinkle the wedges on both sides with the salt mixture. Bake until the pita chips are golden brown and crispy, 12 to 15 minutes. Cool the chips to room temperature. These can be stored in an airtight container at room temperature for up to 5 days.

7 To serve, place the hummus in a bowl or on a platter and top with a drizzle with olive oil and a sprinkle of paprika. Serve with the baked pita chips.

Topping Ideas

You can add all kinds of toppings to your hummus to make it even more dressed up for a party. Here are some of my favorites:

- Toasted pine nuts, chopped fresh parsley, squeeze of fresh lemon juice

- Chopped cucumber, fresh dill, feta cheese

- Chickpeas, za'atar, a drizzle of olive oil

- Pepitas and a sprinkling of smoked paprika

- Sun-dried tomatoes and chopped fresh basil

- Chopped cucumber, tomatoes, Kalamata olives, feta, fresh parsley

- Chopped roasted red peppers

- Pomegranate arils

- Everything-Bagel Seasoning (page 87 or store-bought)

- Spinach-Basil Pesto (page 186 or store-bought pesto)

- Chopped marinated artichokes

- Olive tapenade

- Roasted garlic

- Roasted chickpeas

go-to guacamole

prep: **10 MINUTES** | total: **10 MINUTES** | serves **4 TO 6**

• •

3 ripe Hass avocados (see page 95)

¼ cup diced red onion

1 small jalapeño, seeded and minced

¼ cup chopped fresh cilantro

Juice of 1 large lime

¾ teaspoon kosher salt

¼ teaspoon freshly ground black pepper

Guacamole is one of my all-time favorite foods. Besides cookies, it's proba-bly what I make the most. I aim to make a batch at least once a week so we can all munch on chips and dip on a lazy afternoon. I'll also whip some up to go along with tacos, burrito bowls, quesadillas, enchiladas, and even salads.

This recipe makes the hands-down best guac I've ever had (includ-ing in restaurants). But I also like to get creative: I'll add fun ingredients like diced mango, roasted corn, chipotle peppers, grated cheese, pistachios, or watermelon.

Cut the avocados in half lengthwise. Remove the pits and use a spoon to scoop the avocado flesh into a medium bowl. Discard the skins. Add the onion, jalapeño, cilantro, and lime juice. Mash with a fork to your desired consistency. Season with the salt and pepper.

easy blender salsa

prep: **5 MINUTES** | total: **5 MINUTES** | makes **ABOUT 6 CUPS**

• •

2 (10-ounce) cans Ro*Tel diced tomatoes with green chilies with juices

1 (15-ounce) can diced tomatoes, slightly drained

1 garlic clove, minced

¾ cup packed fresh cilantro

½ cup chopped white onion

Juice of 1 large lime

1 chipotle pepper in adobe sauce (see Note) or 1 small jalapeño, seeded and chopped

¼ teaspoon ground cumin

½ teaspoon kosher salt

Freshly ground black pepper

When I say easy, I mean *easy*. All you need to do is throw all the ingredients in the blender and you'll have salsa that's every bit as good as at your favorite Mexican restaurant—and *way* better than anything you can buy at the store (which, let's be honest, is never as fresh or tasty as you want it to be). Our tradition is to blend up a batch on Sundays after church so we can munch on chips while we watch football, and then we have leftovers for the week to spoon on quesadillas, tacos, and even eggs. Don't worry about this recipe making a lot of salsa—it will keep in the fridge for up to 10 days—but you'll be surprised at how quickly it goes!

In a blender or food processor, combine the Ro*Tel tomatoes, diced tomatoes, garlic, cilantro, onion, lime juice, chipotle in adobo sauce, cumin, salt, and pepper to taste. Blend until smooth. Season with additional salt, if desired.

NOTE: *We use chipotle peppers in adobo sauce a lot in our cooking because we love the mild spice and deep, smoky flavor of the sauce. Since this recipe only calls for one pepper, for mild salsa (or more, depending on how spicy you like your food), you can freeze any remaining peppers and sauce. Just remove them from the can and transfer to a freezer bag or freezer-safe container. For this recipe, you could also use a chopped jalapeño.*

How to Tell If Your Avocados Are Ripe

One of the most important tips I have for making the best guacamole possible is using perfectly ripe (but not overripe!) avocados. Here's a mini avocado ripeness guide:

- The skin of a ripe avocado will be dark green to purplish brown.

- Peel back the small stem or cap at the top of the avocado—if it comes off easily and is green underneath, the avocado is ripe and ready to eat. If the stem doesn't come off, it isn't ripe yet, and if it's brown underneath, it's overripe.

- Press down on the avocado with your thumb. A ripe one will have a little give instead of feeling rock solid. If your thumbprint stays indented, it's overripe.

Other tips:

- **You can ripen hard avocados at home:** Place them in a brown paper bag with bananas and close the bag. Store at room temperature for about 2 days, when the avocados should be ripe.

- If your avocados are ripening too quickly, store them in the refrigerator.

- To keep avocados from browning once they've been sliced, sprinkle with lime or lemon juice. You could also press plastic wrap against a cut avocado (or against the surface of guacamole) to prevent oxygen exposure, which is what causes browning.

More Than Just Lettuce

SALADS

• •

Before we get into this chapter, let's be clear about one thing: While some salads can be boring, these are definitely *not* those salads! We are big salad eaters and so we are always challenging ourselves to come up with new flavor and texture combinations that go well beyond a sad pile of greens. Especially as a vegetarian, I think salads can be the ultimate blank canvas for just about anything salty, sweet, crunchy, or creamy with delicious dressings that will give anything store-bought a run for its money, such as Maple-Mustard Vinaigrette, Lemon-Herb Dressing, and Basil Vinaigrette. And salads don't even have to include lettuce in the first place, especially in the case of the Chickpea, Avocado, and Feta Salad or our Creamy Cucumber Salad.

Think of these salads any time you need to pack a lunch for work, want to make a quick bite in advance for grabbing from the fridge, would like a portable main dish for a picnic, or are put on salad duty for a dinner party or potluck. You never want to be the person showing up with a bag of iceberg lettuce from the store—have your salad be the talk of the town! I guarantee that if you go with any salad in this chapter, at least one person will ask you for the recipe.

everyday butter lettuce salad

prep: **10 MINUTES** | total: **10 MINUTES** | serves **4**

●●

LEMON VINAIGRETTE

¼ cup extra-virgin olive oil

2 tablespoons fresh lemon juice
(1 large lemon)

1 tablespoon golden balsamic
vinegar or Champagne vinegar

1 teaspoon honey

1 garlic clove, minced

Kosher salt and freshly ground
black pepper

BUTTER LETTUCE SALAD

8 cups chopped butter lettuce
(2 large heads)

2 ripe avocados, pitted, peeled,
and sliced

⅓ cup grated Parmesan cheese

¼ cup sliced almonds

Everyone should have a recipe for a great basic salad in their back pocket, whether you need something light and fresh to go alongside a dinner or lunch entrée or a simple foundation for layering in other ingredients. With its bright lemon vinaigrette, crunchy almonds, creamy avocado, and a sprinkle of salty Parmesan, this salad is simple and versatile—but *not* boring. You can make it into a meal by adding heartier ingredients like chicken, shrimp, or canned beans. And I highly recommend taking a few minutes to whisk together the lemon vinaigrette to stash in the fridge because it is more delicious (and nutritious) than anything you can buy at the store, plus it pairs well with just about everything. You could even drizzle it over a plate of steamed, sautéed, roasted, or grilled veggies and call it a dish.

1 Make the vinaigrette: In a small bowl, whisk together the olive oil, lemon juice, vinegar, honey, and garlic. You could also combine all of the ingredients in a jar, cover with a lid, and shake. Season with salt and pepper to taste.

2 Assemble the salad: In a large bowl, combine the lettuce, avocado slices, Parmesan, and almonds. Drizzle the vinaigrette over the salad and toss. Serve immediately.

kale and wild rice salad
with maple-mustard vinaigrette

prep: **15 MINUTES** | total: **15 MINUTES** | serves **4**

MAPLE-MUSTARD VINAIGRETTE

¼ cup extra-virgin olive oil

2 tablespoons balsamic vinegar

1 tablespoon fresh lemon juice

1 teaspoon pure maple syrup

1 teaspoon Dijon mustard

Kosher salt and freshly ground
 black pepper

SALAD

1 large bunch lacinato or dinosaur
 kale, stemmed and chopped

1 teaspoon extra-virgin olive oil

1 tablespoon fresh lemon juice

Pinch of kosher salt

1 cup cooked wild or brown rice

1 large apple, cored and chopped
 (we like Honeycrisp, but Fuji or
 Gala will also work)

1 medium ripe avocado, pitted,
 peeled, and chopped

¼ cup dried cranberries

¼ cup toasted slivered almonds

3 ounces goat cheese, crumbled,
 or feta

This salad is inspired by my favorite menu item at Cubby's, a kid-friendly restaurant here in Utah that I love because they always have something the boys want to eat, and I can get something hearty yet vegetarian—plus a side of their incredible sweet potato fries (salad + fries = balance). The secret to recreating the salad at home is to start by massaging the kale, breaking down all the fibers with your hands so that it gets nice and tender and the flavor mellows out. Then you load it up with sweet, salty, crunchy, creamy deliciousness. And while it's a salad best eaten the day it's made, you could store it in the fridge overnight if you want to pack up something super filling to take to work.

1 Make the vinaigrette: In a small bowl or jar, combine the olive oil, vinegar, lemon juice, maple syrup, and mustard. Whisk or shake until smooth. Season with salt and pepper to taste.

2 Assemble the salad: In a large bowl, combine the kale, olive oil, lemon juice, and salt. Massage the kale with your hands until the leaves soften, about 2 minutes. Add the rice, apple, avocado, dried cranberries, almonds, and goat cheese. Gently toss. Drizzle the vinaigrette over the salad, toss, and serve.

go green quinoa salad

prep: **20 MINUTES** | cook: **20 MINUTES** | total: **40 MINUTES** | serves **4 TO 6**

1 cup white quinoa

2 cups vegetable broth or water

Kosher salt and freshly ground black pepper

2 cups chopped spinach leaves

1 large English cucumber, chopped

1 cup halved cherry or grape tomatoes

1 large ripe avocado, pitted, peeled, and chopped

2 scallions (white and green parts), sliced

½ cup shelled pistachios, chopped (optional)

1 cup Basil Vinaigrette (recipe follows)

This grain salad makes it into my lunch routine almost every single week—and for good reason: I love all things green! Spinach, cucumber, scallions, avocado, and, of course, a vividly verdant basil vinaigrette. It's bright, fresh, and an excellent excuse to eat more cookies—life's about balance, my friends! And if you prep ahead some cooked quinoa (something that takes 20 minutes, tops), then this salad is a breeze to throw together. Top it all off with some pistachios (also green!) for crunch.

1   Rinse the quinoa under cold water in a fine-mesh strainer. Drain well. In a medium saucepan, combine the quinoa with the broth or water (the broth has a touch more flavor, but water is fine) and a pinch of salt. Bring to a boil, reduce the heat to low, and cover. Cook for 15 minutes. Remove the pot from the heat and let the quinoa stand for 5 minutes, covered. Fluff the quinoa with a fork and let it continue to cool, uncovered, to room temperature. You can do this in the fridge to speed up the process.

2   In a large bowl, combine the cooked quinoa, spinach, cucumber, tomatoes, avocado, scallions, and pistachios (if using). Season with salt and pepper to taste. Drizzle the basil vinaigrette over the salad and toss to combine. Serve immediately.

Basil Vinaigrette

prep: **10 MINUTES**
total: **10 MINUTES**
makes **1 CUP**

2 cups packed fresh basil leaves

1 garlic clove, minced

2 tablespoons minced shallot (about 1 small shallot)

½ cup extra-virgin olive oil

2 tablespoons white balsamic vinegar or red wine vinegar

2 teaspoons fresh lemon juice

1 teaspoon kosher salt

Freshly ground black pepper

Combine the basil, garlic, shallot, olive oil, vinegar, lemon juice, and salt in a blender or food processor and blend until smooth. Taste and season with additional salt and some pepper, if necessary. The vinaigrette can be stored in the fridge for up to 5 days.

grilled shrimp salad
with pineapple and cilantro vinaigrette

prep: **20 MINUTES** (30, IF SOAKING SKEWERS) | cook: **10 MINUTES** | total: **30 MINUTES** | serves **4 TO 6**

SHRIMP AND MARINADE

1 pound large shrimp, peeled and deveined

3 tablespoons extra-virgin olive oil

Juice of 1 large lime

2 garlic cloves, minced

Kosher salt and freshly ground black pepper

CILANTRO VINAIGRETTE

2 cups packed fresh cilantro leaves

1 small shallot, minced

½ cup extra-virgin olive oil

1 large garlic clove, minced

1 tablespoon red wine vinegar

1 tablespoon fresh lime juice

¾ teaspoon kosher salt

¼ teaspoon freshly ground black pepper

SALAD

6 cups chopped romaine lettuce

1½ cups chopped fresh pineapple

1 hothouse cucumber, chopped

1 cup grape tomatoes, halved

½ red onion, thinly sliced

2 ripe avocados, pitted, peeled, and sliced

Fresh cilantro, for garnish

Thanks to its light, bright flavors and gorgeously colorful ingredients, this is the ultimate salad for summer dinner parties. When we bring it out on a big platter, we always hear a huge "Wow!" from our guests, and the compliments keep coming long after the last bite is gone. In addition to the smoky-sweet combination of grilled shrimp and pineapple, the star of the show is the cilantro vinaigrette, which has a beautiful green color and tons of fresh-herb flavor. It's delicious with just about any other salad, in addition to burrito bowls and tacos, or drizzled over grilled chicken, fish, or veggies, which is why I love keeping a batch in the fridge pretty much at all times.

1   If using wooden skewers, soak them in water for 30 minutes before grilling. This will keep them from burning.

2   Marinate the shrimp: First, pat the shrimp with a paper towel until dry. In a large bowl, combine the shrimp, olive oil, lime juice, and garlic. Season with a sprinkling of salt and pepper. Toss to coat and set aside so the shrimp can marinate while you make the vinaigrette.

3   Make the vinaigrette: In a blender or food processor, combine the cilantro, shallot, olive oil, garlic, vinegar, lime juice, salt, and pepper. Blend until smooth. Set aside or store in the fridge for up to 3 days.

4   Grill the shrimp: Thread the shrimp on skewers. Heat a grill or grill pan over medium heat. Add the skewered shrimp and cook until opaque, 2 to 3 minutes per side. If you are using a grill pan inside, you will need to cook the shrimp in batches to avoid overcrowding your pan.

5   Assemble the salad: Arrange the lettuce on a large platter and top with the shrimp, pineapple, cucumber, tomatoes, onion, and avocado. Drizzle with the vinaigrette and garnish with the cilantro.

chickpea, avocado, and feta salad

prep: **10 MINUTES** | total: **10 MINUTES** | serves **4**

• •

1 (15-ounce) can chickpeas, drained and rinsed

2 medium ripe avocados, pitted, peeled, and chopped

⅓ cup chopped fresh cilantro

2 tablespoons chopped scallion (white and green parts)

⅓ cup crumbled feta cheese

Juice of 1 lime

Extra-virgin olive oil

Kosher salt and freshly ground black pepper

Here at Two Peas it's a pretty safe bet that if we're eating a lot of something at home, there's going to be a lot of it on the website. Cookies are certainly one example, and salads are another. Especially come January, when we're winding down from our oven being on 24/7 for all manner of cakes, pies, casseroles, and other decadent treats, our meals feature many more salads than usual. This salad has quickly risen through the ranks as one of our favorite lunches because it takes all of 10 minutes to throw together, is light enough to make you feel like you're getting something healthy, but is hearty and creamy enough to satisfy that mid-day craving for something from the drive-thru. It's great heaped over a bed of greens, stuffed into pita bread, scooped up with crackers or pita chips, or eaten straight from the mixing bowl.

In a medium bowl, combine the chickpeas, avocado, cilantro, scallion, feta, and lime juice. Stir until mixed well. Drizzle with olive oil, season with salt and pepper to taste, and serve.

baby potato salad
with bacon and simple lemon-herb dressing

prep: **15 MINUTES** | cook: **30 MINUTES** | total: **45 MINUTES** | serves **6 TO 8**

• •

LEMON-HERB DRESSING

⅓ cup extra-virgin olive oil

Grated zest of 1 small lemon

¼ cup fresh lemon juice (2 to 3 lemons)

1 large garlic clove, minced

⅓ cup fresh basil leaves, chopped

2 tablespoons chopped fresh dill

1 tablespoon honey or brown sugar

Kosher salt and freshly ground black pepper

POTATO SALAD

2 pounds baby Yukon Gold potatoes (see Notes)

Kosher salt

6 slices bacon, cooked and chopped

2 cups grape tomatoes, sliced in half

2 scallions (white and green parts), thinly sliced

3 cups arugula

In my book, no summer barbecue, picnic, or potluck is complete without potato salad. That said, the gloppy mayo-heavy versions with mushy potatoes aren't my idea of a good time. So I came up with a lighter take featuring perfectly tender and bite-sized baby potatoes and a sunny citrus vinaigrette with lots of fresh herbs. Folded in are summer-staple tomatoes, scallions, and arugula, and the winning touch: crispy bacon. I know I have nailed the recipe because, without fail, the bowl is scraped clean after every party.

1   Make the dressing: In a small bowl or jar, whisk or shake together the olive oil, lemon zest, lemon juice, garlic, basil, dill, and honey. Season with salt and pepper to taste.

2   Make the salad: Place the potatoes in a large saucepan, cover with cold water, and add 1 tablespoon salt. Bring to a low boil and cook until the potatoes are tender but not overdone. They are ready when they can be easily pierced with a fork, 20 to 25 minutes. Drain and let cool slightly.

3   When cool enough to handle, cut the potatoes in half or quarters, depending on their size. Place in a large bowl and add the bacon, tomatoes, scallions, and arugula.

4   Pour the dressing over the salad and gently stir to combine. Let the salad sit for at least 10 minutes before serving to absorb the dressing. Serve at room temperature or cold.

NOTES: *You can make this salad with just about any kind of baby potato. I like Yukon Golds, but also will use a colorful medley (red, white, purple) for even more color (and a sort of patriotic look for the Fourth of July!). And you can of course make it vegetarian by omitting the bacon. This salad is great for preparing a few hours ahead; just wait to fold in the arugula until right before serving or it will wilt.*

fruit salad with citrus–poppy seed dressing

prep: **20 MINUTES** | total: **20 MINUTES** | serves **10 TO 12**

• •

CITRUS–POPPY SEED DRESSING

1 teaspoon grated orange zest

3 tablespoons fresh orange juice

1 teaspoon grated lime zest

2 tablespoons fresh lime juice (1 to 2 limes)

2 tablespoons honey

2 tablespoons chopped fresh mint

1 teaspoon poppy seeds

SALAD

1 large pineapple, peeled, cored, and chopped

2 cups blackberries

2 cups strawberries, hulled and sliced

2 cups blueberries

4 kiwi, peeled, halved, and sliced

Fresh mint leaves, for garnish

I love getting assigned salad duty for summer parties and potlucks because it means I can bring this bright update on regular old fruit salad. Believe me, every time this fun dish shows up, so do the rave reviews! There's nothing complicated to it—it's just a mix of fresh fruit—but a citrus–poppy seed dressing and a touch of fresh mint make it feel extra special. Plus, it looks as vibrant on the table as it tastes—like edible decoration.

1 Make the dressing: In a small bowl or jar, combine the orange zest and juice, lime zest and juice, honey, mint, and poppy seeds. Whisk or shake together until the honey is dissolved.

2 Assemble the salad: In a large bowl, combine the pineapple, blackberries, strawberries, blueberries, and kiwi. Drizzle the dressing over the fruit and toss to coat. Garnish with fresh mint and serve.

creamy cucumber salad

prep: **10 MINUTES** | total: **10 MINUTES** | serves **6**

1 cup plain Greek yogurt

½ cup crumbled feta cheese

1 tablespoon fresh lemon juice

1 tablespoon red wine vinegar

2 tablespoons finely chopped fresh dill

2 large English cucumbers, sliced

½ small red onion, thinly sliced

Kosher salt and freshly ground black pepper

I came up with this recipe as a way of putting cucumbers to good use in the summer. Our garden is always overflowing with them, and so is the farmers market. So I thought about the traditional cucumber salads that you find on most cookout tables in the warmer months, which are usually made with sour cream and mayonnaise. I wanted to satisfy the itch for something creamy, but I didn't want to hide all that crunchy, juicy freshness of the cucumbers. So my recipe calls for a combination of tangy Greek yogurt and briny feta cheese, which gives you the same decadent texture but with an extra zip of flavor and none of the heaviness. It's the perfect side dish for just about any meal, whether it's something meaty off the grill or a light lunch.

In a large bowl, combine the yogurt, feta, lemon juice, vinegar, and dill. Stir until combined. Fold in the cucumber slices and red onion and season to taste with salt and black pepper. Serve.

grilled balsamic chicken and peach salad

prep: **45 MINUTES** | cook: **15 MINUTES** | total: **1 HOUR** | serves **4**

● ●

BALSAMIC MARINADE AND DRESSING

⅓ cup balsamic vinegar

⅓ cup extra-virgin olive oil

1½ tablespoons honey

3 garlic cloves, minced

Kosher salt and freshly ground black pepper

CHICKEN AND PEACHES

4 boneless, skinless chicken breasts

Nonstick cooking spray or extra-virgin olive oil

2 large ripe peaches, halved and pitted

SALAD

6 cups mixed greens

6 ounces (about 1¼ cups) blackberries

½ small red onion, thinly sliced

¾ cup crumbled goat or feta cheese

Kosher salt and freshly ground black pepper

When Utah peaches are in season, you better believe that Josh is grilling up this chicken and peach salad nonstop. A balsamic-honey marinade brings out the best flavor of the chicken and smoky caramelized grilled peaches, which are then paired with pops of bright blackberries and a sprinkling of tangy, creamy goat cheese. It's pretty much summer salad perfection. We serve it all up on a big platter at barbecues for our guests to enjoy, and it's always a huge hit. And because you can easily make the salad vegetarian by leaving out the chicken, I also get to indulge.

1 Make the marinade: In a medium bowl, whisk together the vinegar, olive oil, honey, and garlic. Season with salt and pepper to taste.

2 Make the chicken and peaches: Place the chicken in a gallon-sized zip-top bag. Add ½ cup of the marinade and seal the bag. Let the chicken marinate for at least 30 minutes at room temperature, or up to overnight in the refrigerator, turning occasionally. Refrigerate the remaining marinade to use for the peaches and to dress the salad.

3 When ready to cook, remove the chicken from the marinade and discard the marinade.

4 Preheat the grill to medium heat. Coat the grill with nonstick cooking spray or olive oil. Grill the chicken for 5 to 6 minutes per side, until cooked through (a meat thermometer inserted into the thickest part should register 165°F). Allow the chicken to rest for 10 minutes before slicing across the grain (i.e., in the opposite direction of the muscle fibers).

5 Brush the peach halves with some of the reserved marinade. Grill the peaches, cut side down, for 4 to 5 minutes, until they are soft and have nice grill marks. Let the peaches rest for 2 minutes, then slice.

6 Assemble the salad: Arrange the greens on a large platter and top with the sliced chicken and peaches, the blackberries, onion slices, and cheese. Drizzle with the remaining balsamic marinade/dressing and season with a sprinkle of salt and pepper.

SOUPS

S oup is pretty much the ultimate family meal. First, there's the fact that just about everyone loves a warming bowl of soup after a long day or on a chilly afternoon. Second, it's so easy to throw together a pot of something delicious or, better yet, make a pot of something delicious and freeze it for nights when cooking something from scratch is too much of a stretch. All you need is a crusty loaf of bread or a good salad and you have yourself a meal. Third, there are all sorts of ways to dress up a humble pot of soup and turn it into the perfect family or crowd-pleasing dish: homemade croutons, tortilla strips, candied pepitas for crunch; or mini grilled cheeses for dipping and dunking; or garnishes like fresh herbs, dollops of sour cream or crème fraîche, or sprinklings of just about any cheese. Letting everyone do up their own bowl just the way they like it is just as fun as it is delicious.

And soup is great for entertaining too! We love hosting Soup Sundays, when everyone brings over their favorite one-bowl dish. We set out mugs and bowls so everyone can try each offering, along with tons of toppings and garnishes. Then we pack up all the leftovers so everyone can swap. Lunch for the week: done and done!

creamy roasted cauliflower chowder

prep: **10 MINUTES** | cook: **45 MINUTES** | total: **55 MINUTES** | serves **6**

1 large head cauliflower, cored and roughly chopped

3 garlic cloves

1 tablespoon extra-virgin olive oil

Kosher salt and freshly ground black pepper

4 tablespoons unsalted butter

1 medium yellow onion, chopped

2 medium carrots, chopped

2 celery stalks, chopped

1 dried bay leaf

½ teaspoon dried thyme

¼ cup all-purpose flour (you can use gluten-free flour)

3½ cups vegetable broth

1¼ cups milk

½ cup shredded cheddar cheese (we prefer white cheddar)

We get a lot of snow here in Salt Lake City, which is great for two things: ski season and soup days. While I would rather stay inside where it's warm and toasty, Josh loves getting outside when there's been a big snowstorm. He and the boys hit the slopes as often as possible, or just spend the morning building snow forts in the yard. When they come in, they're all ready for a steaming bowl of comfort food—and this chowder always hits the spot. Instead of potatoes, we use roasted cauliflower, which adds deep, caramelized flavor while keeping the soup a little lighter.

1   Preheat the oven to 400°F.

2   Arrange the chopped cauliflower and garlic cloves on a large baking sheet. Drizzle with the olive oil, season with a pinch of salt and pepper, and toss until well coated. Spread out the cauliflower and garlic in a single layer to avoid steaming. Roast for 20 to 25 minutes, stirring once, until the cauliflower is tender. Set aside to cool. When cool enough to handle, remove the garlic from its skin and finely chop.

3   In a large pot, melt the butter over medium-high heat. Add the onion and cook for 2 to 3 minutes, until just beginning to soften. Add the carrots and celery and cook for 5 minutes, stirring occasionally. Stir in the chopped garlic, cauliflower, bay leaf, and dried thyme. Sprinkle the flour over the vegetables and mix to combine. Cook until the flour disappears, about 2 minutes. Pour in the broth, stir, and bring to a simmer. Cook for 10 minutes. Stir in the milk and cheese and continue mixing until the cheese is melted and the chowder is creamy, 2 to 3 minutes. Season with salt and pepper to taste. Discard the bay leaf. Ladle the chowder into bowls and serve warm.

mushroom-farro soup

prep: **10 MINUTES** | cook: **35 MINUTES** | total: **45 MINUTES** | serves **4 TO 6**

1 ounce dried porcini mushrooms

1½ cups boiling water

3 tablespoons unsalted butter

1 yellow onion, chopped

1 large carrot, chopped

1 celery stalk, chopped

4 garlic cloves, minced

1 pound baby bella mushrooms, cleaned (see Notes) and sliced

½ cup white cooking wine or your favorite variety of white wine

6 cups vegetable broth

1 cup uncooked farro (see Notes)

2 teaspoons reduced-sodium soy sauce

2 teaspoons chopped fresh thyme

¼ cup chopped fresh parsley

1¼ teaspoons kosher salt

¼ teaspoon freshly ground black pepper

Nutty, chewy farro is one of my favorite whole grains, and I've found that it's the ideal addition to soups because it doesn't get mushy like rice can. That's why when I wanted to come up with an updated version of mushroom and rice soup, I immediately thought of farro. I especially like pairing farro with mushrooms, which give just about any dish earthy flavor and great meaty texture. The combination is hearty and flavorful—whether or not you're a vegetarian. I regularly reach for this recipe on cold, dreary days and serve it with plenty of Parmesan cheese and crusty bread for sopping up the rich broth.

1   Place the dried porcini in a large bowl with the boiling water. Let them sit for 5 minutes to rehydrate.

2   Meanwhile, melt the butter in a large pot over medium-high heat. Add the onion, carrot, and celery and cook until tender, about 5 minutes. Add the garlic and baby bella mushrooms and cook for 3 minutes, until the mushrooms are tender. Pour in the wine and cook for 5 minutes to let the wine reduce.

3   Drain the porcini and add to the pot along with the broth, farro, soy sauce, and thyme. Bring to a boil, then reduce the heat and cook at a low simmer for 20 minutes, until the farro is cooked. You want the farro to still be slightly chewy and not mushy. Stir in the parsley and season with the salt and pepper. Ladle the soup into bowls and serve immediately.

NOTES: *You can find farro in the bulk section of the grocery store or in the aisle where other grains are sold. And feel free to use any kind of mushrooms that you love. Using dried mushrooms is one of the easiest ways to get really deep, mushroomy flavor in a dish. They might look all shriveled and strange in the package, but don't worry, they plump right up after a soak in hot water. If you want to make this dish vegan, just swap out the butter for olive oil. It will still be delicious!* **Mushroom cleaning tip:** *The easiest way to clean mushrooms is to gently wipe them with a damp paper towel to remove any dirt. Never put them under running water—they'll soak it up like a sponge!*

chipotle–sweet potato chili

prep: **15 MINUTES** | cook: **40 MINUTES** | total: **55 MINUTES** | serves **4**

2 tablespoons extra-virgin olive oil

1 large sweet potato, peeled and diced

1 medium red onion, diced

1 red bell pepper, cored, seeded, and diced

3 garlic cloves, minced

2 (15-ounce) cans black beans, drained and rinsed

1 (15-ounce) can diced tomatoes with juices

1¾ cups vegetable broth

1 medium chipotle pepper in adobo sauce, chopped, plus 2 teaspoons of the adobo sauce

1½ tablespoons chili powder

1 tablespoon ground cumin

1 teaspoon kosher salt

Optional toppings: diced avocado, sliced scallions, chopped fresh cilantro, shredded cheese (cheddar, Mexican blend, Monterey Jack, or pepper Jack work well), crumbled queso fresco, plain Greek yogurt or sour cream, tortilla chips

Chipotles in adobo sauce is one of my favorite secret weapons in the kitchen because they add the most amazing smokiness to a dish without a ton of spice. You can find them in just about every grocery store. I especially love adding them to chili because the smokiness rounds out the flavor and makes the stew taste that much more robust. Plus, the combination of chipotle and sweet potato is *super* tasty. I put out a big pot of this chili on game days with *all* the toppings, including, *of course,* avocado. I don't mention to anyone that it's completely healthy, but that hasn't seemed to make any difference! I highly recommend making a double batch because it freezes really nicely.

1 In a large pot, heat the olive oil over medium-high heat. Add the sweet potato, onion, and red pepper and cook for 5 minutes, until the onion is softened. Add the garlic and cook for 2 minutes.

2 Stir in the black beans, tomatoes, broth, chipotle and adobo sauce, chili powder, cumin, and salt. Cover the pot and reduce the heat to low. Simmer for 30 minutes, until the sweet potato is soft and cooked through. Taste the chili and season with additional salt, if desired. Ladle into bowls and top with all the toppings!

NOTE: *Since you won't need the entire can of chipotles in adobo sauce, stash any leftovers in the freezer for up to 2 months.*

minestrone with parmesan crisps

prep: **25 MINUTES** | cook: **40 MINUTES** | total: **1 HOUR 5 MINUTES** | serves **6**

• •

2 tablespoons extra-virgin olive oil

1 small yellow onion, chopped

2 medium carrots, peeled and diced

2 celery stalks, diced

1 medium zucchini, diced

1 cup fresh green beans, ends trimmed and cut into 1-inch pieces, or frozen cut green beans

4 garlic cloves, minced

2 dried bay leaves

2 tablespoons tomato paste

6 cups vegetable broth

1 (28-ounce) can diced tomatoes with juices

1 (14-ounce) can cannellini beans, drained and rinsed

1 cup whole-wheat elbow macaroni (or gluten-free pasta or regular pasta)

1 teaspoon dried basil

1 teaspoon dried thyme

½ teaspoon dried oregano

Pinch of crushed red pepper flakes

Kosher salt and freshly ground black pepper

1 cup grated Parmesan cheese (the good stuff!)

When I know we're going to have a cold, wet day playing in the snow, my mind starts working on what kind of warm, hearty soup I can serve up afterward. This mix of veggies, beans, and whole-wheat pasta is a mainstay in our rotation—I feel great about it because of the wholesome ingredients, and the boys are fans because it warms their hands and fills their bellies. They're also crazy for the Parmesan crisps I sprinkle over the top, which makes the soup extra special.

1 Heat the olive oil in a large pot over medium-high heat. Add the onion, carrots, and celery and cook until tender, about 5 minutes. Add the zucchini, green beans, garlic, and bay leaves and cook for 3 minutes. Stir in the tomato paste, coating the vegetables. Add the broth, tomatoes, cannellini beans, pasta, basil, thyme, oregano, pepper flakes, ½ teaspoon salt, and ¼ teaspoon black pepper. Bring to a boil and then simmer on low until the vegetables and pasta are tender, 25 to 30 minutes.

2 While the soup is simmering, make the Parmesan cheese crisps: Preheat the oven to 400°F. Line a large baking sheet with parchment paper. Use a tablespoon to scoop mounds of the grated cheese onto the baking sheet, making sure they are 2 inches apart. Lightly pat down the cheese mounds with your fingers. Bake for 3 to 6 minutes, until golden and crisp. Let cool.

3 Taste the soup and season with additional salt and pepper, if necessary. Discard the bay leaves. Ladle the soup into bowls and serve warm with the Parmesan crisps. Store any leftovers in the fridge for up to 5 days, or in the freezer for up to 1 month. If you have any crisps left, you can store them in an airtight container for up to 1 week on the counter.

NOTE: *This recipe is a great canvas for just about any veggies, especially ones that have been sitting in the crisper patiently waiting their turn. I love using bell peppers, yellow squash, butternut squash, spinach, kale, and potatoes—just to name a few options.*

sausage, kale, and gnocchi soup

prep: **10 MINUTES**   cook: **25 MINUTES**   total: **35 MINUTES**   serves **8**

1 pound Italian sausage, removed from casings

6 slices bacon, chopped

1 medium yellow onion, chopped

3 garlic cloves, minced

¼ teaspoon crushed red pepper flakes

4 cups chopped stemmed kale

7 cups chicken broth

1 pound store-bought mini potato gnocchi (we love DeLallo)

1 cup heavy cream

Kosher salt and freshly ground black pepper

Grated Parmesan cheese, for serving (optional)

This is Josh's favorite soup, a take on *zuppa Toscana,* the classic Tuscan dish made with kale, cannellini beans, potatoes, and bacon. To make a quicker version that's still just as hearty and delicious, we swapped out the potatoes for store-bought gnocchi, a nugget-shaped pasta made with potatoes and flour that cooks up in minutes. Then we added sausage and a dash of heavy cream to make it even more filling. I serve this with crusty bread and plenty of Parmesan for sprinkling, and all my boys are very happy campers.

1   Set a large skillet over medium heat. Add the sausage meat and cook, breaking it up with the back of a wooden spoon, until browned and no longer pink, 5 to 7 minutes. Transfer to a plate that has been lined with paper towels and let drain.

2   In a large pot, cook the bacon over medium heat and let it slowly start to render and crisp up, about 2 minutes. Add the onion and cook for 3 to 5 minutes, stirring occasionally. Stir in the garlic, red pepper flakes, and kale and cook for 2 minutes, until the kale is wilted and softened. Add the sausage and stir to combine. Pour in the broth and bring to a low boil. Stir in the gnocchi and cook until the gnocchi float to the top, 3 to 5 minutes.

3   Reduce the heat to low and stir in the cream. Season the soup with salt and pepper to taste. Continue simmering until the soup is warmed through. Ladle into bowls and garnish with Parmesan cheese, if desired.

roasted butternut squash and pear soup
with candied pepitas

prep: **15 MINUTES** | cook: **1 HOUR** | total: **1 HOUR 15 MINUTES** | serves **4 TO 6**

● ●

CANDIED PEPITAS

¼ cup sugar

1 cup pepitas

¼ teaspoon kosher salt

BUTTERNUT SQUASH SOUP

1 butternut squash (about
   3 pounds), peeled, seeded,
   and cut into 1-inch pieces

2 small pears, cored and chopped

2 tablespoons extra-virgin olive oil

Kosher salt and freshly ground
   black pepper

1 small yellow onion, diced

3 garlic cloves, minced

3 cups vegetable broth, plus more
   as needed

¼ teaspoon ground cinnamon

⅛ teaspoon ground nutmeg

Squash soup is an essential fall dish, so of course I had to put my own spin on it. I realized that by roasting the squash until it was tender and caramelized, combining it with pear for just a tiny bit of sweetness and body, and adding a pinch of classic fall spices (cinnamon and nutmeg), I could achieve an elegant, velvety soup without a drop of cream. (Though I certainly won't tell if you add a drizzle!) Since this soup is so special, I wanted to give it the perfect accessory: candied pepitas, which are a perfect mix of sweet and salty with great crunchy texture.

1 Preheat the oven to 400°F.

2 Make the candied pepitas: In a medium skillet over medium heat, melt the sugar, shaking the pan to distribute it in an even layer. When the sugar turns amber in color, after 3 to 5 minutes, remove the pan from the heat and add the pepitas. Stir to combine and sprinkle with the salt. Transfer the pepitas to a parchment-lined plate or baking sheet and let them cool completely. Break the brittle into pieces and store in an airtight container for up to 3 weeks.

3 Make the soup: Arrange the squash and pears in a single layer on a large baking sheet. Drizzle with 1 tablespoon of the olive oil and toss until well coated. Season with a pinch of salt and pepper and roast for 35 minutes, until the squash and pears are soft and tender.

4 In a large pot, heat the remaining 1 tablespoon olive oil over medium-high heat. Add the onion and cook until softened, about 5 minutes. Add the garlic and cook for 2 minutes longer. Stir in the roasted squash and pears along with the broth, cinnamon, and nutmeg. Reduce the heat to low and let the soup simmer for 10 minutes. Remove the pot from the heat.

5 Use an immersion blender to blend the soup right in the pot until smooth. (Alternatively, let the soup cool slightly, then transfer it to a blender to blend until smooth. Return to the pot and heat over medium heat until heated through.) If the soup is too thick, add a little more broth until the desired consistency is reached. Ladle the soup into bowls and top with the candied pepitas.

tomato basil soup with cheesy garlic dunkers

prep: **10 MINUTES** | cook: **30 MINUTES** | total: **40 MINUTES** | serves **4 TO 6**

• •

1 tablespoon extra-virgin olive oil

1 tablespoon unsalted butter

1 medium yellow onion, diced

2 garlic cloves, minced

1 dried bay leaf

½ teaspoon dried thyme

Pinch of crushed red pepper flakes

2 (28-ounce) cans fire-roasted tomatoes with juices

1 (12-ounce) jar roasted red peppers, drained and chopped

1 cup low-sodium vegetable broth

⅓ cup heavy cream

1 tablespoon balsamic vinegar

⅓ cup chopped fresh basil, plus more for garnish

Kosher salt and freshly ground black pepper

Cheesy Garlic Dunkers (recipe follows)

It doesn't get more classic than tomato soup, and this version is often bubbling away on our stove—especially because its ingredients are easy to stash in the pantry for whenever the mood (or the need for a quick and popular dinner!) strikes. The addition of cheesy garlic toasts—a baguette that's been slathered with easy garlic butter and broiled with (you guessed it) loads of cheese—makes this a very convincing reason to gather around the table.

1   In a large pot, heat the olive oil and butter over medium-high heat. Add the onion and cook until soft, about 5 minutes. Add the garlic and cook for 2 minutes. Stir in the bay leaf, thyme, and pepper flakes, plus the tomatoes, roasted red peppers, and broth. Reduce the heat to low and simmer for 15 to 20 minutes.

2   Stir in the cream, vinegar, and basil. Season with salt and pepper to taste. Turn off the heat, remove the bay leaf, and use an immersion blender to puree the soup in the pot. (Alternatively, let the soup cool slightly, then transfer to a blender and blend until smooth. Return to the pot and heat over medium heat until heated through.)

3   Ladle the soup into bowls, garnish with basil, if desired, and serve with the dunkers. You could also let the soup cool completely and refrigerate for up to 5 days or freeze for up to 2 months.

Cheesy Garlic Dunkers

prep: **10 MINUTES**
cook: **5 MINUTES**
total: **15 MINUTES**
makes **ABOUT 24 DUNKERS**

1 baguette, cut into ½-inch slices

4 tablespoons unsalted butter, at room temperature

4 garlic cloves, minced

½ cup finely shredded cheddar cheese

½ cup grated Parmesan cheese

1   Preheat the oven broiler.

2   Arrange the baguette slices on a large baking sheet in a single layer. In a small bowl, combine the butter and minced garlic. Stir until the garlic is well incorporated. Spread each slice of bread with the garlic butter and top with the cheddar and Parmesan. Broil until the cheese is melted and the bread is golden brown around the edges, 3 to 5 minutes. Let cool.

slow cooker chicken tortilla soup
with spiced tortilla strips

prep: **10 MINUTES** | slow cook: **3 TO 4 HOURS ON HIGH OR 6 TO 8 HOURS ON LOW**
total: **3 TO 8 HOURS** | serves **6 TO 8**

SOUP

1 pound boneless, skinless chicken breasts

1 small yellow onion, diced

3 garlic cloves, minced

1 red bell pepper, cored, seeded, and diced

1 poblano pepper, cored, seeded, and diced

4 cups low-sodium chicken broth

2 (14.5-ounce) cans diced tomatoes with juices

2 (15-ounce) cans black beans, drained and rinsed

1½ cups frozen corn kernels

1 (4-ounce) can diced green chiles

2 teaspoons ground cumin

2 teaspoons chili powder

1 teaspoon smoked paprika

¼ teaspoon dried oregano

1 teaspoon kosher salt

Juice of 1 lime

¼ cup chopped fresh cilantro

I'm all for letting my slow cooker make dinner—and this is the ultimate "set it and forget it" recipe. This warm, cozy soup is great to throw together before we head out for an adventure-filled afternoon, or on those crazy days when our schedule is packed with after-school activities or meetings. It's so comforting knowing that whatever you're doing that day, you get to come home to warm, delicious soup topped with spiced, crunchy tortilla strips. Or better yet, knowing that anyone could pop by for dinner and you'll be ready with a hearty meal to share.

SPICED TORTILLA STRIPS

10 corn tortillas

1½ tablespoons canola or vegetable oil

1 teaspoon chili powder

½ teaspoon garlic powder

½ teaspoon onion powder

½ teaspoon paprika

½ teaspoon kosher salt

Optional toppings: shredded cheese, diced avocado, sour cream or plain Greek yogurt, chopped fresh cilantro, sliced scallions, lime wedges

1 Make the soup: In a 6-quart slow cooker, combine all the soup ingredients except the cilantro and stir to combine.

2 Cover the slow cooker and cook for 3 to 4 hours on high heat or 6 to 8 hours on low heat, until the chicken is cooked through. Use two forks to shred the chicken and stir to distribute. Stir in the cilantro.

3 Make the tortilla strips: While the soup is cooking, preheat the oven to 400°F. Line a large baking sheet with aluminum foil.

4 With the tortillas in a single stack, cut them into 1 × ¼-inch strips. Scatter the strips over the baking sheet and drizzle with the oil. Toss until all of the strips are well coated.

5 In a small bowl, mix together the chili powder, garlic powder, onion powder, paprika, and salt. Sprinkle the seasoning over the tortilla strips and toss until they are evenly coated.

6 Arrange the strips in an even layer. Bake for 5 minutes. Use a spoon or spatula to give the tortilla strips a toss. Place the baking sheet back in the oven and bake for an additional 5 minutes, until the strips are crispy. Set aside to cool. Use immediately or store in an airtight container at room temperature for up to 5 days.

7 Ladle the soup into bowls and serve with the spiced tortilla strips and other desired toppings.

NOTE: *This is a great recipe for making in the Instant Pot:*

Set the Instant Pot to the Sauté function. Add 2 tablespoons of olive oil and sauté the onion for 3 to 5 minutes, or until tender. Add the garlic and peppers and cook for an additional 3 minutes, stirring frequently.

Stir in the chicken broth, diced tomatoes, black beans, green chiles, ground cumin, chili powder, smoked paprika, oregano, salt, and lime juice. Add the chicken breasts, stir, and secure the lid. Select "high pressure" and set the time to 18 minutes. When the soup is done cooking, manually release the pressure with quick release and, using an oven mitt or towel, carefully remove the lid.

Use tongs or a slotted spoon to transfer the chicken to a clean plate or cutting board. Use two forks to shred the chicken. Return the chicken to the soup along with the corn and cilantro. Season with additional salt and pepper, if necessary. Ladle the soup into bowls and serve with your desired toppings.

---

slow cooker lentil vegetable soup

prep: **30 MINUTES** | slow cook: **5 HOURS ON HIGH OR 7 TO 8 HOURS ON LOW**
total: **5½ TO 8½ HOURS** | serves **8 TO 10**

1 small yellow onion, chopped

1 large sweet potato, peeled and chopped (about 2 cups)

2 small russet potatoes, peeled and chopped (about 2 cups)

2 medium carrots, peeled and chopped

2 celery stalks, chopped

1 red bell pepper, cored, seeded, and chopped

4 garlic cloves, minced

2 dried bay leaves

1½ cups green lentils, rinsed

7 cups vegetable broth

1 teaspoon ground turmeric

½ teaspoon ground coriander

½ teaspoon dried thyme

¼ teaspoon dried rosemary

Kosher salt and freshly ground black pepper

1 to 2 tablespoons fresh lemon juice

2 cups stemmed, chopped kale or spinach

Grated Parmesan cheese, for serving (optional)

This is the perfect soup for when you're feeling under the weather or just in need of a steaming bowl of nourishing soup. It's loaded with vegetables—sweet potatoes, carrots, peppers, and greens—plus lentils, which are packed with good-for-you protein. The secret to making this a household favorite, though, is pureeing it until it's just about smooth with a little bit of texture from the veggies. All the boys know is that they're eating a creamy, delicious soup that they can top with handfuls of Parmesan cheese. In the colder months, I always have a batch of this soup in the freezer so I can reheat a bowl for lunch.

1 In a 6-quart slow cooker, combine the onion, sweet potato, russet potatoes, carrots, celery, bell pepper, garlic, bay leaves, lentils, broth, turmeric, coriander, thyme, rosemary, 1½ teaspoons salt, and 1 teaspoon black pepper. Stir to combine. Cover the slow cooker and cook on high heat for 5 hours or on low for 7 to 8 hours.

2 Stir in the lemon juice and discard the bay leaves. Puree the soup in the slow cooker with an immersion blender. (Alternatively, let the soup cool slightly, then transfer to a blender to blend.) Blend until the soup reaches your desired consistency. I like to leave mine a little chunky, but you could go for completely smooth. Stir in the kale and season to taste with salt and pepper. Serve with Parmesan cheese, if desired. To freeze, let the soup cool completely before pouring it into one large freezer-safe container or several single-serving-sized containers. Freeze for up to 2 months.

NOTE: *You can also make this soup in an Instant Pot:*

Turn the Instant Pot to Sauté and heat the olive oil. Add the onion, carrots, and celery and sauté for 3 to 5 minutes, or until the vegetables are tender. Add the garlic and sauté for an additional 2 minutes.

Add all of the other ingredients, except for the lemon juice and kale, and select Manual/Pressure Cook to cook on high pressure for 15 minutes. When the cooking cycle is complete, let the pressure naturally release for 10 minutes. With a towel or hot pad, carefully move the steam release valve to vent to release any remaining pressure. Remove the Instant Pot lid and stir in the lemon juice and kale.

Cooking It Forward

To me, there's nothing more special than feeding someone. It's the purest expression of love, really. That's why we don't just cook for our family, but also for our community. Whether it's contributing a dish to church and school events, neighborhood barbecues, and fundraisers; sending care packages to loved ones abroad, kids who have gone off to college, and soldiers who have been deployed; or filling the freezer for those in need of some support and a nourishing meal (new moms, the sick or elderly, grieving families), we believe that cooking is a form of charity.

When it comes to cooking it forward, there's nothing complicated to it. Once you've picked out a recipe that's well suited for traveling and/or freezing, you only need to pack it up, label it (and include reheating instructions, if applicable), and pass it on with a full heart.

Here are some of my favorite recipes in this book for sharing with others:

TRAVELS WELL

- Best-Ever Granola (page 41)
- Our Favorite Chocolate Chip Cookies (page 241)
- Toasted Coconut, White Chocolate, and Macadamia Cookies (page 245)
- Mega Monster Cookies (page 251)
- Peanut Butter Caramelitas (page 277)
- Triple-Chip Chocolate Cookies (page 259)
- Brown Butter–Salted Caramel Snickerdoodles (page 255)

POTLUCK-APPROVED

- Artichoke, Sun-Dried Tomato, and Feta Egg Casserole (page 34)
- Cinnamon Rolls (page 50)
- Creamy Hummus with Baked Pita Chips (page 90)
- Everyday Butter Lettuce Salad (page 98)
- Kale and Wild Rice Salad with Maple-Mustard Vinaigrette (page 101)
- Baby Potato Salad with Bacon and Simple Lemon-Herb Dressing (page 109)
- Fruit Salad with Citrus–Poppy Seed Dressing (page 110)
- Roasted Butternut Squash Farro with Kale-Walnut Pesto (page 168)
- Brown Butter Banana Cake with Brown Butter–Cream Cheese Frosting (page 281)
- Lemon–Poppy Seed Bundt Cake (page 269)

FREEZER-FRIENDLY

- Perfect Buttermilk Pancakes (page 46)

- Belgian Waffles (page 292)

- Chocolate Banana Bread (page 61)

- Chewy No-Bake Granola Bars (page 37)

- Mushroom-Farro Soup (page 120)

- Minestrone with Parmesan Crisps (page 124)

- Chipotle–Sweet Potato Chili (page 123)

- Roasted Butternut Squash and Pear Soup (page 128)

- Tomato Basil Soup (page 131)

- Slow Cooker Chicken Tortilla Soup (page 132)

- Slow Cooker Lentil Vegetable Soup (page 134)

- Black Bean–Quinoa Enchilada Bake (page 188)

- Baked Chicken Taquitos (page 198)

- Salsa Verde–Chicken Stacked Enchiladas (page 217)

- Chicken Pot Pie (page 219)

- Slow Cooker Meatballs (page 226)

- Our Favorite Chocolate Chip Cookies (page 241)

- Dad's Famous Frozen Cookies (page 244)

- Toasted Coconut, White Chocolate, and Macadamia Cookies (page 245)

SIDE DISHES

One of the most frequent topics that people ask Josh and me about is vegetables—what our favorite simple preparations are and, most importantly, how we get our kids to eat them! We're lucky because our kids are great eaters and pretty open-minded when it comes to trying new things. But like all kids—and a lot of adults!—they want food that tastes good. When it comes to vegetables, it's essential to making a dish that everyone loves: It just has to taste *good*. Since we're not fans of fussy food—vegetables or otherwise—we use a really basic rule of thumb when it comes to vegetable side dishes: Keep it fresh; keep it simple. By using the freshest produce possible, you're already ahead of the game in the flavor department. Vegetables that are in season locally will always taste better than those that are flown halfway around the world. And don't forget about frozen veggies! Since they're picked and flash-frozen at their peak freshness, it's possible to find great options year-round.

As for keeping it simple, we don't get too fancy when it comes to cooking techniques. You can get the most flavor out of vegetables when you either roast, grill, or sauté them. So each recipe in this section uses one of these techniques. From there, it's just a matter of pairing the vegetables with other ingredients that bring out their delicious natural flavor. We promise that if you give a couple of these a try, your family will be veggie fans in no time!

veggie roasting 101

• •

Roasting vegetables is seriously magic: It turns ordinary, plain vegetables into something that not only everyone—even the pickiest of eaters—will eat, but actually *crave!* Even those sad, slightly limp vegetables that have spent a little too much time in the crisper can be totally revived by roasting.

Every single week, I meal-prep a pan of roasted veggies that I can have for lunch with cottage cheese (just try it—you'll be amazed!), or tuck into salads, omelets, tacos, quesadillas, egg scrambles, and veggie bowls, or serve with dips like Creamy Hummus (page 90) and Avocado Green Goddess Dip (page 80). And roasting vegetables is beyond easy. Once you know the basics, there's nothing to it. Here's everything you need to know.

WHAT TO ROAST

Some of my favorite veggies to roast include:

Asparagus, ends trimmed

Beets, whole or halved

Bell peppers, cored and cut into thick strips

Broccoli, cut into florets

Brussels sprouts, whole or halved

Butternut squash, cubed

Cabbage, roughly chopped

Carrots, sliced

Cauliflower, cut into florets

Eggplant, cubed

Green beans, whole

Mushrooms, whole or halved

Onions, sliced

Potatoes, cubed

Sweet potatoes, cubed

Yellow squash, sliced into thick rounds

Zucchini, sliced into thick rounds

You can roast different veggies at the same time, but in order for them to cook evenly, make sure they are (a) similar in density and (b) cut into the same size pieces. Think hard versus soft, for example: Sweet potatoes and butternut squash (hard) will take longer to cook than zucchini and bell peppers (soft). You could also start the longer-roasting veg first, then add quicker cooking vegetables part of the way through. For example, you can start roasting beets and then add asparagus spears at the end. Just make sure you leave room on the pan!

GET STARTED

1 Cut the vegetables into uniform pieces so they cook evenly.

2 Line a large baking sheet with high-heat parchment paper or aluminum foil (for easy cleanup!). Place the veggies on the baking sheet.

3 Generously coat the veggies with olive oil—typically about 2 tablespoons per baking sheet, though porous veg like eggplant and mushrooms may need a little more. You want everything nicely coated, but not swimming in oil. Just drizzle it over and use your hands to work the oil into all the nooks and crannies. You can do this in a large bowl or right on your baking sheet (which is what I like to do because it's one less dish to wash!).

4 Add your favorite herbs and seasonings (see "Add Flavor," page 142).

recipe continues

5 Don't crowd the baking sheet! After you've coated everything in olive oil and seasonings, make sure your vegetables are spread in an even layer on the sheet with space between them. This will help the veggies get nice and crispy instead of steaming. If you need to use more than one baking sheet, go for it!

Roasting brings out incredible flavor, so you don't have to add a ton of seasonings. Sometimes I'm in the mood for simple kosher salt and black pepper, while other times I go bold with some of my favorite flavors, which include fresh herbs like rosemary, basil, or thyme; Everything-Bagel Seasoning (page 87); lemon juice; balsamic vinegar; paprika; smoked paprika; garlic; turmeric; and crushed red pepper flakes.

• The best temperature for roasting vegetables is 425°F. Cooking times will vary depending on the vegetable: Starchier or harder vegetables like winter squash (butternut, acorn, pumpkin), roots (carrots, potatoes), and onions take longer to roast, whereas mushrooms and other soft vegetables take less. If you're cooking both, begin with the veggies that take longer. After about 20 minutes, add the softer vegetables and continue cooking until crispy. See below for suggested cook times for different types of vegetables.

• For even browning and caramelization, flip the vegetables halfway through the cook time. You want to make sure all sides are perfectly crispy!

• Suggested roasting times: This will vary depending on your particular oven and the size of your vegetables. You want them to be tender in the middle but have a nice amount of char on the outside. Learn to trust your instincts!

• Just a heads-up: While roasted cauliflower, broccoli, and Brussels sprouts are my favorite, the boys tell me that they're "stinky." Now I light a candle as soon as they go in the oven so there are no complaints!

• After the vegetables are done roasting, taste for seasoning. You may want to sprinkle them with more salt and pepper before serving.

• You can easily reheat roasted vegetables, whether in the oven, skillet, air fryer, or microwave (my least favorite option because it makes them a little mushy, but it gets the job done!).

VEGETABLE (cut into equal-sized pieces)	TIME TO ROAST (at 425°F)
Root vegetables: sweet potatoes, potatoes, carrots, butternut squash	35 to 45 minutes
Winter squash: butternut squash, acorn squash, pumpkin	30 to 50 minutes
Crucifers: broccoli, cauliflower, Brussels sprouts	15 to 30 minutes
Soft vegetables: zucchini, summer squash, bell peppers, mushrooms	15 to 20 minutes
Thin vegetables: asparagus, green beans	10 to 20 minutes

shredded brussels sprouts with parmesan and hazelnuts

prep: **20 MINUTES** | cook: **5 MINUTES** | total: **25 MINUTES** | serves **4 TO 6**

1 pound Brussels sprouts

2 tablespoons unsalted butter

2 tablespoons minced shallot

3 garlic cloves, minced

½ teaspoon grated lemon zest

Juice of 1 lemon

½ cup grated Parmesan cheese

½ cup chopped hazelnuts
(almonds or pecans would work
here too)

¼ cup dried cranberries or cherries
(optional)

½ teaspoon kosher salt

If you think you don't like Brussels sprouts, think again. These aren't the gray, mushy, overcooked sprouts you had as a kid. It's hard to believe it's the same vegetable when you shred them up, quickly sauté in butter, shallots, and garlic, then finish with a bright squeeze of lemon juice and a tuft of salty Parmesan and buttery nuts! To take it to the next level, I sometimes add a sprinkling of dried cranberries or cherries for a great salty-sweet combination—not to mention pretty jewel-tone color. I love making this dish for the holidays (especially if I know there won't be other vegetarian items to eat!). To save time, you can shred the Brussels sprouts in advance: Store them in the fridge in a zip-top bag with a damp paper towel for up to a day.

1 Trim the tough ends off the Brussels sprouts. Peel off and discard any brown, wilted, or blemished outer leaves. Cut the sprouts in half from top to bottom and thinly slice. A sharp knife will be really helpful here. Or, if you have a food processor, you can shred the sprouts with the large slicing attachment. Fluff the pile of shredded sprouts with your hands.

2 In a large skillet, melt the butter over medium heat. Add the shallot, garlic, lemon zest, and shredded sprouts. Cook, stirring occasionally, until the sprouts are tender but still bright green, 4 to 5 minutes.

3 Remove the pan from the heat and stir in the lemon juice, Parmesan, hazelnuts, and dried fruit (if using). Season with salt and serve immediately.

mexican charred corn

prep: **15 MINUTES** | cook: **10 MINUTES** | total: **25 MINUTES** | serves **6 TO 8**

● ●

5 ears sweet corn, husked

1 small poblano pepper

½ cup chopped fresh cilantro

½ cup cotija cheese or queso fresco

3 scallions (white and green parts), sliced

Juice of 2 limes

1 tablespoon extra-virgin olive oil

½ teaspoon chili powder

½ teaspoon kosher salt

It's pretty much a summer rite of passage to pick up a bushel full of sweet corn from the market. You can't have a proper barbecue without grilled corn! And we especially love Mexican street food–inspired corn, where you toss charred kernels with smoky grilled poblano pepper, fresh cilantro, and creamy cotija cheese. It's the perfect summer side dish that goes great with pretty much anything else coming off the grill, or it can be served on its own with tortilla chips. Feel free to tailor the spice factor to your liking—I only use half a poblano pepper, but if you like things hot, go for the whole thing!

1   Preheat your grill to high heat.

2   Place the corn and the poblano pepper directly on the hot grill. Grill the corn for about 5 minutes, turning every minute until evenly charred. Let cool to room temperature. Grill the poblano pepper, turning, for about 10 minutes, until the skin begins to blister and char. Place the poblano in a zip-top bag and let it sit for 5 minutes. Carefully remove the skin with your fingers. Chop the poblano and discard the seeds.

3   Cut the corn kernels from the cob and place in a medium bowl. Add half of the chopped poblano pepper (or all of it!), the cilantro, cotija, scallions, lime juice, olive oil, chili powder, and salt. Stir to combine. Serve immediately at room temperature, or refrigerate and serve chilled.

stir-fried snap peas
with orange, ginger, and sesame seeds

prep: **10 MINUTES** | cook: **10 MINUTES** | total: **20 MINUTES** | serves **4**

• •

4 garlic cloves, minced

1½ teaspoons grated fresh ginger (see Notes)

1 teaspoon grated orange zest

⅓ cup fresh orange juice

3 tablespoons soy sauce

1½ teaspoons toasted sesame oil

1½ teaspoons brown sugar

1 teaspoon cornstarch

1 pound snap peas, strings removed

1 tablespoon toasted sesame seeds (see Notes)

¼ teaspoon crushed red pepper flakes

The Two Peas love peas! With their fresh, sweet flavor, snap peas are by far the favorite vegetable around here in the springtime. When the weather warms up and we find them piled high at the farmers market or grocery store, we know we have to stir-fry. I don't like to do too much because the peas are pretty perfect just the way they are, so I just toss them in a simple Asian-inspired sauce with orange juice and fresh ginger that brings out their bright flavor, and then cook them super-quick so they're still nice and crisp. I serve them up as a side dish with fish, chicken, beef, tofu—pretty much anything!—or I just make a panful and serve them on their own for us to eat with our fingers. They're that good!

1   In a small bowl, combine the garlic, ginger, orange zest and juice, soy sauce, sesame oil, brown sugar, and cornstarch. Whisk until smooth.

2   Heat the garlic mixture in a large skillet over medium heat until the sauce thickens, 2 to 3 minutes. Add the snap peas and stir-fry, stirring occasionally, for 3 to 5 minutes, until the peas are tender but still crisp. Remove the pan from the heat and garnish with the toasted sesame seeds and pepper flakes. Serve immediately.

NOTES: *We keep fresh ginger in the freezer—that way we always have some handy, and it's much easier to grate with a Microplane or finely chop. Just peel it first! To toast sesame seeds, place in an even layer in a small skillet and heat over medium heat for 2 to 3 minutes, shaking or stirring constantly until they're nice and toasty brown.*

sweet potato fries
with magic green tahini sauce

prep: **10 MINUTES** | cook: **30 MINUTES** | total: **40 MINUTES** | serves **4 TO 6**

SWEET POTATO FRIES

2 large sweet potatoes

2 tablespoons grapeseed or olive oil

Kosher salt

MAGIC GREEN TAHINI SAUCE

1 cup packed fresh cilantro leaves

½ cup packed fresh parsley leaves

½ cup tahini

3 garlic cloves, minced

Juice of 1 large lemon

½ teaspoon kosher salt

Pinch of crushed red pepper flakes (optional)

We make these crispy, tender fries all the time because the whole family loves getting in on the dipping action! Using sweet potatoes instead of white potatoes means sneaking in a little more nutrition, but I actually think the crunchy orange treats are so much more delicious, thanks to their sweet-salty flavor. They're the perfect side for any meal, especially served with my magic green tahini sauce. At first Caleb and Maxwell were suspicious because it wasn't ketchup or Fry Sauce (page 73), but once they tried it, they became as hooked as Josh and I are. The combination of rich, creamy tahini with herbs, garlic, and lemon juice makes it essentially like a brighter, fresher hummus. It gets a lot of use in our house as a dip for veggies, pita chips, and crackers or thinned out as a dressing for tossed greens. It's magic!

1 Make the fries: Preheat the oven to 425°F. Line two large baking sheets with parchment paper.

2 You can peel the sweet potatoes if you wish, but I always leave the skins on. Cut the sweet potatoes into ¼-inch-thick sticks or wedges. Place them in a large bowl and toss with the oil until well coated. Spread the fries in a single layer on the baking sheets. Make sure they don't overlap or touch; they need space to get crispy.

3 Roast the fries for 15 minutes. Remove the pans from the oven and use a spatula to flip the fries. Make sure, once again, that they're not touching. Return the fries to the oven, rotating the pans, and continue to roast until the fries are tender on

the inside and crispy on the outside, 10 to 15 minutes more. Season generously with salt, then let the fries cool for 5 minutes.

4 Make the tahini sauce: In a blender or food processor, combine the cilantro, parsley, tahini, garlic, lemon juice, salt, and pepper flakes (if using) with ¼ cup water. Blend until smooth. If the sauce is too thick, add a little more water and blend again. Transfer to a bowl and serve with the potato fries.

NOTE: *There's not much involved in making this recipe, but you do have to be sure to not salt the fries until after they come out of the oven. Salting before roasting will leave you with limp fries.*

simple skillet green beans with lemon and garlic

prep: **5 MINUTES** | cook: **10 MINUTES** | total: **15 MINUTES** | serves **4 TO 6**

1 tablespoon extra-virgin olive oil

⅛ teaspoon crushed red pepper flakes

1 pound fresh green beans, ends trimmed

3 garlic cloves, minced

1 teaspoon grated lemon zest

1 tablespoon fresh lemon juice

Kosher salt and freshly ground black pepper

Green beans are the one vegetable that I can always count on—they take no time to cook, have a mild, sweet taste that even the toughest of vegetable critics will like, and pair really nicely with other fresh flavors, especially the kick of bright lemon and garlic. Whenever I cook this dish, it's a great reminder that simplicity is best.

1   In a large skillet with a fitted lid, heat the olive oil over medium-high heat. Add the pepper flakes and green beans and toss with tongs or a spoon until the green beans are coated with the olive oil. Cover the pan and reduce the heat to medium. Cook for 7 minutes, stirring every minute or two so the green beans don't burn. You want them to be blistered and tender, but still have a little "snap."

2   Remove the lid and add the garlic, stirring to coat the green beans. Add the lemon zest and juice, toss, season with salt and pepper to taste, toss again, and serve immediately.

crispy garlic-rosemary smashed potatoes

prep: **10 MINUTES** | cook: **1 HOUR 10 MINUTES** | total: **1 HOUR 20 MINUTES** | serves **6**

Nonstick cooking spray

2 pounds small red (or purple or golden) potatoes, scrubbed

Kosher salt

½ cup grated Parmesan cheese

5 garlic cloves, minced

1½ teaspoons finely chopped fresh rosemary

3 tablespoons extra-virgin olive oil

¼ teaspoon freshly ground black pepper

3 tablespoons unsalted butter, melted

This is one of my favorite recipes to share with people because they're always amazed that they can re-create the rich, buttery, crispy-yet-creamy potatoes that they usually order at a restaurant. The first secret is using baby potatoes, which are nice and tender. (I usually buy the red ones, but small purple or golden potatoes are fine too.) The second is boiling the potatoes so they're perfectly creamy on the inside. Then you *gently* smash them (this is *not* the time to get out all of your frustrations!) and top with a savory mix of Parmesan, rosemary, and garlic. And simply roast until they're golden and crisp. Oh, and don't forget to baste with butter! It's not hard to imagine why we get a *lot* of requests for this recipe whenever we have people over.

1   Preheat the oven to 450°F. Grease a large baking sheet with nonstick cooking spray and set aside.

2   Place the potatoes in a large pot and add just enough cold water to cover. Season with a generous pinch of salt and bring to a boil over high heat. Reduce the heat to medium and cook uncovered for 30 minutes, until the potatoes are fork-tender. Drain.

3   Arrange the potatoes on the prepared baking sheet. Using the bottom of a jar or glass, gently press down on the potatoes until they are smashed but still in one piece. You want them to hold together, so don't press too hard!

4   In a small bowl, mix together the Parmesan, garlic, and rosemary.

5   Drizzle the potatoes evenly with the olive oil, season with 1 teaspoon salt and the pepper, and sprinkle with the Parmesan topping. Roast for 30 minutes. Drizzle the potatoes evenly with the melted butter and return them to the oven for 10 to 12 minutes, until the potatoes are crispy. Serve warm.

brown butter–honey carrots
with fresh thyme

prep: **10 MINUTES** | cook: **10 MINUTES** | total: **20 MINUTES** | serves **6 TO 8**

2 tablespoons unsalted butter

2 pounds medium carrots, peeled
    and sliced diagonally into
    ¼-inch slices

3 garlic cloves, minced

1 tablespoon honey

Kosher salt and freshly ground
    black pepper

1 tablespoon fresh thyme leaves

Caleb and Maxwell both love raw carrots, but whenever I make this dish, they call it their "special carrots." When I let them pick the vegetable that will go with dinner—a great way to get kids excited about eating their veggies, by the way—they almost always ask for these. The carrots get cooked in browned butter until they're tender and sweet, and then glazed with honey. A little salt, pepper, and fresh thyme keep things on the savory side, but this could almost be dessert it's so delicious. And the best part is that it's easy and quick enough to make during the week (especially because it goes with just about anything), but also elegant enough for a more special supper.

1 In a large skillet, melt the butter over medium-high heat. Whisk until it starts to get frothy and brown, about 2 minutes. Add the carrots and garlic and reduce the heat to medium. Cook for 5 to 7 minutes, stirring occasionally, until the carrots are tender but still crisp.

2 Turn off the heat and drizzle the honey over the carrots. Stir to coat, then season with a pinch of salt and pepper plus the fresh thyme. Serve warm.

VEGETARIAN MAIN DISHES

People always ask me what we *really* eat at our house. They have a hard time believing that we really do cook all these meals (we do!), and also that we don't really eat that much meat. There's this thinking that in order to have a filling meal, you need to have meat on your plate. Well, I'm here to officially let you know that that's just not true. We don't eat meat every single night for a few reasons: It's super budget-friendly; I'm a vegetarian; and over the years I've learned how to cook hearty, satisfying dishes that don't need meat to be completely delicious. No crazy "specialty" ingredients required. Believe me when I tell you that there's not a peep from the peanut gallery when I serve something that doesn't have any beef, pork, or chicken—only cleaned plates! And I have the same experience when we have people over. Sometimes someone will say, "Oh, I just realized that we didn't even have any meat!" But it's only because they're so impressed that the meal was so deeply satisfying and just so happened to be vegetarian. The recipes in this section include some of our most popular dishes on the blog (there's about a bajillion comments for our Black Bean–Quinoa Enchilada Bake, about how much their families can't get enough of it), along with a bunch more of our favorites that are completely kid- and carnivore-approved.

greek salad pita pizzas

prep: **20 MINUTES** | cook: **5 MINUTES** | total: **25 MINUTES** | serves **4**

TZATZIKI SAUCE

1 cup plain Greek yogurt

½ cup diced seedless English cucumber

1 tablespoon fresh lemon juice

1 tablespoon finely chopped fresh dill

1 garlic clove, minced

½ teaspoon kosher salt

¼ teaspoon freshly ground black pepper

PITA PIZZAS

4 (6-inch) white or whole-wheat pitas

1 cup Creamy Hummus (page 90) or store-bought hummus

2 cups chopped romaine lettuce

1 cup halved grape tomatoes

1 cup chopped English cucumber

½ cup pitted Kalamata olives

½ small red onion, thinly sliced

⅓ cup crumbled feta cheese

Chopped fresh dill and parsley, for garnish (optional)

As much as we love making our own pizza dough from scratch (pages 173, 201), sometimes you need a quick store-bought alternative. I came up with these easy pita pizzas to give traditional pizza night a Greek twist, complete with warmed pitas as the crust, hummus instead of tomato sauce, and a whole bunch of fresh toppings like tomatoes, Kalamata olives, red onion, and of course, feta cheese. Then I top 'em off with freshly stirred-up tzatziki sauce, the yogurt-y, herb-y condiment you'll find served with most Greek dishes. You could serve these for dinner or put them out as a starter for parties—either way, there won't be leftovers!

1 Make the tzatziki: In a small bowl, combine the yogurt, cucumber, lemon juice, dill, garlic, salt, and pepper. Stir and set aside.

2 Assemble the pita pizzas: Preheat the oven to 400°F. Place the pita breads on a large baking sheet and bake until warmed through, 5 to 7 minutes.

3 Spread each pita with ¼ cup hummus. Top with the romaine, tomatoes, cucumber, olives, onion, and feta. Drizzle the tzatziki sauce over the tops and garnish with fresh dill and parsley, if desired. Cut into triangles and serve immediately.

bbq chickpea–quinoa bowls

prep: **30 MINUTES** | cook: **30 MINUTES** | total: **1 HOUR** | serves **4 TO 6**

BBQ CHICKPEAS

1 (15-ounce) can chickpeas, rinsed, drained, and skins removed (see page 90)

1 tablespoon extra-virgin olive oil

¾ teaspoon smoked paprika

¾ teaspoon garlic powder

¼ teaspoon onion powder

¼ teaspoon kosher salt

¼ teaspoon freshly ground black pepper

¼ cup of your favorite barbecue sauce

CILANTRO-LIME QUINOA

1 cup quinoa, rinsed under cold water

2 cups vegetable broth or water

⅓ cup fresh cilantro, chopped

3 tablespoons fresh lime juice (2 limes)

Kosher salt

Why should only meat eaters get to have all the barbecue fun? I decided to take the classic barbecue chicken salad and swap in roasted chickpeas instead. They give you that same meaty texture with a great crispy crunch. And of course, barbecue flavor. It's so easy and versatile, and even the most hardcore carnivore won't miss their chicken.

I love serving these bowls for company because everyone can mix-and-match their own toppings. Or if you want a healthy lunch or dinner waiting for you in the fridge, a great time-saver is building bowls in individual containers, so you can just grab them. Just wait to add the avocado and dressing until you're ready to eat.

1 Make the BBQ chickpeas: **Preheat the oven to 425°F.**

2 In a medium bowl, combine the chickpeas, olive oil, paprika, garlic powder, onion powder, salt, and pepper. Stir until the chickpeas are well coated. Arrange the chickpeas on a large baking sheet, making sure they are spread out evenly and not touching (which will help them get crispy). Roast for 15 minutes. Stir and roast for 15 to 20 minutes longer, until the chickpeas are crispy. In a medium bowl, combine the roasted chickpeas with the barbecue sauce and toss to coat. Set aside.

3 Meanwhile, make the quinoa: **In a large pot, combine the quinoa and broth and bring to a boil. Cover, reduce the heat to low, and cook until the liquid is evaporated and the quinoa is tender, about 15 minutes. Remove the pot from the heat and let stand, covered, for 5 minutes. Remove the lid and fluff the quinoa with a fork. Stir in the cilantro and lime juice and season with salt to taste. Keep the quinoa covered until ready to assemble the bowls.**

recipe continues

1 cup plain Greek yogurt

½ cup buttermilk

2 teaspoons fresh lemon juice

1 teaspoon white wine vinegar

1 jalapeño, seeded and diced
   (optional)

1 garlic clove, minced

3 tablespoons chopped fresh
   parsley

2 tablespoons chopped fresh
   chives

2 tablespoons chopped fresh dill
   or ¾ teaspoon dried dill

¼ teaspoon onion powder

Kosher salt and freshly ground
   black pepper

TO ASSEMBLE

2 to 3 cups chopped romaine
   lettuce

1 cup shredded purple cabbage

1 cup halved grape or cherry
   tomatoes

1 cup fresh, frozen, or canned
   sweet corn

1 to 2 ripe avocados, pitted,
   peeled, and sliced

3 scallions (white and green parts),
   thinly sliced

½ cup shredded cheddar cheese
   (optional)

Chopped fresh cilantro, for garnish

Tortilla chips, for serving (optional)

4 Make the ranch dressing: In a medium bowl, whisk together the yogurt, buttermilk, lemon juice, vinegar, jalapeño (if using), garlic, parsley, chives, dill, and onion powder. Season to taste with salt and pepper.

5 Assemble the bowls: Divide the quinoa among four to six bowls and top with BBQ chickpeas, lettuce, cabbage, tomatoes, corn, avocado, scallions, and cheese (if using). Drizzle with the ranch dressing and garnish with fresh cilantro. Serve with tortilla chips, if desired.

enchilada-stuffed sweet potatoes

prep: **20 MINUTES** | cook: **1 HOUR** | total: **1 HOUR 20 MINUTES** | serves **4**

• •

4 medium sweet potatoes, scrubbed

1 tablespoon extra-virgin olive oil

½ cup chopped red onion

2 garlic cloves, minced

1 red bell pepper, cored, seeded, and diced

1 (15-ounce) can black beans, drained and rinsed

¼ cup packed chopped fresh cilantro, plus more for serving

1 tablespoon fresh lime juice

Kosher salt and freshly ground black pepper

2 cups Enchilada Sauce (recipe follows) or store-bought enchilada sauce

1 cup shredded Mexican blend or pepper Jack cheese

Plain Greek yogurt or sour cream, for serving

1 ripe avocado, pitted, peeled, and diced; or Go-To Guacamole (page 92), for serving

Crumbled queso fresco, for serving

Sweet potatoes are in my top five favorite foods of all time (along with avocado, watermelon, peanut butter, and cookies). I can't live without them! They're just so creamy and sweet and filling. But as delicious as they are on their own, nothing beats loading them up with homemade enchilada sauce, cheese, black beans, veggies, and *all* the toppings. These stuffed sweet taters are seriously the queen of both loaded baked potatoes *and* enchiladas! Plus, they're so easy to put together (especially if you bake the sweet potatoes and make the enchilada sauce ahead of time) that I pretty much could make them every night and no one—including myself—would be sad about it.

1   Preheat the oven to 400°F. Line a large baking sheet with aluminum foil. Use a fork to pierce the sweet potatoes all over. Place them on the lined baking sheet and bake for 50 to 60 minutes, until soft. Time will vary depending on the size of the sweet potato. Keep the oven on and do not remove the foil from the baking sheet.

2   Heat the olive oil in a large skillet over medium-high heat. Add the onion and sauté for 2 minutes. Add the garlic and bell pepper and cook for 2 minutes. Stir in the black beans, cilantro, and lime juice. Season with salt and pepper to taste, then continue cooking for 3 minutes. Set aside.

3   Slice the baked sweet potatoes in half lengthwise. Use a fork to smash down the flesh so you have more room to fill them. Pour about ¼ cup enchilada sauce over each potato half. Spoon the black bean filling over the sauce and sprinkle evenly with cheese. Arrange the sweet potatoes on the same baking sheet and bake for 5 to 10 minutes, until the cheese has melted.

4   Top with yogurt or sour cream, avocado or guacamole, cilantro, and queso fresco. Serve hot.

NOTE: *You can easily make these vegan by leaving out the cheese and yogurt or sour cream, or using nondairy versions of these ingredients.*

recipe continues

Enchilada Sauce

prep: **5 MINUTES**

cook: **15 MINUTES**

total: **20 MINUTES**

makes **ABOUT 2 CUPS**

You'll wonder where this enchilada sauce has been your whole life. There's rarely a time when we don't have a batch waiting for us in the freezer because there's just no way we can go back to the store-bought stuff—we've gotten too spoiled!

3 tablespoons vegetable oil

3 tablespoons all-purpose flour

¼ cup chili powder

1 teaspoon ground cumin

¼ teaspoon cayenne

¼ teaspoon dried oregano

¼ teaspoon onion powder

½ teaspoon kosher salt, plus more to taste

1 garlic clove, minced

2 tablespoons tomato paste

2 cups vegetable broth

Heat the oil in a large saucepan over medium heat. Add the flour and whisk for 1 minute. Add all the spices, the salt, and garlic and stir for another minute. Whisk in the tomato paste, then slowly pour in the broth, whisking constantly until the mixture is smooth. Let the sauce simmer over medium-low heat for 10 to 12 minutes, until slightly thickened. The sauce will thicken more as it cools. Taste and season with additional salt, if necessary. Store in the fridge for up to 1 week, or in the freezer for up to 2 months.

goat cheese pasta
with spinach and artichokes

prep: 10 MINUTES | cook: 15 MINUTES | total: 25 MINUTES | serves 4

Kosher salt and freshly ground black pepper

8 ounces dried orecchiette or your favorite short pasta

1 tablespoon extra-virgin olive oil

2 tablespoons minced shallot

3 garlic cloves, minced

Pinch of crushed red pepper flakes

Grated zest of 1 lemon

6 cups packed fresh spinach leaves

1 (14-ounce) can quartered artichoke hearts, drained

5 ounces (1 small log) goat cheese (see Note)

2 tablespoons fresh lemon juice (1 large lemon)

3 tablespoons chopped fresh basil, for garnish

Cheesy pasta that takes less than 30 minutes to make? Can I get a high five?! This easy pasta dish is a weeknight wonder—it's exceptionally tasty and comes together in no time. Plus, I'm a sucker for anything with both spinach and artichokes! The secret is tangy, creamy goat cheese, which instantly melts into the pasta and makes the most amazing sauce. If you think you don't like goat cheese, try this pasta and think again—I promise you'll change your mind.

1   Bring a large pot of water to a boil. Generously salt the water and cook the pasta according to package directions until al dente. Reserve ½ cup of the cooking water and drain the pasta. Set aside.

2   Heat the olive oil in a large skillet over medium-high heat. Add the shallot and garlic and cook for 2 minutes. Add the pepper flakes and zest, along with the spinach. Cook until the spinach wilts, about 3 minutes. Stir in the artichoke hearts.

3   Add the pasta to the spinach and artichoke mixture. Crumble the goat cheese over the top and stir in the lemon juice along with ¼ cup of the reserved pasta water. Continue stirring until a creamy sauce coats the pasta. If the pasta isn't creamy enough, add additional pasta water. Season with salt and pepper to taste and garnish with fresh basil.

NOTE: *Be sure to buy goat cheese in log form, which is creamier than pre-crumbled.*

roasted butternut squash farro
with kale-walnut pesto

prep: **25 MINUTES** | cook: **45 MINUTES** | total: **1 HOUR 10 MINUTES** | serves **4 TO 6**

ROASTED BUTTERNUT SQUASH

1 medium butternut squash, peeled, seeded, and cubed (about 6 cups)

1 tablespoon extra-virgin olive oil

Kosher salt and freshly ground black pepper

FARRO

2 cups uncooked farro

5 cups vegetable broth

KALE-WALNUT PESTO

2 cups packed stemmed Tuscan or dinosaur kale

1 cup packed fresh basil leaves

1 garlic clove, minced

2 tablespoons fresh lemon juice (1 large lemon)

Kosher salt and freshly ground black pepper

½ cup extra-virgin olive oil

½ cup whole walnuts

There is nothing better than comfort food that also happens to be really good for you. The star here is my favorite whole grain: chewy, hearty farro, which has a similar taste and texture as barley. And because I'm all about sneaking greens into meals, I added kale to a bright walnut pesto, which puts the flavor of the dish over the top. I love cozying up to a big bowl of this for dinner in the fall, or I'll even serve it as a side dish at Thanksgiving gatherings. It always gets rave reviews!

1 Roast the squash: Preheat the oven to 400°F.

2 Arrange the squash cubes on a large rimmed baking sheet, drizzle with the olive oil, and season with a pinch of salt and a few cracks of black pepper. Roast for 40 to 45 minutes, until the squash is tender. Set aside.

3 Meanwhile, make the farro: In a large saucepan, combine the farro and broth, bring to a boil, and cover. Reduce the heat to low and simmer for 20 minutes, until the farro is cooked and tender, but not mushy. There should still be broth in the pan, even when the farro is done. Drain the farro and return it to the pan.

4 Make the pesto: In a food processor or high-speed blender, combine the kale, basil, garlic, lemon juice, ½ teaspoon salt, and ¼ teaspoon pepper and blend until smooth. With the machine running, slowly stream in the olive oil and blend until the pesto is nice and thick. Stop the machine and add the walnuts. Blend again until smooth. Season with additional salt and pepper, if necessary.

5 Assemble the dish: Add the squash to the pan with the farro. Drizzle over the pesto and stir until the farro and squash are well coated. Heat over medium-low heat just until the dish is warm. Season with salt and pepper, if necessary, and serve.

NOTE: *I always make Josh cut the butternut squash, but to save time you can buy it precut at the store. If you want to bulk up the soup, you can add white beans or chicken.*

sweet and spicy tofu with zucchini noodles

prep: **20 MINUTES** | cook: **20 MINUTES** | total: **40 MINUTES** | serves **4**

TOFU

1 (16-ounce) package extra-firm tofu

2 tablespoons soy sauce

½ cup cornstarch

SAUCE

¼ cup packed brown sugar

Grated zest and juice of 1 medium orange (always zest before juicing!)

2 tablespoons soy sauce or tamari soy sauce

1 tablespoon tomato paste

1 tablespoon rice wine vinegar

1 tablespoon cornstarch

STIR-FRY

2 tablespoons vegetable or canola oil, plus more if needed

2 garlic cloves, minced

2 teaspoons grated fresh ginger

1 teaspoon grated orange zest

¼ teaspoon crushed red pepper flakes

ZUCCHINI NOODLES

1 teaspoon toasted sesame oil

4 small zucchini, spiralized, *or* 4 cups store-bought zucchini noodles

4 scallions (white and green parts), thinly sliced, for garnish

Sesame seeds, for garnish

Think tofu isn't for you? Listen up: This isn't any old tofu; it is crispy, sticky, sweet, spicy *perfection!* I'd say it's as good as Chinese takeout, but it's *way* better because it doesn't get all steamed and soggy on its way to your house, and you can make the sauce as spicy or mild as you like. It's also not all greasy and heavy, thanks to serving the tofu over a bed of zucchini noodles. The flavors are light and fresh, and even the most meat-friendly eaters have loved this dish (no need to point out that it's vegan).

1   Make the tofu: To get your tofu nice and crispy, you need to drain it first: Wrap the tofu block in paper towels and set on a plate. Place a heavy object on top of the tofu to press it down. (A large skillet with a few cans or books on top works well.) Let the tofu sit for 15 to 20 minutes so the excess water can drain. Unwrap the paper towels and cut the tofu into 1-inch cubes.

2   Transfer the tofu cubes to a large zip-top bag. Add the soy sauce and gently mix until the tofu is well coated. Add the cornstarch and gently toss to coat the tofu. It will get pasty, and that is okay. Set aside.

3   Make the sauce: In a medium bowl, combine the brown sugar, orange zest and juice, soy sauce, tomato paste, vinegar, and cornstarch. Whisk until the mixture is smooth and the cornstarch is dissolved. Set aside.

4   Make the stir-fry: In a large non-stick skillet, heat the oil over medium-high heat. Working in batches so you

don't crowd the pan, add the tofu and cook for 3 minutes on each side, until browned and crispy. Transfer the cooked tofu to a plate or bowl. If you need to add more oil in between batches, you can.

5   When all the tofu has been cooked, add the garlic, ginger, orange zest, and pepper flakes to the pan. Cook for 2 minutes. Return all of the tofu to the pan and slowly pour in the sauce. Reduce the heat to low and cook for 5 minutes, until the sauce thickens. Turn off the heat.

6   Make the noodles: In a second large skillet, heat the sesame oil over medium-high heat. Add the zucchini noodles and cook for 1 minute, tossing with tongs so all of the zucchini noodles soften slightly. Don't overcook them—they'll get mushy.

7   Divide the zucchini noodles among four plates and top with the tofu, sliced scallions, and sesame seeds.

veggie-full fried rice

prep: **15 MINUTES** | cook: **15 MINUTES** | total: **30 MINUTES** | serves **6**

2 tablespoons canola oil or other neutral-tasting oil

4 large eggs, whisked

1 small white or yellow onion, chopped

2 carrots, chopped

1 red bell pepper, cored, seeded, and chopped

8 ounces button mushrooms, sliced

1 cup frozen peas

1 cup frozen shelled edamame

4 garlic cloves, minced

1 tablespoon toasted sesame oil

2 cups chilled cooked brown or white rice, any clumps broken up (see Notes)

1 cup cauliflower rice (see Notes)

2 scallions (white and green parts), sliced

3 tablespoons reduced-sodium soy sauce or tamari soy sauce

Pinch of crushed red pepper flakes (optional)

Kosher salt and freshly ground black pepper

This is one of my favorite ways to eat my veggies, and it doesn't hurt that the rest of the family agrees. It's almost unbelievable how you're able to stuff this dish full of all kinds of vegetables—mushrooms, carrots, bell peppers, peas—and yet it doesn't feel like you're just eating a bowl full of them thanks to perfectly crisped-up rice. My little secret is mixing together brown rice with cauliflower rice. (Shhh, don't tell the boys!) It's a cinch to cook up for a healthy weeknight meal, and trust me when I say that you won't miss the take-out version.

1 Heat ½ tablespoon of the canola oil in a large sauté pan or wok over medium-low heat. Swirl the pan so the bottom is completely coated. Pour the whisked eggs into the middle of the pan; as the eggs begin to set, gently pull the eggs across the pan with a spatula, forming large soft curds. Continue cooking, pulling, lifting, and folding the eggs until they are thickened but barely set, about 3 minutes. Transfer the scrambled eggs to a plate and set aside.

2 Add the remaining 1½ tablespoons oil to the pan and heat over medium-high heat. Add the onion, carrots, bell pepper, and mushrooms and sauté for 5 minutes, until the vegetables are soft. Stir in the peas, edamame, and garlic and cook for an additional 3 minutes.

3 Stir in the sesame oil, brown rice, cauliflower rice, scallions, soy sauce, and pepper flakes (if using). Continue stirring for 3 minutes to fry the rice. Add the scrambled eggs and stir until combined. Season with salt and pepper to taste and serve immediately.

NOTES: *The crispy fried rice really is the star of this dish. Whenever we make rice for another dish, we always toss in extra so we have leftovers to make this. In order to get yours super crispy, make sure you use cooked rice that's been chilled. Fresh, warm rice won't work because it'll stick together in the pan, resulting in soggy, clumpy rice. If you don't have time to chill the rice overnight, make a fresh batch, spread it over a large baking sheet, and chill it in the fridge until it's completely cooled, about 30 minutes. We like long-grain brown rice, but white rice works too. I mix it with cauliflower rice, which you can buy at the store—or make it yourself by just pulsing raw cauliflower florets in a food processor until it resembles rice.*

potato, fontina, and rosemary pizza
with whole-wheat crust

prep: 45 MINUTES   cook: 20 MINUTES   total: 1 HOUR 5 MINUTES, PLUS 30 MINUTES RISING   serves 6 TO 8

● ●

WHOLE-WHEAT PIZZA DOUGH

1 cup warm water

2¼ teaspoons (one ¼-ounce packet) active dry yeast

1 teaspoon sugar

2½ cups whole-wheat flour (we use white whole-wheat flour)

1 tablespoon extra-virgin olive oil

1 tablespoon honey

1½ teaspoons kosher salt

TOPPINGS

2 medium Yukon Gold potatoes, scrubbed and dried

1 tablespoon plus 1 teaspoon olive oil

1 garlic clove, minced

3 cups shredded fontina cheese (see Note, page 174)

2 teaspoons minced fresh rosemary

Sea salt, for sprinkling

2 cups arugula

Juice of ½ lemon

This recipe is inspired by a pizza we couldn't get enough of at a restaurant in Salt Lake City. Sadly, the restaurant closed, but luckily Josh and I figured out how to re-create the pizza at home. You might be surprised to see potatoes on pizza, but when they roast in the oven and get crispy on the outside and creamy in the middle, they're the most amazing topping—and carbs on carbs is *always* a good idea. The fontina adds a salty punch, while rosemary adds its herb-y freshness. And when the pie comes out of the oven, it gets topped with arugula and lemon juice, which brightens the whole thing up—and makes the argument that this is pizza *and* a salad!

The pizza dough—whole-wheat with a touch of sweetness from honey—is really versatile and freezes well, so I highly recommend making it ahead or preparing an extra batch to stash away for later use.

1 Make the dough: In the bowl of a stand mixer fitted with the dough hook attachment, combine the warm water, yeast, and sugar. Stir and let sit until the yeast starts to foam and bubble, about 5 minutes.

2 With the mixer on low, slowly add 1¼ cups of the flour plus the olive oil, honey, and kosher salt. When combined, add the remaining 1¼ cups flour. Once a dough starts to form, increase the speed to medium. Mix for 3 to 5 minutes, until the dough is well combined.

3 Turn out the dough onto a floured work surface and knead it a few times to form a ball. The dough should be smooth and shiny. Place the dough in a lightly greased bowl, cover loosely with a towel, and let rise for 30 minutes, until doubled in size. At this point you can cover the bowl with plastic wrap and refrigerate for up to 48 hours. Or freeze the dough in a freezer bag for up to 3 months; make sure to squeeze out all the air before freezing. To defrost, let the dough sit in the fridge overnight.

recipe continues

4 Prepare the toppings: Slice the potatoes very thin using a mandoline or sharp knife. Place the slices in a medium bowl and toss with 1 teaspoon of the olive oil. Set aside.

5 In a ramekin or small bowl, combine the remaining 1 tablespoon olive oil with the minced garlic.

6 Preheat the oven to 450°F.

7 Roll the dough into a 14- to 16-inch round, depending on how thick you like your crust and the size of your pan. Carefully transfer the dough to a baking sheet.

8 Brush the dough evenly with the garlic olive oil and top with the fontina. Arrange the potato slices evenly over the cheese and sprinkle with the rosemary and sea salt.

9 Bake the pizza for 18 to 20 minutes, until the crust is golden brown, the potato is cooked through, and the cheese has melted. Top with the arugula, lemon juice, and a little sea salt. Slice and serve warm.

NOTE: *If you can't find fontina cheese, shredded mozzarella will work well too.*

crispy bean tostadas with smashed avocado and jicama-cilantro slaw

prep: 25 MINUTES | cook: 10 MINUTES | total: 35 MINUTES | serves 3 TO 6

PICKLED RED ONIONS

½ medium red onion, thinly sliced

Juice of 1 lime

1 tablespoon white vinegar

Pinch of kosher salt

JICAMA-CILANTRO SLAW

2 cups shredded green cabbage

½ cup packed fresh cilantro leaves

½ cup ¼-inch-thick slices peeled jicama

Juice of 1 lime

½ teaspoon ground cumin

½ teaspoon chili powder

Kosher salt and freshly ground black pepper

TOSTADAS

6 corn tortillas

Nonstick cooking spray or extra-virgin olive oil

Kosher salt

2 (16-ounce) cans vegetarian refried beans

3 large ripe avocados, pitted and peeled

Juice of 1 lime

½ cup halved grape tomatoes

½ cup crumbled queso fresco

This simple meal has everything going for it: crispy baked tortillas topped with refried beans, a creamy avocado spread, and a refreshing crunchy slaw. I also top off the tostadas with easy pickled onions—and when I say easy, I mean it! There's nothing to be intimidated about when it comes to making them and they add major flavor to the tostadas (or salads, sandwiches, grain bowls, tacos—anything!). The boys love the idea of eating big chips for dinner, and we all just dig in with our hands. Sure, things get a little messy, but that's just how we roll at our house.

1 Make the pickled onions: In a medium bowl, combine the sliced onions with the lime juice, vinegar, and salt and stir until the onions are well coated. Let the onions sit while you make the slaw and tostadas. The pickled onions can be stored in a jar in the fridge for up to 1 week.

2 Make the slaw: In a large bowl, combine the cabbage, cilantro, jicama, lime juice, cumin, and chili powder. Season with salt and pepper to taste and set aside.

3 Assemble the tostadas: Preheat the oven to 425°F.

4 Spray both sides of each tortilla generously with nonstick cooking spray or brush with olive oil, season with salt, and arrange in a single layer on a large baking sheet. Bake for 4 minutes, then flip and bake for 4 to 6 more minutes, until the tortillas are crispy.

5 Gently heat the refried beans in the microwave or on the stovetop. In a medium bowl, smash the avocados with a fork. Stir in the lime juice and season with salt to taste.

6 Spread refried beans evenly over each tortilla. Add a layer of smashed avocado and top with the slaw, pickled onions, tomatoes, and queso fresco. Serve immediately.

NOTE: *If you want to ensure that these tostadas are vegetarian, make sure you buy vegetarian refried beans. To make them vegan, just skip the queso fresco or use a nondairy version.*

garlic-bread eggplant-parmesan sandwiches

prep: **20 MINUTES** | cook: **15 MINUTES** | total: **35 MINUTES** | serves **4**

• •

1 cup panko bread crumbs

1¼ cups grated Parmesan cheese

½ teaspoon dried basil

½ teaspoon dried oregano

½ teaspoon garlic powder

¼ teaspoon kosher salt

¼ teaspoon freshly ground black pepper

1 large egg

1 eggplant, cut into ¼-inch-thick slices

2 tablespoons extra-virgin olive oil, plus more if needed

4 tablespoons unsalted butter, at room temperature

2 garlic cloves, minced

2 (8-inch) Italian-style sandwich rolls, cut in half lengthwise

1 cup Classic Marinara Sauce (recipe follows) or your favorite store-bought sauce

1 cup shredded mozzarella cheese

2 tablespoons chopped fresh parsley or basil

I know that people either love or hate eggplant, so I found a way to ensure that even the most anti-eggplant person will love these open-faced sandwiches. My boys were never big fans, but once they had eggplant slices fried up until golden and crispy, bathed in homemade marinara sauce, topped with melty, gooey cheese, and heaped on top of garlic butter-slathered Italian rolls…let's just say this meal gets requested a *lot*. We'll just keep it a secret that the key to this filling, meaty-tasting dish is none other than eggplant!

1   In a shallow pie plate or baking dish, combine the panko, 1 cup of the Parmesan, the dried basil, oregano, garlic powder, salt, and pepper.

2   In a separate shallow dish, beat the egg with 1 tablespoon water.

3   One at a time, dip the eggplant slices into the egg mixture, then dredge in the panko mixture, pressing on the crumbs gently to adhere and shaking off the excess.

4   Heat the olive oil in a large skillet over medium-high heat. Carefully lay the eggplant slices in a single layer in the hot pan. You may need to do this in batches. Fry the eggplant until deep golden brown, 2 to 3 minutes per side. Transfer the eggplant to a paper towel–lined plate. Repeat with the remaining slices, adding more oil to the pan if necessary.

5   Preheat the oven broiler.

6   In a medium bowl, combine the softened butter and garlic. Spread the garlic butter evenly onto the cut surfaces of the sandwich rolls. Arrange the rolls on a large baking sheet, butter side up. Divide the eggplant slices between the rolls. Spoon the marinara sauce evenly over the eggplant slices and top with the mozzarella and remaining ¼ cup Parmesan.

7   Place the baking sheet under the broiler on the middle rack of the oven and broil for 1 to 2 minutes, until the cheese has melted. Keep an eye on the sandwiches to make sure they don't burn. Top the sandwiches with fresh parsley or basil and serve warm.

recipe continues

Classic Marinara Sauce

prep: 10 MINUTES
cook: 40 MINUTES
total: 50 MINUTES
makes 5 CUPS

There is not a moment when there's not a batch of this traditional red sauce in our freezer. Whether we're making lasagna, chicken or eggplant parm, or just boiling up a pot of noodles or frozen ravioli, homemade marinara is what makes the dish feel like a true home-cooked meal.

2 tablespoons extra-virgin olive oil

1 yellow onion, diced

1 carrot, diced

1 celery stalk, diced

4 garlic cloves, minced

¼ teaspoon crushed red pepper flakes

⅛ teaspoon fennel seeds

1 bay leaf

2 (28-ounce) cans crushed San Marzano tomatoes

½ teaspoon dried oregano

½ teaspoon dried basil

Kosher salt and freshly ground black pepper

¼ cup chopped fresh basil

1   Heat the olive oil in a large pot over medium-high heat. Add the onion, carrot, and celery and cook for 5 minutes, until the vegetables are soft. Stir in the garlic, pepper flakes, fennel seeds, and bay leaf and cook for 2 minutes. Stir in the tomatoes, oregano, dried basil, 1 teaspoon salt, and ¼ teaspoon black pepper. Simmer, uncovered, for 30 minutes.

2   Remove the pot from the heat and discard the bay leaf. Using an immersion blender in the pot, blend the sauce until smooth or to your desired consistency. You can also let the sauce cool slightly, then transfer to a blender to blend. Stir in the fresh basil and season with additional salt and pepper, if necessary. Store in the fridge for up to 1 week or in the freezer for up to 2 months.

NOTE: *I highly recommend using San Marzano tomatoes because I like their flavor more than other canned tomatoes. Whenever I see them on sale I stock up!*

cauliflower and chickpea curry

prep: **15 MINUTES** | cook: **20 MINUTES** | total: **35 MINUTES** | serves **6 TO 8**

2 teaspoons coconut oil

3 garlic cloves, minced

1 teaspoon grated fresh ginger

2 large carrots, peeled and sliced

1 large red bell pepper, cored, seeded, and sliced

¼ cup red curry paste

1 tablespoon tomato paste

2 (13.5-ounce) cans coconut milk

2 tablespoons soy sauce

1 medium head cauliflower, cut into florets

1 (8-ounce) can bamboo shoots, drained

1 (15-ounce) can chickpeas, drained and rinsed

Grated zest and juice of ½ large lime

¾ teaspoon kosher salt

½ teaspoon crushed red pepper flakes

½ cup chopped fresh basil

Cooked basmati rice, for serving

This is my take on Curry in a Hurry—it's just as aromatic and flavorful as what you'd get from a restaurant, yet it's ready in just over 30 minutes. When I put this on the table with plenty of steaming-hot basmati rice, our guests never believe that I didn't order in!

Melt the coconut oil in a large pot over medium heat. Add the garlic and ginger and cook for 2 minutes, until fragrant. Add the carrots and bell pepper and sauté for 2 minutes. Add the curry paste and tomato paste and cook for 1 minute, stirring to coat the veggies. Stir in the coconut milk, soy sauce, cauliflower florets, and bamboo shoots and bring to a boil. Reduce the heat to a simmer and add the chickpeas, lime zest and juice, salt, and pepper flakes. Cook until the cauliflower is tender, 10 to 15 minutes. Remove the pot from the heat and fold in the basil. Serve over basmati rice.

spiced cauliflower and chickpea tacos

prep: **10 MINUTES** | cook: **35 MINUTES** | total: **45 MINUTES** | serves **4**

● ●

SPICED CAULIFLOWER AND CHICKPEAS

Nonstick cooking spray

1 tablespoon extra-virgin olive oil

1 tablespoon fresh lime juice

2 teaspoons chili powder

1 teaspoon ground cumin

1 teaspoon kosher salt

¼ teaspoon garlic powder

¼ teaspoon onion powder

1 (15-ounce) can chickpeas, drained and rinsed

1 small head cauliflower, cut into bite-sized florets

LIME CREMA

1 cup plain Greek yogurt or sour cream

2 tablespoons fresh lime juice (1 to 2 limes)

¼ cup chopped fresh cilantro

Kosher salt and freshly ground black pepper

FOR SERVING

Corn tortillas—I'd say at least 8

1 cup finely chopped red cabbage

1 jalapeño, seeded and sliced

1 large ripe avocado, pitted, peeled, and diced

Chopped fresh cilantro

Throughout my entire pregnancy with Maxwell, I did not stop craving Mexican food. Burritos, tostadas, enchiladas, taco salads—you name it, I *needed* it. That said, I wanted to figure out something new and fresh to add to the rotation, especially because we vegetarians have to get a little more creative when it comes to fillings if we don't want to settle for beans and cheese. I knew that roasted chickpeas made an awesome taco filling, so I started with that and added cauliflower, which gets almost meat-like when it's seasoned and roasted. The finishing touch was a lime crema—Greek yogurt brightened up with lime juice and cilantro—which brought the whole dish together. You heap everything onto warmed corn tortillas with all your favorite toppings, and it's like having the best taqueria in your own home.

1 Make the cauliflower and chickpeas: Preheat the oven to 400°F. Spray a large baking sheet with nonstick cooking spray and set aside.

2 In a medium bowl, whisk together the olive oil, lime juice, chili powder, cumin, salt, garlic powder, onion powder, and 1 tablespoon water. Stir in the chickpeas and cauliflower florets until evenly coated.

3 Arrange the seasoned chickpeas and cauliflower on the prepared baking sheet in a single layer. Roast for 30 to 35 minutes, stirring occasionally, until the chickpeas are slightly crispy and the cauliflower is tender. Set aside.

4 Make the crema: In a medium bowl, combine the yogurt with the lime juice and cilantro. Stir well and season with salt and pepper to taste.

5 To serve: If you want to warm the tortillas first, you can use my trick, which is to use tongs to heat them directly over a gas burner on low; this usually takes 10 to 20 seconds per side, depending on the strength of your burner. Or you can use Josh's trick: Working with two tortillas at a time, place them between two damp paper towels and microwave for 20 to 30 seconds. Or you can just enjoy them fresh! Mound each tortilla with cauliflower and chickpea mixture. Top with cabbage, jalapeño slices, avocado, and cilantro. Drizzle with the lime crema and enjoy!

NOTE: *You can make these tacos vegan by using vegan sour cream or yogurt in the crema.*

pesto-havarti mac and cheese

prep: **5 MINUTES** | cook: **15 MINUTES** | total: **20 MINUTES** | serves **6**

● ●

Kosher salt and freshly ground black pepper

3 cups (12 ounces) whole-wheat elbow macaroni (orecchiette also works well)

4 tablespoons unsalted butter

¼ cup all-purpose flour

2 cups whole milk, at room temperature

2 cups shredded Havarti or mozzarella cheese

3 tablespoons Spinach-Basil Pesto (recipe follows) or store-bought pesto

I usually make a salad for myself on mac and cheese night, unless this version is on the menu—then I grab a bowl and join my boys. This easy "gourmet" version of the classic is my personal favorite, and yet it takes just as little time as the boxed kind to prepare. It gets its creaminess from Havarti cheese (a soft cow's milk cheese that is super melty and gooey—you could also use mozzarella), plus a boost from fresh spinach-basil pesto. At first the boys were wary because their mac wasn't orange, but after one bite they were yelling for more. Now it's a family favorite that we all get excited for.

1   Bring a large pot of salted water to a boil. Add the pasta and cook just until al dente, about 8 minutes. Drain the pasta and set aside.

2   In a large pot, melt the butter over medium heat. Reduce the heat to low and whisk in the flour to create a paste. Add the milk and whisk until smooth. Increase the heat to medium and continue whisking until the sauce starts to thicken, about 2 minutes. Stir in the shredded cheese and continue stirring until the cheese is melted and the sauce is smooth. Fold in the pesto.

3   Add the pasta, stirring to combine, and cook just until the pasta is warmed through. Season with salt and pepper to taste. Serve immediately.

NOTE: *This dish is a great blank canvas for all kinds of mix-ins, such as cooked chicken, broccoli, or frozen peas. And a fun variation is to turn the mac and cheese into a crunchy-topped baked casserole: Just pour the finished mac and cheese into a baking dish, sprinkle panko bread crumbs and Parmesan cheese over the top, and broil for 3 minutes, until the bread crumbs are golden brown.*

Spinach-Basil Pesto

prep: **5 MINUTES**
total: **5 MINUTES**
makes **1 CUP**

In the summer, when our basil is growing like weeds, we make a big batch of pesto and keep it in the fridge or freezer to dig into pretty much at all times, whether we're dolloping it on chicken, pasta, veggies, homemade pizzas, or fish; putting it out as a spread; or schmearing it on sandwiches. Our version gets an extra dose of green from spinach, which doesn't take away from the fresh basil flavor and yet gives you an even more vibrant color and a sneaky serving of vegetables. What you won't find here are nuts—which are traditional in pesto—because Josh is allergic. Not to worry, you won't miss them!

4 cups packed spinach leaves

2 cups packed fresh basil leaves

½ cup extra-virgin olive oil, or more for a thinner pesto

¼ cup grated Parmesan cheese

2 tablespoons fresh lemon juice (1 large lemon)

2 garlic cloves, peeled

½ teaspoon kosher salt, plus more to taste

¼ teaspoon freshly ground black pepper, plus more to taste

1   In a food process or blender, combine all the ingredients and blend for 30 seconds. Scrape the sides down with a spatula and blend again until smooth. If you want a thinner pesto, add more olive oil. Taste and add more salt and pepper, if necessary.

2   Store in a jar or container in the fridge for up to 2 weeks or pour into ice cube molds to freeze for up to 6 months.

NOTE: *One of my favorite tricks is to freeze the pesto in ice cube trays, so all I need to do is pop out a few cubes and toss them in a pan for a perfectly flavorful dish.*

shells with cheese and trees

prep: **10 MINUTES** | cook: **15 MINUTES** | total: **25 MINUTES** | serves **4 TO 6**

½ teaspoon kosher salt, plus more for cooking the pasta

3 cups (12 ounces) pasta shells (we use whole-wheat)

2 cups broccoli florets

4 tablespoons unsalted butter

¼ cup all-purpose flour

2 cups whole milk, at room temperature

2 cups shredded cheddar cheese

¼ teaspoon freshly ground black pepper

Once you try this almost-instant homemade version, you'll never buy a box of mac and cheese again. It's as simple as whisking up the creamy (real!) cheese sauce while the pasta boils, and throwing some broccoli florets—oops, I mean *trees!*—in with the pasta during the last couple minutes of cooking. In total, it takes just about as much time and only slightly more ingredients than making a boxed version, and yet it's so much more flavorful and delicious—with a few veggies thrown in for good measure. Our boys love this mac and cheese, but it isn't just for kids—it's a huge hit when we pull it out for grown-up company, too.

1 Bring a large pot of salted water to a boil. Add the pasta and cook just until al dente, about 10 minutes. Add the broccoli to the pot and continue cooking for 2 minutes. Drain the pasta and broccoli and set aside.

2 Meanwhile, melt the butter in a large pot over medium heat. Reduce the heat to low and whisk in the flour to create a paste. Whisk in the milk until smooth. Increase the heat to medium and whisk until the sauce begins to thicken, about 2 minutes. Fold in the shredded cheddar and stir until the cheese is melted and the sauce is smooth.

3 Add the drained pasta and broccoli to the sauce and stir until evenly coated. Season with the salt and black pepper. Serve immediately.

black bean–quinoa enchilada bake

prep: **15 MINUTES** | cook: **1 HOUR** | total: **1 HOUR 15 MINUTES** | serves **8 TO 10**

Nonstick cooking spray

1 cup quinoa, rinsed with cold water

1 tablespoon extra-virgin olive oil

1 small yellow onion, diced

3 garlic cloves, minced

1 jalapeño, seeded and diced

1 red bell pepper, cored, seeded, and diced

1 orange or yellow bell pepper, cored, seeded, and diced

1 cup frozen corn kernels

Juice of 1 small lime

1 tablespoon chili powder

1 teaspoon ground cumin

⅓ cup chopped fresh cilantro

Kosher salt and freshly ground black pepper

2 (15-ounce) cans black beans, drained and rinsed

2 cups Enchilada Sauce (page 164) or store-bought

2 cups shredded Mexican cheese

For garnish (optional): sliced scallions, sliced radishes, sliced avocado, sour cream

For serving (optional): tortilla chips

This is one of our favorite family meals and one of the most popular recipes on the blog. It miraculously satisfies everyone: meat-lovers, vegetarians, kiddos. It blends fresh veggies like corn, bell peppers, garlic, and onions (take a tip from Josh and wear your ski goggles to keep from crying while chopping!) with hearty, filling quinoa and black beans to make the kind of dinner that's easy to pull together on a weeknight but also freezes really nicely if you're planning ahead. The boys recommend that you serve it with tortilla chips for scooping up all its cheesy goodness.

1 Preheat the oven to 350°F. Grease a 9 × 13-inch baking dish with nonstick cooking spray and set aside.

2 In a medium saucepan, combine the quinoa and 2 cups water, bring to a boil over medium heat, reduce the heat to low, and simmer for about 15 minutes, until all the water is absorbed. Remove the pot from the heat and fluff the quinoa with a fork. Cover and set aside.

3 In a large skillet, heat the olive oil over medium-high heat. Add the onion, garlic, and jalapeño and sauté until softened, about 5 minutes. Add the bell peppers and corn and cook for 3 to 4 minutes. Stir in the lime juice, chili powder, cumin, and cilantro and remove the pot from the heat. Season with salt and pepper to taste.

4 In a large bowl, combine the cooked quinoa and black beans. Add the sautéed vegetable mixture and enchilada sauce and stir to combine. Fold in ½ cup of the shredded cheese. Pour the mixture into the prepared baking dish. Top with the remaining 1½ cups shredded cheese and cover the pan with aluminum foil. Bake for 20 minutes. Remove the foil and bake for an additional 10 minutes, until the cheese is melted and the edges are bubbling. Let the casserole cool for 10 minutes. Garnish with your toppings of choice and serve warm with tortilla chips, if desired.

spaghetti squash with broccolini, tomatoes, and garlic bread crumbs

prep: **20 MINUTES** | cook: **1 HOUR** | total: **1 HOUR 20 MINUTES** | serves **4 TO 6**

● ●

SPAGHETTI SQUASH

1 large spaghetti squash

1 tablespoon extra-virgin olive oil

Kosher salt and freshly ground black pepper

GARLIC BREAD CRUMBS

½ loaf crusty artisan bread, roughly torn

4 tablespoons unsalted butter

3 garlic cloves, minced

¼ cup finely chopped fresh basil

BROCCOLINI AND TOMATOES

1 pound broccolini, ends trimmed

1 pint grape tomatoes

2 tablespoons extra-virgin olive oil

2 tablespoons balsamic vinegar

Kosher salt and freshly ground black pepper

½ cup grated Parmesan cheese

NOTE: *You can add Classic Marinara Sauce (page 180) or Spinach-Basil Pesto (page 186) to this recipe if you want it saucier.*

Spaghetti squash is magical—you put it in the oven as squash, but when you pull it out, it's spaghetti! This is because the squash flesh has a noodle-like texture and a mild taste, which makes it perfect for treating like pasta. Since it's so nice and light, I love topping it with even more roasted vegetables, such as broccolini (broccoli's skinnier cousin) and oven-blistered tomatoes, plus my favorite homemade garlic bread crumbs. The only thing left to do is sprinkle everything with plenty of Parmesan!

1 Make the squash: **Preheat the oven to 425°F.**

2 Cut the squash in half lengthwise and scoop out the seeds with a large spoon. Place the squash on a large baking sheet cut side up, drizzle the flesh with the olive oil, and season with a pinch of salt and a couple cracks of pepper. Roast for 50 to 60 minutes, until the squash is tender and light golden brown around the edges. Let the squash sit at room temperature until cool enough to handle.

3 Meanwhile, make the bread crumbs: In a food processor, pulse the bread into fine crumbs. Melt the butter in a large skillet over medium heat. Add the garlic and cook for 2 minutes. Stir in the bread crumbs and reduce the heat to medium-low. Toast the bread crumbs for 7 to 10 minutes, stirring constantly and making sure that they get nice and toasty but don't burn. Remove the pan from the heat, stir in the basil, and set aside.

4 Make the broccolini and tomatoes: Arrange the broccolini and tomatoes in a single layer on a large baking sheet. Drizzle with the olive oil and balsamic vinegar and toss until well coated. Season with a pinch of salt and a few cracks of black pepper. After the squash has roasted for 30 minutes, transfer the broccolini and tomatoes to the oven and roast for 20 minutes, until the broccolini is tender and the tomatoes are blistered.

5 Assemble the dish: Use a fork to scrape the spaghetti squash strands away from the skin. Discard the skin and divide the squash among serving plates. Top with the roasted vegetables and garlic bread crumbs and sprinkle with the Parmesan. Serve immediately.

Cooking with Kids

We love cooking with our boys and find that it makes cooking more fun for everyone. We turn on our favorite tunes and have kitchen dance parties while we work. Time is precious with kids, and we love spending as much of it with our little peas as we can. It gives us a chance to share stories about our day, plus we get to teach them kitchen skills so someday they can cook on their own...and maybe even for us!

The kitchen is the perfect place for kids to fall in love with and appreciate food. The more you're willing to let them help, the more involved they'll want to be. And when they feel a sense of ownership in the meal, they're more likely to want to eat it. As any parent can tell you, that's a major score! That all adds up to the kitchen being our happy place.

Here are some of our favorite tips for cooking with kids:

- **Let them help pick the recipes, or pick a recipe you know they love.** It will get them excited about what they're about to cook! It also helps to pick age-appropriate recipes, so maybe no fresh pasta on the first try...And it doesn't have to be dinner! Maybe a simple snack is a better place for you to start.

- **Feed them first!** This is the golden rule—don't expect a hungry kid to wait patiently to be done with the recipe. A small snack before cooking (for kids and adults!) is essential.

- **Don't be a in a rush.** Expect it to take a little longer to make the recipe and plan accordingly. Patience is crucial! If they see you get frustrated, they'll get frustrated too and want to give up.

The more you practice together, the better they'll get, and the more confidence they'll have. Kids need time to play and learn in the kitchen! Weekends are a great time to cook with kids because you won't feel as rushed.

- **Be ready for a mess.** Cooking is messy and so are kids—so embrace it. There's nothing you can't clean up later—or better yet, get the kids involved in that too!

- **Dress accordingly.** Make sure you and your kids are wearing clothes that can get splattered and spilled on. It's a great reason to get everyone their own special apron.

- **Make it easy.** Have a step stool so little ones can comfortably reach the counter, or use the kitchen table as your work area. Look at your recipe beforehand and think

about all the ways little hands can help: mixing, whisking, measuring, grabbing ingredients from the fridge or pantry, even taste testing! Giving kids a job title like Chief Mixer or Head Taster makes them feel important that they play a special role in making the meal.

- **Make it safe.** Before getting started, talk about kitchen safety. If your child is old enough to use a knife (there's no right answer—it's what you feel comfortable with; there are great kid-friendly options available), teach him how to properly hold it. In any case, remove other sharp and any hot objects from reach. And don't forget to wash your hands!

- **Make it interesting.** Read through the recipe, or have older children read the recipe.

Discuss the steps and talk about what you'll be doing—and keep it exciting! When you think of it from a child's perspective (or an adult's!), mixing a whole bunch of ingredients together is like a big science experiment! You can also talk about the individual ingredients, where they come from, and what they taste like. Make sure there are plenty of taste tests along the way!

- **Make it fun.** Get kids involved from the very beginning—seeing the process from start to finish is exciting! Let them help pick out the ingredients at the farmers market or store. Then when you get in the kitchen, embrace the spirit of the project—have a good time! We love music in our kitchen, and we also pull out special spoons, bowls, and measuring cups in bright colors that the kids love.

- **Make it teamwork.** If you have more than one child, make sure your kids take turns and work together. We're always telling the boys that we're a team—everyone has a job and everyone's job is equally important for the meal to come together.

- **Have reasonable expectations.** Your little one might not be ready to help with an entire recipe from start to finish, and some kids have different attention spans. Even if they help a little, that's still enough to make them feel important. Be sure to offer lots of praise and encouragement!

Getting Dinner on the Table

Here in the Two Peas kitchen, dinner is not about fussy dishes that you've had to babysit all day. To us, a great meal is less about what you cook and more about who you share it with. That's the intention that has gone into every recipe in the main dish chapters: It's all about sharing a nourishing meal with the people you love, whether that's your family, friends, roommates, or neighbors. I can't think of anything that makes me happier than pulling out the recipe that my boys helped choose, having Josh chopping up some veggies on one end of the counter, and the boys helping me stir sauce at the other. We turn up the music—we play Maxwell and Caleb's favorite songs—and have a blast making something delicious together.

I like bringing that same casual, laid-back, everyone-pitching-in approach to entertaining—which any of the dishes in the two main dish chapters are perfect for. Between Josh inviting people over anytime he runs into someone at the grocery store and our open-door policy, we're pretty consistently setting extra spots at the table. But that doesn't mean we're stressing out about the house not being clean enough, the kids not being dressed up enough, or the food not being fancy enough. We want people to see how we are as a *real* family, sink full of dirty dishes and all. Nothing is staged! It all looks exactly the way it would if we were just cooking for ourselves—us having a great time and all hands on deck in the kitchen. We might put out an appetizer (or four!) so guests can settle in and make themselves at home, but otherwise, we'll be busy getting dinner on the table, and if anyone wants to join us, the more, the merrier! And even though our main dish recipes are divided into vegetarian and meat/fish chapters, what the recipes have in common is that they all taste better when shared with people you like and love. (They can also all be easily adapted to either include meat or leave it out.)

Of course, there's always going to be those days when Josh and I are racing into the house after a long day hopping between meetings and calls, or we're coming home late after soccer practice. That's why we aim for getting a from-scratch homemade meal on the table four nights a week. The other three nights we either repurpose leftovers, rewarm something from the freezer, or hit up our very handy un-recipes (page 234). So if you're just starting out cooking for yourself or your family, don't be too hard on yourself! As for deciding what to cook, check out page 27 for my meal planning tips. It's a great way to get everyone in the family involved!

HOW TO COOK MORE HOMEMADE MEALS... AND STAY SANE

While I've made it my mission to include many helpful tips and tricks throughout this book to help you realize that cooking at home is not only easy but also fun, I want you to know that dinner's not always going to be a perfect, Instagram-worthy affair. So even though you might have the best-stocked pantry and an arsenal of great recipes, one of the most important tools for cooking more at home—and enjoying it—is also having reasonable expectations of yourself and your family. We use these same guidelines in our family, especially on weeknights:

- **Divide and conquer.** If everyone's home for dinner—which, granted, doesn't always happen owing to busy schedules—we get everyone involved. We get the boys stirring, grabbing ingredients from the pantry, or running items to the table. We put on music, loosen up, and just have fun. It gets dinner on our plates more quickly, and we've also found that getting the boys involved means there's a better chance they'll eat whatever we're making. Plus, kitchen time is quality time.

- **It's okay to keep it quick.** Just because everyone is sitting down to dinner together doesn't mean it has to take all night! Sometimes we just have 10 minutes to grab something before heading out for an activity, but taking that time to sit and spend it together makes it meaningful.

- **Embrace the un-recipes!** Following a recipe doesn't get you more points than whipping up scrambled eggs with some roasted veggies on top. See page 234 for some of our go-to un-recipes, or simple preparations that barely require any time to make and still totally count as a home-cooked meal.

- **Don't be a short-order cook.** This is when menu planning with kids can come in handy—if my boys start to complain about what's for dinner, I remind them that it was our plan and that we all agreed on it. If that doesn't work, we have a rule that you have to try everything and take at least two bites. If someone doesn't like it, they can say "No, thank you" and sit with the rest of the family while we eat. But we are not making them a new meal. Nothing wrong with a little tough love!

MEAT AND FISH MAIN DISHES

Sometimes people don't believe me when I tell them that Josh is just as kitchen-savvy as I am and loves spending just as much time in there as I do. Well, it's true! Josh has been an avid cook and baker since before I met him, and his culinary expertise has only grown since then. Whether it's making the perfect chewy pizza crust, flaky pot pie, or smoked-to-perfection ribs, Josh is my go-to guy. He's the best cooking partner a girl could ask for—and his cleanup skills aren't too shabby either! I'm especially lucky that he's a meat master. Since I'm a vegetarian, that part of the menu isn't my expertise, so I look to Josh to help whip up hearty, meaty (and fishy) dishes that please just about every-one. The recipes in this chapter are his creations, but I can attest to how well loved they are. And I've included some of his tips for how to get them just right.

baked chicken taquitos

prep: **20 MINUTES** | bake: **15 TO 20 MINUTES** | total: **40 MINUTES** | makes **ABOUT 20 TAQUITOS**

Nonstick cooking spray

2 cups shredded rotisserie chicken

½ teaspoon ground cumin

½ teaspoon chili powder

½ teaspoon kosher salt

¼ teaspoon garlic powder

¼ teaspoon paprika

2 teaspoons fresh lime juice

1 cup shredded cheddar or
  Mexican cheese blend

20 corn tortillas

For serving: Go-To Guacamole
  (page 92), Easy Blender Salsa
  (page 93), shredded lettuce,
  diced tomatoes, sour cream,
  chopped scallions, crumbled
  queso fresco

JOSH'S TIP: *Layering the tortillas
in damp paper towels before heating
them creates a steaming effect, which
makes the tortillas easier to roll.*

It's a great feeling when your dinner plan gets a round of cheers from the kids. It helps that the boys love yelling "TAQUITOS!"—but mostly they're excited because it means they get to gobble up a whole bunch of crispy oven-baked taco rolls. These are great served as an appetizer or as a meal, and they're perfect for quick dinners and parties because you can use leftover chicken or shredded store-bought rotisserie chicken, you can bake them in advance and reheat them in the oven or microwave, or you can even freeze them. Then put out all the topping options for guests to add themselves. Just don't forget the special song to sing while making them: "Rolling, rolling, rolling, get those taquitos rolling…"

1 Preheat the oven to 425°F. Spray a large baking sheet with nonstick cooking spray and set aside.

2 In a medium bowl, combine the shredded chicken with the cumin, chili powder, salt, garlic powder, paprika, and lime juice. Stir until the chicken is well coated with the seasonings. Add the shredded cheese and toss to combine.

3 Working with two tortillas at a time, place the tortillas between two damp paper towels and microwave for 20 to 30 seconds. Place a heaping table-spoon of the chicken and cheese mix-ture in the center of each and roll up tightly. Place the taquitos seam side down on the prepared baking sheet. Continue softening the tortillas and rolling taquitos until the tortillas and filling are gone. You should have about 20 taquitos.

4 Spray the taquitos generously with nonstick cooking spray. Bake for 15 to 20 minutes, until the taquitos are golden brown and crispy. Serve warm with the toppings of your choice.

5 To freeze, place the baked taqui-tos on a baking sheet and freeze com-pletely before transferring to a freezer bag and storing in the freezer for up to 1 month. When ready to reheat, place the frozen taquitos on a large baking sheet, spray with nonstick cooking spray, and bake in a 425°F oven for 15 to 20 minutes, until completely heated through.

bbq chicken pizza

prep: **30 MINUTES**   bake: **25 TO 30 MINUTES**   total: **1 HOUR, PLUS 2 HOURS RISING**   makes **12 SQUARE SLICES**

● ●

JOSH'S PIZZA DOUGH

1 cup whole milk

1 tablespoon unsalted butter, plus more for greasing

1 tablespoon sugar

1 teaspoon kosher salt

2¼ teaspoons (one ¼-ounce package) active dry yeast

5 cups all-purpose flour, plus more if needed

TOPPINGS AND SAUCE

2½ cups chopped cooked chicken

½ cup plus 2 tablespoons of your favorite barbecue sauce

3 cups shredded mozzarella cheese

½ cup chopped cooked bacon

½ cup diced pineapple

½ cup jarred sliced tamed jalapeño peppers (see Note, page 202), drained

2 tablespoons unsalted butter, melted

1 garlic clove, minced

Josh is the pizza master in our house, and he's perfected the art of making dough from scratch. So we throw a lot of pizza parties—for game days, birthdays, holidays, Friday night pizza nights (our boys' favorite night of the week, of course)—and BBQ Chicken Pizza is always on the menu. We sometimes think people come over just so they can eat this sheet-pan pizza, which is loaded with barbecue chicken, tons of cheese, pineapple, bacon, and jalapeño slices, all piled on top of a perfectly pillowy homemade crust. Luckily, Josh has agreed to finally share his secrets to making his world-famous pizza—you're welcome!

1   Make the dough: In a small saucepan, gently warm the milk over medium heat until it's hot to the touch, taking care not to let it boil. Stir in the butter, sugar, and salt. Remove the pot from the heat and allow the milk mixture to cool until it's just warm to the touch. (Make sure it is not too hot or it will kill the yeast.) Add the yeast and mix thoroughly. Let stand until foamy, about 5 minutes.

2   In the bowl of a stand mixer fitted with the dough hook, add the milk mixture. Mix on low speed as you slowly add 1 cup flour, then add ½ cup water. Continue to mix, adding the flour 1 cup at a time. Then add another ½ cup water and mix until the dough pulls away from the side of the bowl and forms a ball. If the dough is still wet, add a little more flour. Continue mixing for 5 minutes, until the dough is silky and smooth. Turn out the dough into a large, butter-greased

bowl. Cover the bowl with a damp clean towel and allow the dough to rise at room temperature for 45 minutes to 1 hour, until doubled in size.

3   Punch the dough down and form the dough back into a ball. Let it rise for another 45 minutes to 1 hour, until again doubled in size.

4   Make the pizza: Preheat the oven to 400°F. Lightly grease an 18 × 13-inch rimmed baking sheet with butter and set aside.

5   Give the dough another punch and knead briefly on a lightly floured surface. Using a rolling pin, roll out the pizza dough to a ½-inch thickness; it should be roughly the same size as the baking sheet. Place the dough on the prepared pan, pushing the dough into the bottom and rolling the edges around the lip of the pan to create a nice crust all the way around the pan.

recipe continues

Pizza Tips from Josh

Over the years I've made it my mission to perfect homemade pizza. At first it was out of necessity—what's less expensive than mixing together flour, water, and yeast?—and then I realized that homemade was always way more delicious than delivery. So I challenged myself to make the best version ever. It takes a little extra work than phoning in an order, but it's like a really neat science experiment that the kids love—you get to mix everything together to make a crazy goo, watch it grow as it rises, and then get your hands all in there to knead it. It's an afternoon activity and dinner all in one!

Here are the secrets I've discovered for making the perfect homemade deep-dish crust:

Let it rise twice: This helps the crust get nice and pillowy with tons of flavor.

Brush the crust with garlic butter halfway through baking: It's like eating the best-ever garlic sticks.

Bake the pizza in a sheet pan: You don't have to worry about shaping the dough pizzeria-style and you can feed a lot more people (or have more leftovers).

Reheat it in an air fryer: It brings the pizza right back to freshly baked status. If you don't have an air fryer, put the pizza in a skillet over medium heat. Cover the pan with a lid and heat for 5 to 8 minutes, until crisped up and warmed through.

6 In a medium bowl, combine the chicken and the 2 tablespoons barbecue sauce. Stir until the chicken is well coated. Evenly spread the remaining ½ cup barbecue sauce over the pizza dough. Top with the mozzarella, barbecue chicken, bacon, pineapple, and jalapeño slices.

7 Bake the pizza on the bottom rack for 10 minutes, until the crust is just starting to brown.

8 In a small bowl, combine the melted butter and garlic and use a pastry brush to generously coat the edge of the pizza crust with the garlic butter. Return the pizza to the bottom rack of the oven and finish baking for 15 to 20 minutes, until the crust is golden brown and the cheese is melted.

9 Let the pizza sit for 5 to 10 minutes before cutting into squares and serving warm.

NOTE: *We use jarred tamed jalapeños, which aren't too spicy and can be found at most grocery stores near the olives and pickles.*

aunt whitney's crispy coconut chicken fingers

prep: **15 MINUTES** | cook: **15 MINUTES** | total: **30 MINUTES** | serves **6**

1 cup all-purpose flour

1 teaspoon kosher salt

1 teaspoon garlic powder

1 teaspoon onion powder

½ teaspoon paprika

2 large eggs

1 cup sweetened flaked coconut, roughly chopped

1 cup corn flakes, slightly crushed

1 cup panko bread crumbs

2 pounds boneless, skinless chicken tenders

Nonstick cooking spray

Your choice of favorite dipping sauces, for serving: ketchup, mustard, barbecue sauce, Fry Sauce (page 73)

My sister-in-law Whitney is my food-loving soul sister. We love cooking, baking, and most importantly, eating together. Every time she comes to visit, our kitchen is full of laughter, good food, and *lots* of boys. Whitney and Josh's brother, Ben, have four boys of their own, so when we get together, there are a half dozen little Lichty boys running around. That's a lot of busy little bodies to feed! Luckily, whenever Whitney is in town, she always makes these chicken fingers, which feature her secret to a perfectly crispy crust with a tiny hint of sweetness: coconut. We put out a big plate with lots of sauces for dipping and watch as they're gobbled up just about as quickly as it takes to make them.

1   Preheat the oven to 400°F. Arrange two wire racks on two large rimmed baking sheets. Set aside.

2   In a medium bowl, whisk together the flour, salt, garlic powder, onion powder, and paprika. In a separate bowl, beat the eggs with 1 tablespoon water. In a pie plate or shallow dish, combine the coconut, corn flakes, and panko.

3   Dredge the chicken tenders in the seasoned flour, coating both sides. Next, dip in the egg mixture, and then transfer to the dish with the coconut mixture. Coat both sides of the chicken tenders with the mixture, pressing firmly so the crumbs stick. Arrange the chicken tenders on the wire racks, making sure they aren't touching. Repeat the process until all of the chicken tenders are coated.

4   Spray the coated tenders with nonstick cooking spray. Bake for 10 to 15 minutes, depending on how big and thick your tenders are. You want the outside to be golden brown and crispy and the center no longer be pink. Serve warm with your desired dipping sauces.

NOTE: *If you can't find chicken tenders, cut boneless chicken breasts into tender-sized pieces. And if you don't have wire racks for baking the fingers, just use parchment-lined baking sheets. But I recommend the racks for getting them extra crispy.*

grilled salmon with mango-avocado salsa

prep: **15 MINUTES** | cook: **15 MINUTES** | total: **30 MINUTES** | serves **4**

• •

2 medium ripe mangos, pitted, peeled, and chopped

1 large ripe avocado, pitted, peeled, and chopped

½ cup chopped red bell pepper

½ cup chopped red onion

⅓ cup chopped fresh cilantro

1 jalapeño, seeded and minced

Juice of 1 large lime

Kosher salt

SALMON

Extra-virgin olive oil, for the grill or grill pan, plus more for brushing the salmon

2 tablespoons unsalted butter, melted

1 tablespoon honey

2 garlic cloves, minced

½ teaspoon grated lime zest

1 (1½-pound) fresh salmon fillet, skin-on, small pin bones removed

Kosher salt and freshly ground black pepper

It doesn't get much better than a light, healthy meal that takes minutes to prepare, is really delicious, *and* gets requested by your kids. Caleb in particular is a big fan of this dish, so it's become a regular meal for us. Grilling the salmon with honey and garlic butter produces tender, flaky, and flavorful fish in almost no time. And topping it with a fresh, colorful salsa brings an extra touch of brightness to the meal. It's also the perfect dish to make for company.

1　Make the salsa: In a medium bowl, combine the mango, avocado, bell pepper, onion, cilantro, jalapeño, and lime juice. Give everything a gentle toss and season to taste with salt. Set aside.

2　Make the salmon: Oil the grates of the grill (or a grill pan) and preheat to medium-high heat. (Or preheat the oven; see Note.) In a small bowl, whisk together the melted butter, honey, garlic, and lime zest. Set aside.

3　Brush the salmon with olive oil and sprinkle with salt and pepper. Place the salmon on the hot grill (or grill pan) flesh side down and cook until grill marks form, about 6 minutes. Using two spatulas, carefully flip the salmon and drizzle with the honey-lime butter. Cook for an additional 5 to 6 minutes, until the fish flakes easily. (Timing will vary depending on how thick your salmon is.) Carefully transfer the salmon to a large platter and top with the mango avocado salsa. Serve immediately.

NOTE: *You could also make this dish in the oven. Line a large baking sheet with a piece of aluminum foil that is large enough to fold over the fish. Place the salmon fillet on the foil, skin side down. Pour the butter mixture evenly over the salmon and season with a pinch of salt and pepper. Create a packet by folding the sides of the foil over the fish, and then fold or roll the edges together to create a solid seal (so the juices don't leak out). Bake in a 375° oven until the salmon is solid pink through the center, 18 to 23 minutes. Cooking time will vary depending on the thickness of your salmon fillet. Be careful not to overcook or the salmon will be dry. Carefully open up the foil packet and broil the salmon for 2 minutes. Watch the fish carefully so it doesn't burn; you just want the top to crisp up a little. Serve immediately, drizzling the salmon with a little of the cooking sauce and topping with the mango-avocado salsa.*

honey-mustard sheet-pan chicken
with brussels sprouts

prep: 15 MINUTES | cook: 35 MINUTES | total: 50 MINUTES | serves 4

Nonstick cooking spray

¼ cup plus 2 tablespoons extra-virgin olive oil

2 tablespoons fresh lemon juice (1 lemon)

1 tablespoon Dijon mustard

1 tablespoon whole-grain mustard

1 tablespoon honey

3 garlic cloves, minced

Kosher salt and freshly ground black pepper

2 pounds bone-in, skin-on chicken thighs (4 medium thighs)

1½ pounds Brussels sprouts, halved

¼ large red onion, sliced

Josh and I came up with this recipe because, like you, we wanted a really, really easy way to whip up a delicious chicken dish that didn't involve roasting for an hour or dirtying up a bunch of pans. Enter the sheet pan! Instead of starting with a whole chicken, we use bone-in, skin-on chicken thighs, which don't need very long to cook and stay extra juicy while the skin gets nice and crispy. They would be delicious roasted with just a little salt and pepper, but we like to dunk them first in a simple honey-mustard sauce. Brussels sprouts get caramelized and browned right next to the chicken, so they soak up all those delicious pan juices. There's barely any prep, the oven does all the work, and when you pull out the pan, your family and friends will be amazed by this impressive almost-instant dinner. As for the dishes, done and done!

1   Preheat the oven to 425°F. Grease a large baking sheet with nonstick cooking spray and set aside.

2   In a medium bowl, whisk together the ¼ cup olive oil, 1 tablespoon of the lemon juice, the Dijon mustard, whole-grain mustard, honey, and garlic. Season with salt and pepper to taste.

3   Use tongs to dip the chicken thighs in the sauce, coating both sides. Place the thighs on the prepared baking sheet. Discard any remaining sauce.

4   In a medium bowl, combine the Brussels sprouts and red onion. Drizzle with the remaining 2 tablespoons olive oil and 1 tablespoon lemon juice and toss until well coated. Arrange the sprouts around the chicken on the baking sheet, making sure they aren't overlapping. Season with salt and pepper.

5   Roast for 30 to 35 minutes, until the chicken is golden brown and has an internal temperature of 165°F and the Brussels sprouts are crispy. Serve hot.

asian pork lettuce wraps

prep: **20 MINUTES** | cook: **10 MINUTES** | total: **30 MINUTES** | serves **4**

SAUCE

¼ cup hoisin sauce

2 tablespoons reduced-sodium soy sauce or tamari soy sauce

2 tablespoons fresh lime juice (1 to 2 limes)

1 tablespoon chili garlic sauce

1 tablespoon finely chopped fresh mint

1 teaspoon ground ginger

1 garlic clove, minced

PORK

1 tablespoon coconut oil or vegetable oil

1 pound ground pork

1 (8-ounce) can water chestnuts, drained and diced

LETTUCE WRAPS

1 large head Boston or butter lettuce, leaves separated

1 cup shredded red cabbage

1 medium carrot, julienned

4 scallions (white and green parts), sliced

½ cup chopped fresh cilantro

½ cup chopped fresh mint

½ cup chopped cashews

These fun little wraps are a lot like tacos, but wrapped in crisp lettuce and with a great sweet and salty Asian-inspired sauce made with hoisin, soy sauce, ginger, garlic, and mint. We love serving them in the summer because they're not too heavy and have a nice refreshing crunch from the toppings—water chestnuts, red cabbage, carrots, and scallions—plus tons of fresh mint and cilantro. You can put out all the ingredients and let people top their own, taco bar–style, or assemble a tray and put them out as appetizers. Feel free to substitute ground chicken for the pork, or use chopped peanuts instead of the cashews. And for an even heartier meal, serve with a side of rice.

1   Make the sauce: In a small bowl, whisk together all the sauce ingredients.

2   Make the pork: Heat the oil in a large skillet over medium-high heat. Add the pork and cook, breaking it up with a wooden spoon, for 5 minutes. Add the water chestnuts and pour in the sauce. Cook for 5 more minutes, until the pork is completely cooked through.

3   Assemble the lettuce wraps: Spoon pork mixture into the center of each lettuce leaf. Top with the shredded cabbage, carrot, scallions, cilantro, mint, and cashews. Serve immediately.

grilled steak tacos with chimichurri

prep: 30 MINUTES, PLUS 30 MINUTES MARINATING | cook: 15 MINUTES
total: 1 HOUR 15 MINUTES | serves 6 TO 8

● ●

CHIMICHURRI

1 poblano pepper, halved, stemmed, and seeded

3 garlic cloves, minced

1 cup packed fresh cilantro leaves

1 cup packed fresh parsley leaves

¼ cup plus 2 tablespoons extra-virgin olive oil

2 tablespoons fresh lime juice (1 to 2 limes)

2 tablespoons red wine vinegar

1 teaspoon kosher salt

STEAK

1 (1½-pound) flank steak

Juice of 2 large limes

Grated zest of 1 large lime

1 tablespoon kosher salt

1½ teaspoons sugar

¾ teaspoon freshly ground black pepper

¾ teaspoon chili powder

¾ teaspoon ground cumin

¾ teaspoon paprika

¾ teaspoon garlic powder

¾ teaspoon dried oregano

¼ teaspoon ground cinnamon

Extra-virgin olive oil, for grilling

Josh makes these tacos all summer long, and we know they're a hit because friends are always requesting them when they come over for dinner. It's no surprise to us—a flavorful smoky steak fresh off the grill is always a crowd-pleaser, then add a bright, fresh sauce packed with parsley and cilantro and wrap it all up in a tortilla? A no-brainer! It's the perfect meal for entertaining because the steak takes almost no time to cook, and you can make the chimichurri in advance—which I highly recommend because the flavor gets even better as it sits. All that's left to do is put out a bunch of avocado, red onion, and queso fresco for sprinkling, and everyone will be in taco heaven.

1 Make the chimichurri: Roast the poblano under the broiler for about 5 minutes, until the skin has started to char. Transfer to a paper bag or a bowl covered with plastic wrap to cool for about 15 minutes. Use your fingers to peel off the skin—it should slip off easily.

2 In a blender or food processor, combine the roasted poblano with the remaining chimichurri ingredients and blend until smooth. You might have to stop and scrape down the sides with a spatula and blend again. Transfer the sauce to a lidded container and store in the fridge until ready to use, or up to 2 days. Give the sauce a shake or a stir before using.

3 Make the steak: Place the steak in a 9 × 13-inch pan. Pour the lime juice over the steak and marinate at room temperature for 30 minutes.

4 Meanwhile, in a medium bowl, combine the lime zest, salt, sugar, black pepper, chili powder, cumin, paprika, garlic powder, oregano, and cinnamon.

5 Lightly pat dry the steak with paper towels to remove any excess juice, then rub both sides with the spice mixture, pressing with your fingers to help the rub adhere to the meat.

6 Preheat the grill (or a grill pan) over medium-high heat. Lightly coat a paper towel with the oil. Using a pair of long tongs, rub the oiled towel over the grill rack (or pan). Place the steak directly on the grill (or pan) and cook for 5 minutes on each side. Let the steak rest on a cutting board, covered with aluminum foil, for 10 minutes.

Corn tortillas

½ small red onion, chopped

2 large ripe avocados, pitted, peeled, and sliced

Chopped fresh cilantro

⅓ cup crumbled queso fresco

7 While the steak is resting, warm the corn tortillas on the grill or use a gas flame to char them slightly.

8 Cutting against the grain of the meat, slice the steak into strips. Serve with the steak strips between the tortillas and top with chimichurri, red onion, avocado, cilantro, and queso fresco.

skillet chicken parmesan

prep: **25 MINUTES** | cook: **20 MINUTES** | total: **45 MINUTES** | serves **4**

• •

2 boneless, skinless chicken breasts, halved horizontally

Kosher salt and freshly ground black pepper

3 large eggs

1 cup all-purpose flour

2 cups panko bread crumbs

1 cup grated Parmesan cheese

2 tablespoons finely chopped fresh basil, plus more for garnish

Grated zest of 1 lemon

½ teaspoon garlic powder

¼ teaspoon onion powder

3 tablespoons extra-virgin olive oil

1 tablespoon unsalted butter

2 cups Roasted Tomato Sauce (recipe follows), Classic Marinara Sauce (page 180), or your favorite store-bought sauce (see Note)

8 ounces fresh mozzarella, sliced into 4 pieces

Spaghetti, zucchini noodles, or spaghetti squash, for serving (optional)

Chicken Parmesan is a classic that's surprisingly easy to make at home and also happens to be one of Josh's favorite meals. His secret to a great restaurant-quality chicken Parm is cooking it in a skillet on the stove first so the chicken gets nice and golden brown, then finishing it off in the oven so the cheese gets nice and bubbly. Plus, you get the extra wow-factor of serving it right from the skillet. Josh usually enjoys this over spaghetti, but it's also great with zucchini noodles or spaghetti squash. And when we have company, we whip up a batch of our Caprese Garlic Bread (page 74) for a full-on Italian feast. It always gets rave reviews!

1   Preheat the oven to 350°F.

2   Place the chicken breasts between two sheets of plastic wrap and pound with a meat mallet until ¼ inch thick. Season with salt and pepper on both sides. Set the cutlets aside.

3   Beat the eggs with 1 tablespoon water in a shallow dish. Place the flour in a second shallow dish. In a third shallow dish, combine the panko, ¾ cup of the Parmesan, the basil, lemon zest, garlic powder, and onion powder.

4   Dip the chicken cutlets first into the flour, then into the egg mixture, and finally into the panko mixture, pressing to ensure the crumbs adhere.

5   Heat the olive oil and butter in a large ovenproof skillet over medium-high heat. Add the chicken cutlets and cook until golden brown, about 3 minutes per side. Remove the chicken, wipe out the skillet, then return the chicken to the pan. Spoon the sauce

over the cutlets, sprinkle with the remaining ¼ cup Parmesan, and cover each with 1 slice of mozzarella.

6   Transfer the skillet to the oven and bake for 10 to 15 minutes, until the chicken is cooked through (a meat thermometer registers an internal temperature of 165°F) and the cheese has melted. Serve warm with pasta, zucchini noodles, or spaghetti squash, if desired.

NOTE: *You have a few options when it comes to the sauce: I especially love using our Roasted Tomato Sauce because of its deep, rich flavor, but our Classic Marinara Sauce is super delicious when you're short on time. And of course, you could always use your favorite jarred sauce! If you already have a homemade sauce on hand or go for the store-bought, prepping the Chicken Parm takes barely any time.*

Roasted Tomato Sauce

prep: **10 MINUTES**
cook: **55 MINUTES**
total: **1 HOUR 5 MINUTES**
makes **3½ TO 4 CUPS**

This is our favorite summer sauce, when tomatoes and fresh herbs are basically taking over the garden and we have more than we know what to do with. Roasting the tomatoes brings out their deep, sweet flavor and makes it seem like you spent hours babysitting the pot on the stove—not the case! I particularly love making several batches and freezing them for the winter when I crave the fresh taste of summer. Just be sure to use the best, ripest tomatoes in order to get the most delicious flavor.

3 pounds ripe Roma tomatoes, halved and cored

10 medium garlic cloves, peeled

¼ cup extra-virgin olive oil

3 tablespoons balsamic vinegar

1 tablespoon fresh oregano leaves

1 tablespoon fresh thyme leaves

Kosher salt and freshly ground black pepper

NOTE: *Yes, the recipe calls for 10 cloves of garlic, but don't be scared. It gives the sauce really great, complex flavor but isn't overpowering. I promise!*

1 Preheat the oven to 400°F.

2 Arrange the tomatoes cut side up in a 9 × 13-inch pan. Add the garlic cloves, oil, vinegar, oregano, thyme, 1½ teaspoons salt, and 1 teaspoon pepper and toss to combine. Roast for 25 minutes. Stir the tomato mixture, return the pan to the oven, and roast for an additional 30 minutes, until the tomatoes are caramelized and some of the liquid has evaporated. Allow the tomatoes to cool slightly.

3 Puree the tomatoes and garlic in a blender until the sauce reaches your desired consistency (we like ours smooth, but go with chunky if that's what you prefer!). Season with more salt and pepper, if necessary. Store the sauce in the fridge for up to 1 week or the freezer for up to 2 months.

He Said, She Said: The Perfect Stay-In Date Night

Josh and I always make sure to include a date night in our entertaining rotation. A lot of people forget that taking the time to make something special for themselves is just as important and fun as having people over. At the end of a long day, we usually don't feel like doing much more than putting on our comfiest pj's (for me that's always one of Josh's soft hooded sweatshirts—what's his is mine, right?), making one of our favorite meals, cozying up on the sofa for a movie, and finishing off the night with a homemade dessert.

HIS

The Menu: Huevos Rancheros (page 49). Breakfast for dinner is my favorite.

The Movie: Action adventure or comedy. Maria usually falls asleep 10 minutes into the movie, but she always—without fail—manages to wake up just in time for dessert.

The Special Treat: Our Favorite Chocolate Chip Cookies (page 241) with a glass of cold milk. I always pour an extra-tall glass because I know Maria will end up dunking her cookies in my milk too!

HERS

The Menu: A cheese board or crudité platter (page 78). Snacks for dinner are my favorite—I love adulting!

The Movie: Drama or romantic comedy. I love watching movies over and over again, but Josh always wants something new. I don't know why he doesn't want to watch *Pretty Woman* for the hundredth time . . .

The Special Treat: Deep-Dish Brownie Cookies (page 252) served warm out of the oven with vanilla ice cream. It's better than any dessert you could get at a restaurant, plus you get to eat it in your pj's.

salsa verde–chicken stacked enchiladas

prep: **15 MINUTES** | cook: **35 MINUTES** | total: **50 MINUTES** | serves **8 TO 10**

●●

Nonstick cooking spray

2½ cups Roasted Salsa Verde (recipe follows) **or store-bought salsa verde**

14 (6-inch) corn tortillas, cut in half

4 cups shredded rotisserie chicken

3 cups shredded Monterey Jack or Mexican blend cheese

For serving: queso fresco, jalapeño slices, avocado slices, chopped fresh cilantro, pepitas

Enchiladas are one of our favorite family dinners, but we wanted to come up with a way to make them even easier to make. We discovered that instead of rolling up individual tortillas with filling, you can just layer all of the ingredients in a baking dish casserole-style. But since I don't really like the word "casserole" (it makes me think of mysterious concoctions that usually involve canned cream-of-something soup—yikes!), I call this creation Stacked Enchiladas. We cheat and use rotisserie chicken, but you can cook chicken and shred it, or use leftovers. Since you can layer up everything in advance and bake it off a half hour before dinnertime, this is great not only for weeknight meals but also for entertaining. You can also bake the enchiladas, let them cool to room temperature, and freeze them for a night when making dinner isn't in the cards.

1 Preheat the oven to 350°F. Spray a 9 × 13-inch casserole dish with nonstick cooking spray.

2 Spread ½ cup of the salsa verde on the bottom of the prepared dish. Arrange 4½ corn tortillas in a single layer over the sauce. (I find 4½ is the magic number in my pan, but add enough tortilla halves to cover the sauce and comfortably fit in the dish.) Top with 2 cups shredded chicken, 1 cup salsa verde, and 1 cup shredded cheese. Repeat with another layer of tortillas, chicken, salsa, and cheese, then finish with a third layer of tortillas and the remaining 1 cup cheese. You may have a leftover tortilla half or two, and that's fine.

3 Use nonstick cooking spray to coat the shiny side of a sheet of aluminum foil, turn over, and use to cover the enchiladas. Bake for 30 minutes. Carefully remove the foil and bake for 5 minutes longer, until the cheese is melted and bubbly.

4 Garnish the enchiladas with any desired toppings, slice into squares, and serve warm.

NOTE: *We use our homemade salsa verde because it's beyond easy and, honestly, better than most jarred versions. But if you need to buy yours at the store, I won't tell anyone!*

Roasted Salsa Verde

prep: 15 MINUTES
cook: 10 MINUTES
total: 25 MINUTES
makes 2½ CUPS

Homemade green salsa is completely underrated, mostly because people don't know how easy it is to make. All it takes is roasting the tomatillos under the broiler—which really brings out their flavor and gives them a little charred smokiness—then popping them in the blender or food processor. The salsa is bright and fresh, and not too spicy, so the kids love it.

1 pound tomatillos, papery husks removed, rinsed, and dried

½ medium white onion

2 serrano peppers, stemmed and seeded

2 Anaheim peppers, stemmed and seeded

3 garlic cloves

½ teaspoon extra-virgin olive oil

½ cup packed fresh cilantro

Juice of 1 large lime

1 teaspoon kosher salt, plus more to taste

¼ teaspoon ground cumin

1   Preheat the broiler with an oven rack about 4 inches below the heat source. Line a large baking sheet with aluminum foil.

2   Arrange the tomatillos, onion, and peppers on the prepared baking sheet. Set the garlic cloves in a little square of aluminum foil, drizzle with the olive oil, fold into a packet, and place on the baking sheet. Broil until the vegetables are blackened in spots and softened, about 5 minutes. Remove the pan from the oven and turn all the vegetables over. Return the pan to the oven and broil the other sides until blackened and tender, about 5 minutes more. Let cool slightly.

3   Carefully unwrap the garlic cloves from the foil packet, remove and discard their skins, and transfer to a blender or food processor. Add the roasted tomatillos, onion, and peppers, along with the cilantro, lime juice, salt, and cumin. Blend until smooth, scraping down the sides, if necessary. Season to taste with additional salt, if desired. Store in the fridge for 7 to 10 days, or freeze for up to 1 month.

chicken pot pie

prep: **40 MINUTES** | bake: **45 MINUTES** | total: **1 HOUR 25 MINUTES** | serves **8**

• •

PIE DOUGH

2½ cups all-purpose flour

1 tablespoon sugar

1 teaspoon kosher salt

1 cup (½ pound) cold unsalted butter, cut into tablespoon-sized cubes

½ cup cold buttermilk

Up to 2 tablespoons cold water

FILLING

4 tablespoons unsalted butter

⅓ cup diced yellow onion

2 medium carrots, sliced (about 1 cup)

1 celery stalk, sliced (about ½ cup)

2 garlic cloves, minced

⅓ cup all-purpose flour, plus more for dusting

1¾ cups chicken broth

½ cup heavy cream

1 tablespoon minced fresh parsley

1½ teaspoons minced fresh thyme

1 teaspoon kosher salt

½ teaspoon freshly ground black pepper

3 cups shredded cooked chicken or turkey

1 cup frozen peas

1 large egg, beaten

Classic American pot pie is the ultimate comfort food. It's not hard to see why—there's a rich, creamy filling of chicken, veggies, and herbs, all tucked inside a flaky, buttery crust. Luckily, it's easy to make a version at home, crust and all. We pull out this recipe whenever we have leftover roast chicken or turkey (it's perfect for after Thanksgiving!), and we're always sure to keep a small stash in the freezer (either whole or by the slice) since it freezes well. Josh and I especially love heating up a pie whenever we go out for date night—the boys get a cozy hug of a dinner, and the babysitter will definitely want to sit again! (You can also use store-bought pie dough in a pinch!)

1 Make the dough: In a large bowl, combine the flour, sugar, and salt. Add the butter and toss to coat the cubes. Turn out the mixture onto a clean surface and use a rolling pin to flatten the butter into thin sheets, combining it with the flour. Use a bench scraper to scrape the butter off the rolling pin and to bring the mixture back into a pile as necessary. Continue rolling and flattening until all of the butter is incorporated into the flour. The mixture will be very flaky. Return the mixture to the bowl and place in the freezer for 15 minutes to chill the butter.

2 Once chilled, stir in the buttermilk, using a spoon first and then your hands to bring the mixture together into a ball. If the mixture is too crumbly and dry, add 1 tablespoon of water at a time. Divide the dough in half and flatten into disks. Wrap each disk in plastic wrap and chill in the refrigerator while you make the filling.

3 Make the filling: In a large deep skillet, melt the butter over medium-high heat. Add the onion, carrots, celery, and garlic and cook until tender, stirring occasionally, 7 to 10 minutes. Whisk in the flour, followed by the broth, cream, parsley, thyme, salt, and pepper until there are no lumps. Reduce the heat to medium-low and simmer for 10 minutes, until the filling has thickened. Stir in the chicken and peas. Remove the pot from the heat and set aside while you roll out the pie dough.

recipe continues

4   Preheat the oven to 400°F.

5   On a lightly floured surface, use a rolling pin to roll out one piece of dough to a 12-inch round about ¼ inch thick. Carefully transfer to a 9-inch pie pan and pat the dough into the pan with your fingers. Trim the over-hanging dough with a knife and dis-card. Pour the filling into the pie and set aside.

6   Roll out the second disk of dough into a 12-inch round about ¼ inch thick. Carefully drape it over the pie, trim the overhang, and seal the edges by crimping with a fork or your fin-gers. Use a sharp knife to slice a few 1-inch slits in the center of the top crust. Using a pastry brush, brush the top of the pie with the beaten egg. I use a piecrust shield to protect the edges from browning too much too soon, but you could also tent them with alumi-num foil.

7   Bake the pot pie for 45 minutes, until the crust is golden brown. Let the pie cool for 10 minutes before slicing and serving.

sweet and smoky ribs

prep: **30 MINUTES** | cook: **4 HOURS** | total: **4½ HOURS** | serves **6 TO 8**

RIBS

2 tablespoons packed brown sugar

1 tablespoon kosher salt

1 tablespoon paprika

1 tablespoon garlic powder

½ teaspoon dry mustard

2 slabs (about 6 pounds) baby
back ribs

BARBECUE SAUCE

1 teaspoon extra-virgin olive oil

1 teaspoon finely chopped
jalapeño (seeds discarded if you
don't want a lot of heat)

1½ cups peach jam

½ cup tomato paste

½ cup apple cider vinegar

1 teaspoon Worcestershire sauce

2 teaspoons brown sugar

2 teaspoons garlic powder

2 teaspoons dry mustard

1 teaspoon onion powder

1 teaspoon kosher salt

Josh loves making these ribs when we have company because they're always a hit, but I honestly think he'd make them all for himself just so he had an excuse to play with his Traeger grill! The ribs will take about 4 hours to smoke (or 2½ hours to bake in the oven), but I can tell you that they're definitely worth the wait.

1 If using a grill: **Start your grill with the lid open until the fire is established, then leave it open for 5 minutes. Set to 225°F and close the lid to preheat for 15 minutes.**

2 If using an oven: **Preheat the oven to 275°F.**

3 Make the ribs: In a small bowl, combine the brown sugar, salt, paprika, garlic powder, and dry mustard. Set aside.

4 If the ribs still have the silverskin membrane covering the back of the rack, remove it: Use a butter knife and work the tip underneath the membrane over a middle bone, grab the skin with a paper towel, and tear it off.

5 Season both sides of the ribs with the rub and place the ribs, meat side up, directly on the rack of the smoker. Close the lid and smoke for 4 hours, until a meat thermometer registers an internal temperature of 200°F.

6 If cooking in the oven, place the ribs on a large baking sheet and cover tightly with aluminum foil. Bake in the oven for 2½ hours, until a meat thermometer registers an internal temperature of 200°F.

7 While the ribs are cooking, make the barbecue sauce: In a large skillet, heat the olive oil over medium heat. Add the jalapeño and cook for 2 minutes. Stir in the jam, tomato paste, vinegar, Worcestershire, brown sugar, garlic powder, dry mustard, onion powder, and salt with 3 tablespoons water and stir until combined. Reduce the temperature to low and let the sauce reduce for 15 minutes, stirring occasionally, until it reaches the consistency of barbecue sauce.

8 When the ribs have finished cooking, set the oven to broil. Brush the ribs generously with sauce on both sides so they are well coated. Place the ribs, meat side up, on a large foil-lined baking sheet. Set the ribs in the oven on the middle rack and broil for 5 to 7 minutes, until the sauce starts to caramelize. Watch the ribs closely to make sure they don't burn.

9 Let the ribs rest for 5 minutes, then slice in between the bones and serve hot.

josh's favorite double cheeseburger

prep: **25 MINUTES** | cook: **10 MINUTES** | total: **35 MINUTES** | makes **8 BURGERS**

AIOLI

1 cup mayonnaise

1 garlic clove, minced

1 teaspoon smoked paprika

½ teaspoon kosher salt

BURGERS

4 tablespoons unsalted butter, at room temperature

8 hamburger buns (I love brioche.)

1 pound (80 percent lean) ground beef

1 pound mild Italian sausage, removed from casings

1 teaspoon kosher salt, plus more to taste

½ teaspoon onion powder

½ teaspoon garlic powder

1 large red onion, cut into ½-inch-thick rounds

1 tablespoon extra-virgin olive oil

Freshly ground black pepper

8 slices cheddar cheese

8 slices Havarti cheese

Lettuce

Tomato slices

16 slices bacon, cooked

Josh is *serious* about good burgers, and there's barely a summer weekend that goes by that doesn't find him out at the grill, serving 'em up to any neighbor, friend, or relative who's stopped by. According to Josh, the keys to a killer burger are: thin doubled-up patties that are a flavorful combo of beef and Italian sausage; cheddar *and* Havarti cheese (cheddar for the classic sharp flavor, Havarti for its amazing meltiness); bacon (a must for Josh!); a creamy smoked paprika aioli; perfectly caramelized grilled onions; and buttery grilled buns. Hungry yet?

1 Make the aioli: In a small bowl, stir together the mayonnaise, garlic, smoked paprika, and salt. Set aside.

2 Make the burgers: Generously butter the insides of the hamburger buns and set aside.

3 In a large bowl, combine the ground beef, sausage meat, salt, onion powder, and garlic powder. Mix until all the ingredients are well incorporated. Form the meat into 16 patties, about 4½ inches in diameter and ¼ inch thick. You want the patties to be thin because each burger will get two. Separate each patty with a piece of wax paper so they don't stick together and can easily be transferred to the grill.

4 Preheat the grill to medium-high heat.

5 Brush the onion rounds with the olive oil and season with salt and black pepper.

6 Place the patties and onion rounds directly on the hot grill. Cook the onions for 3 minutes on each side, until they are softened and have nice char lines. Cook the patties for 2 to 3 minutes and flip with a spatula. Place a slice of cheese on top of each patty so half of the patties are topped with cheddar and half with Havarti. Cook for 2 to 3 minutes longer, until the patties are no longer pink on the outside and the cheese has melted.

7 Transfer the onion slices and burgers to a serving platter or large baking sheet. Cover with foil to keep warm.

8 Place the buttered hamburger buns cut side down on the grill and grill until toasted, 30 to 60 seconds.

9 To assemble the burgers, spread the aioli on the insides of the toasted buns. Top the bottoms with two patties, one cheddar and one Havarti. Add the grilled onions, lettuce, tomato slices, and bacon and then top with the bun tops. Serve immediately.

slow cooker meatballs

prep: **40 MINUTES** | cook: **3 HOURS ON HIGH OR 6 HOURS ON LOW**
total: **3½ TO 7 HOURS** | **SERVES 8 TO 10**

● ●

MEATBALLS

1 pound lean ground beef

1 pound Italian sausage, removed from casings

1 cup Italian seasoned bread crumbs

½ cup finely grated Parmesan cheese

2 large eggs, beaten

2 garlic cloves, minced

1 tablespoon finely chopped fresh basil

1 tablespoon finely chopped fresh parsley

1 teaspoon dried oregano

1 teaspoon kosher salt

1 teaspoon freshly ground black pepper

3 tablespoons extra-virgin olive oil

My boys love this dinner because it means they can stuff their bellies full of meatballs, and Josh loves the recipe because it means simply tossing a bunch of ingredients in the slow cooker and letting it do all the work. Cooking meatballs in the flavorful marinara means they stay nice and juicy, while the sauce takes on their meaty flavor—which is so good thanks to Josh's trick of blending ground beef with Italian sausage. Everything gets heaped over spaghetti, zucchini noodles, or spaghetti squash and covered with grated Parm, then served up with a side of Caprese Garlic Bread (page 74). But the best part is seeing the boys' faces after dinner—always big marinara smiles thanks to all the noodle slurping.

SAUCE

1 small yellow onion, diced

1 carrot, finely diced

3 garlic cloves, minced

2 (28-ounce) cans crushed San Marzano tomatoes

1 (6-ounce) can tomato paste

2 tablespoons extra-virgin olive oil

2 dried bay leaves

1 tablespoon dried basil

1 teaspoon kosher salt, plus more to taste

1 teaspoon freshly ground black pepper, plus more to taste

½ teaspoon dried oregano

Pinch of crushed red pepper flakes

FOR SERVING

Cooked spaghetti, zucchini noodles, or spaghetti squash

Grated Parmesan cheese

Fresh basil, if desired

1 Make the meatballs: In a large bowl, combine the beef, sausage meat, bread crumbs, Parmesan, eggs, garlic, herbs, salt, and pepper. Mix well. Form the mixture into balls, about 2 tablespoons per meatball. (A small ice cream scooper works well here.)

2 Heat the olive oil in a large heavy-bottomed pot over medium-high heat. When the oil shimmers, add the meatballs in a single layer. You don't want to crowd the pan or the meatballs won't brown, so you may need to work in batches. Brown the meatballs on all sides, 5 to 7 minutes per side. Transfer the meatballs to a paper towel–lined plate and repeat with the remaining meatballs.

3 Make the sauce: Combine all of the sauce ingredients in a 6-quart slow cooker (or see Note) and stir to combine. Add the meatballs, stirring gently to coat with the sauce. Cover and cook on low for 6 hours or on high for 3 hours, until the meatballs are cooked through. Remove and discard the bay leaves. Taste and season with additional salt and pepper, if necessary.

4 To serve, place cooked noodles in a dish or bowl, top with marinara sauce and meatballs, and sprinkle with freshly grated Parmesan cheese and basil, if desired. Serve hot.

NOTES: *Instead of the slow cooker, you could simmer the sauce and meatballs in a large pot on the stove. But the sauce is so much better with a slow cooker because of how long it simmers. The recipe makes a lot of meatballs, so it's a great one for sharing with friends and family. It also freezes nicely—just let the meatballs cool completely in the sauce and transfer everything to a freezer-safe container to freeze for up to 1 month. Defrost, reheat, and serve!*

honey-mustard pork tenderloins with carrots

prep: **15 MINUTES, PLUS 1 HOUR MARINATING** | cook: **50 MINUTES** | total: **2 HOURS 5 MINUTES** | serves **6 TO 8**

● ●

Pork tenderloin is one of Josh's favorite cuts to cook—it's lean and tender, takes on flavor really well, and is easy to cook perfectly. You can't argue with that! After our guests tuck into the perfectly-browned-yet-juicy pork that's been glazed with honey, Dijon, and soy sauce and topped with glazed carrots and caramelized onions, they're *always* begging for the recipe. Because the tenderloins need some time to marinate and about 40 minutes to roast, this is also the perfect dish to make on a laid-back Sunday when you won't be straying far from the kitchen anyway.

PORK TENDERLOINS

½ cup apple cider vinegar

½ cup honey

¼ cup Dijon mustard

2 tablespoons soy sauce

2 tablespoons packed brown sugar

3 garlic cloves, minced

1½ teaspoons finely chopped fresh thyme

2 pork tenderloins (about 2¼ pounds total)

GLAZE

¼ cup honey

3 tablespoons Dijon mustard

2 tablespoons unsalted butter

1½ tablespoons Worcestershire sauce

1 large garlic clove, grated or finely minced

1 teaspoon finely chopped fresh thyme

¾ teaspoon ground coriander

¼ teaspoon kosher salt

TO ASSEMBLE

1½ pounds medium carrots, cut into ½-inch pieces

1 small red onion, peeled, quartered, and layers separated

2 tablespoons plus 2 teaspoons extra-virgin olive oil

Kosher salt and freshly ground black pepper

3 tablespoons roughly chopped fresh parsley

1 Marinate the tenderloins: In a large bowl, whisk together the vinegar, honey, mustard, soy sauce, brown sugar, garlic, and thyme. Place the marinade in a large zip-top plastic freezer bag. Add the pork tenderloins and seal the bag, making sure the pork is covered with the marinade. Refrigerate for at least 1 hour or up to overnight.

2 Remove the pork from the refrigerator and let stand at room temperature while you make the glaze: In a small saucepan over medium heat, whisk together the honey, mustard, butter, Worcestershire, garlic, thyme, coriander, and salt. Cook just until the glaze is heated through, about 3 minutes. Remove from the heat and set aside.

3 Assemble: In a medium bowl, combine the carrots and onions with the 2 teaspoons olive oil. Toss to combine and season with salt and pepper.

4 Preheat the oven to 400°F.

5 Heat the remaining 2 tablespoons oil in a large skillet over medium-high heat. Remove the pork from the marinade and sprinkle with salt and pepper, making sure to cover all sides of the meat. Sear the pork on all sides until a browned crust forms, 2 to 3 minutes per side. (You're just browning the pork, not cooking it all the way through.)

6 Place the seared pork loins in the middle of a large baking dish and scatter the carrots and onion around them. Baste the pork and carrots with the honey glaze. Roast for 20 minutes. Remove the pan from the oven to give the carrots a toss and baste the pork with more glaze from the bottom of the pan. Return the pan to the oven and roast for an additional 20 minutes, until a meat thermometer inserted into the thickest portion registers 150 to 155°F. Remove the tenderloins from the pan and let them stand for 10 minutes before slicing. Sprinkle the vegetables with the parsley and serve alongside the sliced pork.

ginger-garlic shrimp stir-fry

prep: **15 MINUTES** | cook: **10 MINUTES** | total: **25 MINUTES** | serves **4**

2 tablespoons soy sauce

3 tablespoons fresh orange juice

2 teaspoons brown sugar

2 teaspoons cornstarch

1 pound medium shrimp, peeled and deveined

½ teaspoon kosher salt

¼ teaspoon freshly ground pepper

3 teaspoons toasted sesame oil

3 garlic cloves, minced or grated

1½ tablespoons grated fresh ginger

Pinch of crushed red pepper flakes

1 red bell pepper, cored, seeded, and thinly sliced

1 yellow bell pepper, cored, seeded, and thinly sliced

1 cup snow peas

1 (8-ounce) can sliced water chestnuts, drained

¼ cup chopped Thai or regular basil

2 scallions (white and green parts), sliced

Stir-fries are a great colorful, flavorful option for quick dinners because once you get all your (super-simple) ingredients prepped out, it's just a matter of minutes before the meal is on the table. Plus, they're really versatile—just about any veggie can go into a stir-fry, whether sliced mushrooms, broccoli florets, diced eggplant, or sliced or shredded carrots. We typically reach for whatever is in the crisper and needs to get used up. You could also swap out the shrimp for chicken or beef, or go vegetarian and just toss in a few more veggies. Serve over white or brown rice, cauliflower rice, quinoa, or noodles and you'll have a new saucy, satisfying dish to add to your dinner rotation. Just don't forget to pack up leftovers for lunch!

1   In a small bowl, whisk together the soy sauce, orange juice, brown sugar, and cornstarch. Set aside. Pat the shrimp dry with a paper towel and season with the salt and pepper.

2   Heat 1 teaspoon of the sesame oil in a large skillet over medium heat. Add the shrimp and cook on one side for about 1 minute. Turn and cook for 1 more minute, until opaque. You'll know the shrimp are done when they make a "C" shape. You don't want the shrimp to close all the way into an "O" because that means they're overcooked and tough. Transfer the shrimp to a plate or bowl.

3   Add another teaspoon sesame oil to the pan and toss in the garlic, ginger, and pepper flakes. Cook, stirring continuously, for about 30 seconds, until fragrant. Add the remaining 1 teaspoon sesame oil along with the bell peppers, snow peas, and water chestnuts. Cook until tender, 3 to 4 minutes. Add the reserved soy sauce mixture and the shrimp to the pan, stirring to coat thoroughly with the glaze. Cook for 1 minute, then remove the skillet from the heat. Stir in the basil and scallions and serve hot.

asian-glazed sheet-pan salmon and broccoli

prep: 15 MINUTES, PLUS 30 MINUTES MARINATING
cook: 15 MINUTES | total: 1 HOUR | serves 4

• •

4 tablespoons extra-virgin olive oil

⅓ cup soy sauce

¼ cup hoisin sauce

¼ cup honey

¼ cup chopped fresh mint

3 tablespoons chopped fresh cilantro

Grated zest and juice of ½ orange (about 2 tablespoons juice)

3 garlic cloves, minced

2 tablespoons minced fresh ginger

1 teaspoon toasted sesame oil

¼ teaspoon crushed red pepper flakes

4 (6-ounce) boneless salmon fillets, 1½ inches thick

1 large head broccoli, cut into bite-sized florets

¼ teaspoon kosher salt

⅛ teaspoon freshly ground black pepper

2 scallions (white and green parts), thinly sliced

It doesn't get easier during the week (or any night, for the matter) than a sheet-pan dinner, aka all of your dinner components roasted together on a single baking sheet. To take this otherwise simple meal to the next level, we toss together a quick-yet-delicious marinade for the salmon with deeply flavored Asian ingredients—soy sauce, hoisin, sesame oil, garlic, and ginger—plus lots of fresh mint and cilantro. You'll have tender, flaky salmon and crispy broccoli in no time at all—and cleanup is a breeze, especially if you line the pan.

1   In a medium bowl, whisk together 2 tablespoons of the olive oil, the soy sauce, hoisin, honey, mint, cilantro, orange zest and juice, garlic, ginger, sesame oil, and pepper flakes. Reserve ⅓ cup of the marinade and set aside.

2   Place the remaining marinade in a zip-top freezer bag with the salmon fillets and seal, making sure the salmon is covered with the marinade. Marinate in the fridge for 30 minutes.

3   Preheat the oven to 425°F. Line a large rimmed baking sheet with aluminum foil or parchment paper.

4   Remove the salmon from the marinade and arrange the fillets on the baking sheet. Arrange the broccoli florets around the salmon, drizzle them with the remaining 2 tablespoons olive oil, and season with salt and pepper. Bake the salmon and broccoli for 15 minutes, until the broccoli is tender and the salmon is flaky (timing may vary depending on the thickness of your fillets), brushing or drizzling the salmon with the reserved marinade after 7 minutes of cooking. Garnish with the sliced scallions and serve immediately.

NOTE: *If you like your broccoli extra crispy, start roasting the broccoli 5 minutes before adding the salmon.*

oven-baked cod with wine-herb sauce

prep: **15 MINUTES** | cook: **20 MINUTES** | total: **35 MINUTES** | serves *6*

• •

1½ pounds fresh cod, cut into 6 equal pieces

4 tablespoons unsalted butter

¾ cup chicken broth

¾ cup sliced grape tomatoes

½ cup dry vermouth

2 garlic cloves, minced

1 tablespoon minced shallot

1 tablespoon cornstarch

1 tablespoon chopped fresh basil

1 tablespoon chopped fresh parsley

1½ teaspoons fresh lemon juice

1½ teaspoons soy sauce

Crusty bread, for serving

Our sister-in-law's mom, Sherill, makes this fish dish every Christmas, and we're so happy she shared the recipe with us because the secret really is in the sauce. With butter, shallots, a splash of vermouth (a fortified wine), fresh herbs, and tomatoes, it's a throwback to fancy old-school seafood restaurants. This dish also takes almost no hands-on time to make (just whip up the sauce, pour over the fish, and bake), but it has people licking their plates clean. That's why we suggest serving the flaky fish with plenty of crusty bread so everyone can soak up more of that magical sauce.

1   Preheat the oven to 400°F.

2   Place the cod in a 9 × 13-inch pan. Set aside.

3   In a large skillet, melt the butter over medium heat. Add the broth, tomatoes, vermouth, garlic, shallot, cornstarch, basil, parsley, lemon juice, and soy sauce. Let the sauce cook until thickened, about 5 minutes.

4   Pour the sauce over the fish and transfer the pan to the oven. Bake for 15 minutes, until a meat thermometer inserted into the thickest part registers 145°F. Serve immediately with plenty of crusty bread.

Un-Recipes

When I tell people that Josh and I cook almost every night and rarely eat out, they usually can't believe it. How can working parents of two young children manage to consistently get a warm homemade meal on the table?! It's not because we have some kind of super powers or extra-special skills (aside from great organization and meal-planning abilities). It's mainly that we've realized that a nourishing, belly-filling dinner doesn't have to be from a proper recipe. So for the nights when we have about 15 minutes or less to get dinner on the table, we reach for our rotation of "un-recipes," or meals that can be thrown together quickly using whatever ingredients happen to be in the fridge or pantry. Keep these simple preparations in mind—or tacked up on your fridge until you get the hang of it—and you'll find yourself reaching for frozen pizzas or takeout less and less.

Quesadillas: There's nothing to these other than flour tortillas and your favorite fillings. Just heat a little oil in a large skillet, add a tortilla, top with some cheese and your filling, and layer with a second tortilla. Give it a press with your spatula and then flip when the first side is golden. Continue cooking until the second side is nice and browned and the filling has warmed through. Pretty much any cheese will do the trick, though our favorites are cheddar, Monterey Jack, pepper Jack, queso fresco, or a Mexican blend. Some of the other fillings we like include:

- Leftover rotisserie chicken, shredded (add barbecue sauce for a barbecue version, along with red onion, pineapple, and cilantro)

- Leftover grilled veggies (especially peppers, onions, and mushrooms)

- Leftover grilled steak

- Black beans or refried beans (keep a couple cans in the pantry—they last forever)

- Corn (fresh or frozen)

- Black olives

- Spinach or kale

- Mango—really good with black beans and avocado

- Guacamole

- Salsa (see page 93 for our super-quick, no-cook blender salsa)

Grilled cheese: Whip up a stack with your favorite cheese or bread, or go unconventional:

- Pair classic ham with Swiss cheese and whole-grain mustard.

- Add apple or pear slices, which are really good with Gouda or Brie cheese—and the boys like to add bacon or prosciutto.

- Go green by adding pesto, either Spinach-Basil (page 186) or Kale-Walnut (page 168), which are great with mozzarella, fontina, or Havarti cheese.

- Add roasted red peppers and marinated artichokes, which pair well with mozzarella or provolone cheese.

Mini pizzas: Slather a bagel, English muffin, or pita with tomato sauce plus any toppings you'd normally order on a pizza (cheese, veggies, meats) and bake in a 400°F oven until the cheese is nice and melty. Definitely enlist the kids to assemble their own!

Scrambled eggs: There's not much you can't throw into eggs to make them a meal. Any veggies you have in your fridge will do the trick (spinach, red pepper, and mushrooms are always a hit in our house), along with fresh herbs, shredded cheese, chopped bacon, or even thinly sliced cured meats like salami or prosciutto. Heat a large skillet over medium-high heat and add oil or butter. Add the eggs (I recommend 2 to 3 per person), stir in the fillings along with a pinch of salt and pepper, and use a spatula to move the eggs and fillings in the pan until the eggs are light and fluffy.

Clean-out-the-fridge salad: My favorite kind of meal. Grab all the greens, veggies, and fruit that need to be used up and make a massive salad for dinner. Add leftover chicken, steak, fish, or hard-boiled eggs for protein or turn to your pantry for canned beans or nuts. Leftover grains are great here, too. Then let everyone add their favorite dressing and toppings.

Baked potatoes with toppings: Just bake russet or sweet potatoes until tender (which you can do in advance) and add your favorite toppings. Some of our favorites include:

- bacon, cheddar, sour cream, and chives
- leftover barbecue chicken or pork with cheddar cheese and scallion
- leftover roasted veggies with pesto (Spinach-Basil Pesto, page 186; or store-bought) and mozzarella cheese
- steamed broccoli florets and cheddar cheese
- leftover Chipotle-Sweet Potato Chili (page 123) and cheese
- Fajita-style—grilled peppers, mushrooms, chicken, cheese, and salsa
- Greek-style—chickpeas, cucumber, tomatoes, Kalamata olives, feta, and Tzatziki Sauce (page 158)

BLTs: After all, it's basically a meal between two slices of bread! To make it heartier, add avocado and use whole-wheat bread.

Couscous with veggies: Couscous is a quick-cooking grain that is a blank canvas for pretty much anything. I like to toss a steaming, fluffy bowlful with sautéed veggies (or roasted or grilled veggies, if we have leftovers), fresh herbs, and a sprinkling of Parmesan.

Noodles with butter: Enough said, right?! Toss any noodles you have in the pantry with butter, garlic, and Parmesan and serve with a simple green salad.

Ravioli or tortellini: We always have a package of fresh ravioli or tortellini in the freezer, which cooks up in about 5 minutes or less. Then we toss it with our Classic Marinara Sauce (page 180), store-bought pesto, or just olive oil. Serve with your favorite vegetable on the side.

Burrito bowls: Who doesn't love a bowl of rice and beans heaped with their favorite Mexican-inspired toppings? Mix and match your favorite rice (or other grains) with beans (black or pinto are great), sautéed and/or fresh veggies like bell peppers, onions, tomatoes, and lettuces, and other fun additions like guacamole, sour cream, and different salsas, cheeses, and grilled meats.

COOKIES

Make the World a Better Place

• •

Cookies are my favorite dessert. I don't need a fancy cheesecake, crème brûlée, or triple-layer this or that. *Cookies* are the best. They just make the world a better place. You can throw together a batch, put together a cookie care package to make someone's day, or keep dough in the freezer in case you need to pop a couple in the oven for a fresh-cookie fix at 10 p.m. There are few things I love more than creating new, fun cookie recipes (except eating them, of course), and it's the one activity in our kitchen that I usually don't let Josh touch—until they come out of the oven. I don't think there's ever been a week that I haven't made at least one batch of cookies, and our blog has over 200 recipes to show for it. Sometimes Josh will say, "Can't we just have chocolate chip?" And to that I usually say something like, "Why would you do that when you could brown the butter and put toffee in it, or bake it in a skillet, or add a glaze or sprinkle it with sea salt…" You get the idea. He usually just rolls his eyes and thinks, *Here we go again…* That said, he's also the first person in line to eat one of my new creations when they come out of the oven!

So, it's very safe to say that cookies are my obsession. To stick a cookie recipe or two in the dessert chapter and call it day just wouldn't cut it, which is why we've included a chapter devoted entirely to cookies.

Maria's Tips for Cookie Success

- Before you start baking, make sure you have all of your ingredients (it's not fun to discover halfway through that you've run out of sugar) and that your baking powder and baking soda are fresh. (Check the dates—yes, they do expire!)

- I use unsalted butter in my cookie recipes. While salt is a very important ingredient (a small amount makes sweeter flavors taste more balanced), I want to control the amount.

- Make sure your butter is *slightly* soft, but not melted (melted butter will make your cookies flat and greasy). Softened butter will give slightly when pressed but still hold its shape. As a general rule, take it out of the fridge about 30 minutes before baking, but how quickly it softens will depend on the temperature of the room.

- Use a stand mixer or hand mixer to beat butter and sugars together until smooth and combined. This usually takes 1 to 2 minutes, depending on the recipe—you don't want to overbeat the butter and sugars and incorporate too much air; you aren't making a light and fluffy cake!

- Measure your flour correctly: First, use a spoon to "fluff" the flour and then scoop it into the appropriate dry measuring cup. Level off the flour with a butter knife. Never pack the cup with flour—adding too much flour to your dough can make your cookies puffy and too dry.

- *Always* use *pure* vanilla extract. The richer vanilla flavor is definitely worth the extra money. It should say "pure vanilla extract" on the label.

- Once you add your dry ingredients to the wet, don't overmix! It will make your cookies flat and dense. Mix on low until *just* combined, then stir in the chocolate chips or any other mix-ins by hand.

- Line your baking sheets with a silicone baking sheet (such as a Silpat). I love these because you can use them over and over again, your cookies will bake more evenly, and cleanup is easy. You could also use parchment paper.

- I like to hand roll my cookie balls so the cookies are perfectly round, but you could also use a medium-sized (1½- to 2-tablespoon) cookie scoop.

- This might be a (really, really) tough one because it means waiting longer for cookie time, but for some of these cookie recipes—and *especially* my chocolate chip cookies—chill your dough before baking! Chilling the dough in the fridge for 24 to 72 hours concentrates the flavors. It also limits how much the cookies spread while baking, which means a chewier, more "bakery-style" cookie. Even if you can chill it for just 30 minutes, it makes a difference. That said, you'll still end up with a pretty tasty cookie if you decide to not chill the dough first.

- Use light-colored baking sheets so your cookies don't get too dark on the bottoms. I love Williams-Sonoma's Goldtouch half sheet (13 × 18 inches).

- Make sure you space out your cookies evenly on the prepared baking sheet, about 2 inches apart. This keeps them from baking into each other.

- Don't overbake your cookies! Remove them from the oven when they're slightly underbaked in the center, then let them cool on the baking sheet for 2 to 3 minutes before transferring them to a cooling rack. This will allow them to finish baking while keeping them nice and soft. Let them cool completely on the cooling rack. Or eat one warm—for quality control…

- I love sprinkling sea salt flakes on top of most of our cookies after they come out of the oven. It doesn't make the cookies taste super salty; it just makes the sweet flavors pop a little more, and the chocolate taste even more chocolaty. Don't skip it—trust me!

- Store your cookies in an airtight container on the counter. I like to store mine with a piece of bread—a trick my dad taught me! The bread will get rock hard but the cookies will stay super soft.

- You can freeze most cookies after they're baked, or you can freeze the cookie dough balls before baking them. Place the cookie dough balls on a large plate or small baking sheet and freeze until hard. Then transfer to a zip-top freezer bag and return to the freezer. To bake frozen dough balls, add a few additional minutes to the baking time. Frozen cookies and dough will keep in the freezer for up to 2 months.

- When I'm baking a lot of cookies for the holidays, I like to do a dough day and then a baking day. This helps make sure all of the cookies are fresh for delivering to friends and family or serving at parties!

our favorite chocolate chip cookies

prep: **15 MINUTES** | bake: **10 TO 12 MINUTES PER BATCH** | makes **33 COOKIES**

• •

3¼ cups all-purpose flour

1½ teaspoons baking powder

1 teaspoon baking soda

1 teaspoon coarse sea salt

1 cup (½ pound) unsalted butter, at room temperature

1½ cups packed light brown sugar

½ cup granulated sugar

1 large egg

1 large egg yolk

1 tablespoon pure vanilla extract

1 cup (6 ounces) semisweet chocolate chips, plus more for finishing

1 cup semisweet chocolate chunks

Maldon sea salt flakes, for sprinkling

This is a very exciting moment for me: I'm finally sharing my all-time favorite chocolate chip cookie recipe. I have baked a *lot* of chocolate chip cookies over the years, and it's helped me hone the perfect Cookie Monster–approved treat. As a family, we agree that the ultimate CCC should be crisp around the edges, soft in the center, chewy, and have the perfect amount of chocolate chips *and* chocolate chunks. (I like using both because the chips are classic while the chunks make little chocolate puddles throughout the cookies.) Plus there should be a hint of vanilla and a little sea salt to round out the sweetness of the chocolate. And the final secret? Adding an extra egg yolk for an even richer, moister cookie. You're welcome!

My three biggest recommendations for making these cookies are: First, don't be afraid of salt in your cookies! It really does help bring out the flavor of the chocolate. Second, make sure to use good chocolate. It makes a huge difference. (My favorite brand is Guittard.) Third, refrigerate the dough before baking it. I know the wait can be tough, but it makes for a chewier, more flavorful cookie. Aim for 24 to 72 hours—but feel free to bake off just a few right away to satisfy your Cookie Monster appetite. The cookies are still really good without chilling, but they're the *best* after some time in the fridge. Oh, and definitely freeze some of your portioned unbaked cookies! There's nothing better than having a batch ready to go in the oven for fresh-baked cookies on demand.

1   Preheat the oven to 350°F. Line a large baking sheet with a silicone baking mat or parchment paper and set aside.

2   In a medium bowl, whisk together the flour, baking powder, baking soda, and coarse sea salt. Set aside.

3   In the bowl of a stand mixer fitted with the paddle attachment, beat the butter on high speed for 30 seconds so it gets a little creamy. Add both sugars and beat for about 1 minute, stopping about halfway through and scraping down the sides of the bowl with a spatula, until the mixture is smooth and fluffy.

recipe continues

NOTE: *This recipe calls for 1 whole egg and 1 egg yolk, which results in a chewy cookie. If you'd rather have a crispier cookie, use 2 whole eggs instead.*

4 Add the egg, egg yolk, and vanilla and mix until combined. Reduce the mixer to low speed and add the dry ingredients, mixing until just combined. Don't overmix! Use a spoon or spatula to fold in the chocolate chips and chocolate chunks.

5 Wrap the dough in plastic wrap and chill for 24 to 72 hours. (Hang in there!)

6 Remove the dough from the refrigerator. Form the dough into balls the size of 2 heaping tablespoons and arrange 2 inches apart on the prepared baking sheet. Not all the cookies will fit on the sheet for one batch.

7 Bake the cookies for 10 to 12 minutes, until the edges are light golden brown. Gently press a few more chocolate chips into the tops of the cookies. (It makes them look extra-delicious!) Sprinkle the cookies with the salt flakes and let cool on the baking sheet for 2 to 3 minutes before transferring them to a wire cooling rack to cool completely—or eat them gooey and warm, dunked in a glass of cold milk. Once the baking sheet has cooled completely, repeat with the remaining dough.

8 Store the cookies in an airtight container at room temperature for as long as they're around (it won't be long), or in a freezer bag in the freezer for up to 1 month.

dad's famous frozen cookies

prep: **15 MINUTES** | bake: **12 MINUTES PER BATCH** | makes **36 COOKIES**

••

2 cups all-purpose flour (see Notes)

1 teaspoon baking soda

½ teaspoon kosher salt

2½ teaspoons ground cinnamon

½ teaspoon ground nutmeg

¼ teaspoon ground cloves

½ cup (8 tablespoons) unsalted butter, at room temperature

1 cup packed light brown sugar

2 large eggs

1 tablespoon pure vanilla extract

1 cup unsweetened applesauce (chunky, if you can find it—see Notes)

1 cup raisins

2½ cups old-fashioned rolled oats

1 cup (6 ounces) semisweet chocolate chips

NOTES: *You can use white whole-wheat flour instead of all-purpose. If you can find chunky applesauce, I highly recommend using it. It gives the cookies great texture. But if all you can find is smooth, you'll still end up with delicious cookies.*

I grew up on these cookies, so even though I have a lot of favorite cookies on my best-of list, these are at the tippy top. My dad got the recipe from his mom, who would bake the cookies and then hide them in the freezer so the kids couldn't find them. However, they knew there was a stash socked away, so one day when they really wanted a cookie, they ate them straight out of the freezer—and discovered they're even better frozen! Growing up, there was pretty much always a batch in our freezer, so whenever friends came over, that's exactly what we grabbed. Don't get me wrong—they're delicious fresh, but there's something magical that happens when they're icy cold.

1 Preheat the oven to 375°F. Line a large baking sheet with a silicone baking mat or parchment paper and set aside.

2 In a medium bowl, whisk together the flour, baking soda, salt, cinnamon, nutmeg, and cloves. Set aside.

3 In the bowl of a stand mixer, beat together the butter and brown sugar until creamy, about 2 minutes on medium speed. Scrape down the sides of the bowl and add the eggs and vanilla. Beat until combined. Add the applesauce and mix until combined. Stop the mixer and scrape down the sides of the bowl. Mix in the raisins.

4 Slowly add the dry ingredients with the mixer on low and mix just until combined. Use a spoon or spatula to stir in the oats and chocolate chips.

5 Drop spoonfuls of cookie dough, about 2 tablespoons per cookie (not more or they will spread too much!), onto the prepared baking sheet, leaving about 2 inches between each cookie. Not all the cookies will fit on the sheet for one batch. Bake for 12 minutes, until the cookies are golden brown around the edges and only slightly set in the middle. You want them to be a little underbaked.

6 Let the cookies cool on the baking sheet for 2 minutes, then transfer to a wire cooling rack to cool completely. Once the baking sheet has cooled completely, repeat with the remaining dough. Store the cookies in a large freezer bag and freeze for up to 2 months. Enjoy them frozen!

toasted coconut, white chocolate, and macadamia cookies

prep: **20 MINUTES** | bake: **10 TO 12 MINUTES PER BATCH** | makes **36 COOKIES**

1¼ cups shredded sweetened coconut

3¼ cups all-purpose flour

1½ teaspoons baking powder

1 teaspoon baking soda

1 teaspoon sea salt

1 cup (½ pound) unsalted butter, at room temperature

1½ cups packed light brown sugar

½ cup granulated sugar

2 large eggs

2 teaspoons pure vanilla extract

2 cups white chocolate chunks or chips

1 cup chopped macadamia nuts

Maldon sea salt flakes, for sprinkling

Of all the chocolates, white chocolate usually isn't at the top of my list, but Caleb *loves* it and is always begging me to add it to a cookie recipe. I decided to start with a pretty classic flavor combination—white chocolate and macadamia—and then took it up a notch with another favorite: toasted coconut. Because white chocolate can be pretty sweet, I balanced things out with a sprinkling of sea salt at the end. The result: A cookie that made my little guy *so* happy (I got two thumbs up!) and made me a white chocolate fan.

1 Preheat the oven to 350°F. Line a large baking sheet with a silicone baking mat or parchment paper and set aside.

2 Line a second large baking sheet with a silicone baking mat or parchment paper and spread the coconut in an even layer over the top. Place the baking sheet on the middle oven rack and bake for 3 minutes. Gently stir the coconut with a spatula and continue baking until the coconut is golden brown and fragrant, 3 to 4 more minutes. Set aside to cool completely.

3 In a medium bowl, whisk together the flour, baking powder, baking soda, and sea salt.

4 In the bowl of a stand mixer fitted with the paddle attachment, cream together the butter and both sugars for about 2 minutes, scraping down the bowl with a spatula between mixing, if necessary. Add the eggs and vanilla and mix until combined. With the mixer on low speed, slowly add the dry ingredients. Use a spoon or spatula to stir in the white chocolate, macadamia nuts, and cooled toasted coconut.

5 Form the dough into balls the size of 2 tablespoons. Arrange on the prepared baking sheet about 2 inches apart. Not all the cookies will fit on the sheet for one batch. Bake the cookies for 10 to 12 minutes, until the edges are slightly golden brown. Sprinkle the cookies with the salt flakes and let cool on the baking sheet for 3 to 5 minutes before transferring them to a wire cooling rack to cool completely. Once the baking sheet has cooled completely, repeat with the remaining dough.

6 Store the cookies at room temperature in an airtight container for up to 4 days or in the freezer for up to 1 month.

easy frosted sugar cookies

prep: **20 MINUTES** | bake: **8 MINUTES PER BATCH** | makes **24 COOKIES**

COOKIES

2¾ cups all-purpose flour

½ teaspoon baking soda

½ teaspoon cream of tartar

½ teaspoon kosher salt

½ cup (8 tablespoons) unsalted butter, at room temperature

½ cup vegetable or canola oil

¾ cup granulated sugar

½ cup confectioners' sugar

1 large egg

1 teaspoon pure vanilla extract

½ teaspoon almond extract

Nonstick cooking spray

FROSTING

¾ cup (12 tablespoons) unsalted butter, at room temperature

3 cups confectioners' sugar, sifted

3 tablespoons heavy cream or milk

1½ teaspoons pure vanilla extract

¾ teaspoon almond extract

Sprinkles, for decorating (optional)

When there are so many amazing cookie flavor combinations out there (and in this book), sometimes the basic sugar cookie doesn't get its due. So I wanted to come up with a cookie that is perfect in its simplicity. These are just the right amount of sweet and basically melt in your mouth. And the best part? You don't have to roll out the dough! They're the perfect clean-slate cookie, and because you can easily double the recipe, they're great for the holidays and cookie-decorating parties—just add tons of options for sprinkles and toppings! You could also change up the color of the frosting with food coloring if you want something other than white.

1 Make the cookies: Preheat the oven to 350°F. Line a large baking sheet with a silicone baking mat or parchment paper. Set aside.

2 In a large bowl, whisk together the flour, baking soda, cream of tartar, and salt.

3 In the bowl of a stand mixer fitted with the paddle attachment, cream together the butter, oil, ½ cup of the granulated sugar, and the confectioners' sugar until smooth. Add the egg, vanilla extract, and almond extract. Mix until combined. Add the dry ingredients and mix on low until just combined.

4 Roll the dough into about 24 balls, about 2 tablespoons dough per cookie, and arrange on the prepared baking sheet about 2 inches apart. Not all the cookies will fit on the sheet for one batch.

5 Pour the remaining ¼ cup granulated sugar on a small plate. Spray the bottom of a drinking glass with nonstick cooking spray. Press the bottom of the glass into the sugar so that it's evenly coated with sugar. Press the sugared glass bottom on top of each cookie dough ball and press down gently, dipping the glass back into the sugar after each cookie so the glass doesn't stick to the dough and every cookie has an evenly sugared top.

6 Bake the cookies for 8 minutes. Do not overbake! The cookies won't look done—they will still be light in color and soft in the center, and that is okay. They will set up as they cool on the baking sheet. Let them cool for 5 minutes before transferring to a wire cooling rack to cool completely. When the baking sheet has cooled completely, repeat with the remaining dough.

7 **Make the frosting:** In the bowl of a stand mixer fitted with the paddle attachment, beat the butter until smooth. Add the confectioners' sugar and mix until combined. Stream in the cream, vanilla extract, and almond extract. Beat until the frosting is smooth. If the frosting is too thick, add a little more cream. If it is too thin, add a little more sugar.

8 **Assemble the cookies:** Use a butter knife to spread frosting over the tops of the cooled cookies. Decorate with sprinkles, if desired. Store in an airtight container at room temperature for up to 3 days.

chocolate-mint whoopie pies

prep: **60 MINUTES** | bake: **10 MINUTES PER BATCH** | makes **ABOUT 25 MINI WHOOPIE PIES**

MINT FILLING

¾ cup (12 tablespoons) unsalted butter, at room temperature

1¼ cups confectioners' sugar, sifted

1 teaspoon pure vanilla extract

1 teaspoon mint extract

⅛ teaspoon kosher salt

2½ cups marshmallow creme, from a jar

CHOCOLATE COOKIES

2 cups all-purpose flour

½ cup Dutch-process cocoa powder

1 teaspoon baking soda

¾ teaspoon kosher salt

½ cup (8 tablespoons) unsalted butter, at room temperature

1 cup packed brown sugar

1 large egg, at room temperature

1 teaspoon pure vanilla extract

1 cup buttermilk, at room temperature

1 (4.67-ounce) box Andes chocolate mints, finely chopped, *or* 2 cups mint chocolate chips

Whoopie pies are a classic dessert made with two soft, cake-like cookies that sandwich a fluffy marshmallow creme filling. It's basically like cake and cookies in one! I give this standby a twist with a chocolate-mint version, which is one of our family's favorite flavor combos. The finishing touch is rolling the pies in chopped Andes chocolate mints, though you could use mint chocolate chips instead, or even just plain chocolate chips. For the holidays, I use crushed candy canes. So pretty and festive!

This recipe is perfect for making ahead. The filling can be made in advance and refrigerated for up to 2 days, and the cookies can also be baked 2 days in advance. Store them in an airtight container in the fridge, making sure to use parchment paper between the stacks. You can also freeze the assembled cookies; just wrap them individually in plastic wrap.

1 Make the filling: Using a stand mixer fitted with the paddle attachment, beat together the butter and confectioners' sugar on medium speed until light and fluffy, about 2 minutes. Beat in the vanilla extract, mint extract, and salt. Scrape down the sides of the bowl with a spatula, add the marshmallow creme, and mix until combined. Refrigerate the filling for at least 30 minutes.

2 Make the cookies: Preheat the oven to 350°F. Line a large baking sheet with a silicone baking mat or parchment paper and set aside.

3 In a medium bowl, whisk together the flour, cocoa powder, baking soda, and salt. Set aside.

4 In a stand mixer fitted with the paddle attachment, beat together the butter and brown sugar until light and fluffy, about 2 minutes, scraping down the sides of the bowl with a spatula as needed. Add the egg and vanilla and mix until combined. Scrape down the bowl, if necessary.

5 With the mixer on low, alternate adding a third of the flour mixture, half of the buttermilk, a third of the flour mixture, the rest of the buttermilk, and finally the remaining flour mixture. Mix until just combined. Give the batter a final stir with a spatula to make sure there isn't any flour at the bottom of the bowl.

6 Use a small cookie scoop to portion out about 2 teaspoons of batter onto the prepared baking sheet, placing the batter about 2 inches apart. Not all the cookies will fit on the sheet for one batch. Bake for 10 minutes, until the centers spring back when gently touched. Let the cookies cool on the baking sheets for 5 minutes, then transfer to a wire cooling rack to cool completely. Once the baking sheet has cooled completely, repeat with the remaining dough.

7 Assemble the whoopie pies: Spread the mint filling over the flat sides of half of the cookies and top with the remaining cookies. You can also use a pastry bag fitted with a tip to fill the pies.

8 Scatter the chopped Andes mints on a plate. Roll the whoopie pies on their sides to coat the filling with the toppings. Store the whoopie pies in an airtight container in the refrigerator for up to 3 days. If you stack them, make sure to put parchment paper between them.

mega monster cookies

prep: **20 MINUTES** | bake: **14 TO 18 MINUTES PER BATCH** | makes **16 LARGE COOKIES**

● ●

3 cups old-fashioned rolled oats

1½ cups all-purpose flour

1 teaspoon baking soda

1 teaspoon kosher salt

1 cup (½ pound) unsalted butter, at room temperature

1 cup creamy peanut butter

1 cup granulated sugar

1 cup packed light brown sugar

2 large eggs

2 teaspoons pure vanilla extract

1 cup (6 ounces) semisweet chocolate chips

1 cup M&M's candies

1 cup chopped pretzels

Maldon sea salt flakes, for sprinkling

NOTE: *When the cookies come out of the oven, you can stick additional M&M's on top to make these extra colorful. Just press them in gently.*

I say, when it comes to cookies, the bigger, the better! These cookies—as their larger-than-life name suggests—are pretty much as big as they come because they're loaded with peanut butter, oats, chocolate chips, M&M's, *and* chopped pretzels. The sweet and salty combo is pretty tough to beat, and when they're sitting out on the counter, their enormous, bakery-style size make any child's—or grown-up's!—eyes light up. Don't forget a glass of cold milk.

1   Preheat the oven to 350°F. Line a large baking sheet with a silicone baking mat or parchment paper and set aside.

2   In a medium bowl, whisk together the oats, flour, baking soda, and salt.

3   In the bowl of a stand mixer fitted with the paddle attachment, beat together the butter, peanut butter, and both sugars until creamy, about 2 minutes on medium speed. Beat in the eggs and vanilla and mix until well combined. With the mixer on low speed, add the oat mixture and mix until just combined. Use a spoon to stir in the chocolate chips, M&M's, and pretzels.

4   Form the dough into about 16 large round balls, about ⅓ cup of dough per cookie. Arrange the balls on the prepared baking sheet about 2 inches apart. Not all the cookies will fit on the sheet for one batch; I usually put 5 cookies per sheet. Lightly press down on the dough balls with the palm of your hand.

5   Bake for 14 to 18 minutes, until the cookies are lightly browned around the edges but still soft in the middle. Sprinkle the cookies with the salt flakes and let cool on the baking sheets for 5 minutes before transferring them to a wire rack to cool completely. Once the baking sheet has cooled completely, repeat with the remaining dough.

6   Store the cookies in an airtight container at room temperature for up to 3 days or freeze for up to 1 month.

deep-dish brownie cookies

prep: **15 MINUTES** | bake: **18 TO 20 MINUTES** | total: **35 MINUTES** | makes **10 COOKIES**

Nonstick cooking spray

½ cup all-purpose flour

3 tablespoons Dutch-process cocoa powder

½ teaspoon baking powder

¼ teaspoon kosher salt

1 cup semisweet chocolate chunks or chocolate chips

4 tablespoons unsalted butter, cut into cubes

2 large eggs

½ cup packed brown sugar

¼ cup granulated sugar

1 teaspoon pure vanilla extract

½ cup semisweet chocolate chips

Vanilla ice cream (or your favorite flavor), for serving (optional)

Whenever I go out to eat, no matter how much I've had for dinner, I'm always excited to see the dessert menu (because, duh!). But as much as I love the idea of fancy pastries, tarts, mousses, or bread puddings, when it comes down to it, I'll always go for the cookie or brownie option. But if I have to choose between the two? That's *way* too hard a decision! So I came up with the ultimate dessert that combines them. You basically get the deep, rich chocolate flavor of a brownie but in deep-dish cookie form. And I underbake them just a touch so they're gooey and warm, perfect for serving brownie sundae–style with a cold scoop of ice cream.

1 Preheat the oven to 350°F. Grease ten 4-ounce ramekins with nonstick cooking spray and set aside.

2 In a medium bowl, whisk together the flour, cocoa, baking powder, and salt. Set aside.

3 In a large glass bowl, combine the chocolate chunks and butter. Microwave for 1 minute and stir. Microwave for 30 more seconds and stir until smooth. You could also do this over a pot of simmering water.

4 Whisk the eggs, both sugars, and vanilla into the chocolate mixture until smooth. Gently stir in the dry ingredients. The dough will be thick. Fold in the chocolate chips.

5 Evenly divide the cookie dough among the ten greased ramekins and arrange the ramekins on a large rimmed baking sheet. Bake the cookies for 18 to 20 minutes, until they are set around the edges but still soft and gooey in the middle. You want them to be a little underbaked.

6 Let the cookies cool for 5 minutes. Top with ice cream, if desired (but hello!), and serve warm.

NOTE: *These are great to make ahead because you can prep the dough in advance and bake off the cookies when you're ready for dessert. Feel free to add Salted Caramel Sauce (page 70), Peanut Butter Hot Fudge (page 270), or sprinkles. Or change up the flavor by folding peanut butter chips, white chocolate chips, or mint chocolate chips into the dough.*

lemon-almond cookies
with lemon glaze

prep: **15 MINUTES** | bake: **12 TO 14 MINUTES PER BATCH** | makes **ABOUT 30 COOKIES**

● ●

COOKIES

2¼ cups all-purpose flour

½ teaspoon baking powder

½ teaspoon kosher salt

¾ cup granulated sugar

2 tablespoons grated lemon zest

1 cup (½ pound) unsalted butter, at
   room temperature

1 large egg

1 teaspoon pure vanilla extract

¼ teaspoon almond extract

LEMON GLAZE

1 cup confectioners' sugar

1 teaspoon grated lemon zest

3 tablespoons fresh lemon juice
   (2 lemons)

1 cup sliced almonds

These lemony, buttery cookies are like little bursts of sunshine—they always make me happy! They're perfectly soft and chewy with a slight crunch from sliced almonds scattered over the tops, and then there's the simple glaze that gives everything a bright pop of citrus. They also look really pretty on a platter and are a sweet addition to a party spread. I'm always making them for baby showers, bridal showers, Easter brunch, summer garden parties, or just because I want a little lemon love in my life.

1   Make the cookies: Preheat the oven to 350°F. Line a large baking sheet with a silicone baking mat or parchment paper and set aside.

2   In a medium bowl, whisk together the flour, baking powder, and salt.

3   In a small bowl, combine the sugar and lemon zest and rub together with your fingers until fragrant. In the bowl of a stand mixer fitted with the paddle attachment, combine the sugar mixture and butter and beat until light and fluffy, about 3 minutes. Add the egg, vanilla extract, and almond extract and mix until smooth. Slowly beat in the flour mixture on low speed until the mixture comes together into a dough.

4   Drop the dough by the tablespoon, 2 inches apart, onto the prepared baking sheet. Not all the cookies will fit on the sheet for one batch. Gently press down the dough with the palm of your hand.

5   Bake for 12 to 14 minutes, until the cookies are just set and slightly golden brown around the edges. Let the cookies cool on the baking sheets for 2 minutes before transferring them to a wire rack to cool completely. Once the baking sheet has completely cooled, repeat with the remaining dough.

6   Make the glaze: In a medium bowl, whisk together the confectioners' sugar and lemon zest and juice. Once the cookies are completely cool, dip each cookie top into the lemon glaze. Sprinkle sliced almonds on top of each cookie, making sure they stick to the glaze. Let the cookies sit until the glaze has set, 15 to 20 minutes. Store the cookies in an airtight container at room temperature for up to 3 days.

brown butter–salted caramel snickerdoodles

prep: **15 MINUTES, PLUS 30 MINUTES CHILLING** | bake: **8 TO 10 MINUTES PER BATCH**

makes **ABOUT 36 COOKIES**

• •

COOKIES

1 cup (½ pound) unsalted butter, sliced into tablespoon-sized pieces

2½ cups all-purpose flour

1 teaspoon baking soda

½ teaspoon ground cinnamon

2 teaspoons cream of tartar

½ teaspoon sea salt

1¼ cups packed dark brown sugar

½ cup granulated sugar

1 large egg

1 large egg yolk

1 tablespoon pure vanilla extract

1 tablespoon plain Greek yogurt or sour cream

About 18 caramels, cut in half

CINNAMON-SUGAR TOPPING

2 teaspoons ground cinnamon

¼ cup granulated sugar

Maldon sea salt flakes, for sprinkling

This twist on the classic cinnamon snickerdoodle is in my top 10 (okay, maybe 20—there's just so many!) favorite cookie recipes. Inspired by my love for sea-salted caramel, (Trader Joe's Fleur de Sel Caramels are my favorite), I tuck store-bought caramels into a nutty brown-butter dough. The overall effect is a sweet and salty cookie with a rich, gooey center and a dusting of cinnamon and sugar—like a classic snickerdoodle but on a whole new level. They're always the first ones to go at holiday parties!

1   Make the cookies: To brown the butter, heat a heavy-bottomed skillet over medium heat. Add the sliced butter pieces and whisk frequently as they melt. The butter will start to foam and browned specks will begin to form at the bottom of the pan. Continue cooking until the milk solids look like little golden-brown flecks and have a nutty aroma, 1 to 2 minutes. Watch closely because the butter can go from brown to burnt quickly. Remove the pan from the heat and let the butter cool to room temperature.

2   In a medium bowl, whisk together the flour, baking soda, cinnamon, cream of tartar, and sea salt. Set aside.

3   In the bowl of a stand mixer fitted with the paddle attachment, combine the brown butter, brown sugar, and granulated sugar. Mix until blended and smooth. Beat in the egg, egg yolk, vanilla, and yogurt and mix until combined. With the mixer running on low speed, slowly add the dry ingredients and mix until just combined.

4   Form the dough into a large ball and cover with plastic wrap. Chill in the refrigerator for at least 30 minutes or overnight.

5   When ready to bake, preheat the oven to 350°F. Line a large baking sheet with a silicone baking mat or parchment paper.

recipe continues

6 Measure about 2 tablespoons dough and roll into a ball. Flatten the ball slightly with the palm of your hand and place a caramel half in the center. Wrap the cookie dough around the caramel, making sure the caramel is completely covered with dough. Repeat with the remaining dough and caramels.

7 Make the cinnamon-sugar topping: In a small bowl, combine the cinnamon and sugar. Roll the balls in the topping and place on the prepared baking sheet about 2 inches apart. Not all the cookies will fit on the sheet for one batch.

8 Bake the cookies for 8 to 10 minutes, until the edges begin to turn golden brown. The centers will still be soft. Sprinkle the cookies with the salt flakes and cool on the baking sheet for 2 to 3 minutes, until set. Transfer the cookies to a wire cooling rack to cool completely. Once the baking sheet has cooled completely, repeat with the remaining dough.

9 Store the cookies in an airtight container at room temperature for up to 3 days.

triple-chip chocolate cookies

prep: **15 MINUTES** | bake: **10 MINUTES PER BATCH** | makes **33 COOKIES**

• •

2⅓ cups all-purpose flour

¾ cup Dutch-process or unsweetened cocoa powder

1 teaspoon baking soda

½ teaspoon sea salt, plus more for sprinkling

1 cup (½ pound) unsalted butter, at room temperature

1 cup granulated sugar

1 cup packed light brown sugar

2 large eggs

1½ teaspoons pure vanilla extract

¾ cup milk chocolate chips, plus more for finishing

¾ cup semisweet chocolate chips, plus more for finishing

¾ cup white chocolate chips, plus more for finishing

Chocolate lovers are in for a real treat with these rich cocoa cookies made with *three* kinds of chocolate chips: milk, semisweet, and white. It's the kind of cookie that technically will scratch the sweet-tooth itch after eating just one, but let's be honest: Who can stop there? Make sure you have a glass of cold milk nearby for dunking.

1   Preheat the oven to 350°F. Line a large baking sheet with a silicone baking mat or parchment paper. Set aside.

2   In a medium bowl, whisk together the flour, cocoa, baking soda, and sea salt. Set aside.

3   In the bowl of a stand mixer fitted with the paddle attachment, combine the butter and both sugars. Mix until smooth, 2 minutes. Add the eggs one at a time, mixing well after each addition. Add the vanilla and mix until combined.

4   Gradually add the flour mixture and beat on low speed until just combined. Use a spatula to stir in all the chocolate chips.

5   Drop the dough by the rounded tablespoon on the prepared baking sheet, about 2 inches apart. Not all the cookies will fit on the sheet for one batch. Bake for 10 minutes, until the cookies are set but still soft in the center. Don't overbake. Gently press a few more chocolate chips and chunks into the tops of the cookies. Let the cookies cool on the baking sheet for 3 to 5 minutes before transferring to a cooling rack to cool completely. While the cookies are still soft, gently press the extra chocolate chips into the cookies to make them look pretty. Once the baking sheet has cooled completely, repeat with the remaining dough.

6   Store the cookies in an airtight container at room temperature for up to 4 days or in the freezer for up to 1 month.

biscoff oatmeal sandwich cookies

prep: 20 MINUTES | bake: 10 MINUTES PER BATCH | makes 16 SANDWICH COOKIES

● ●

COOKIES

1½ cups old-fashioned rolled oats

¾ cup all-purpose flour

½ teaspoon baking soda

1 teaspoon ground cinnamon

¼ teaspoon kosher salt

½ cup (8 tablespoons) unsalted butter, at room temperature

½ cup Biscoff spread (see Note)

½ cup granulated sugar

½ cup packed light brown sugar

1 large egg

1 teaspoon pure vanilla extract

BISCOFF BUTTERCREAM

3 tablespoons unsalted butter, at room temperature

½ cup Biscoff spread (see Note)

1¼ cups confectioners' sugar, sifted

3 tablespoons whole milk

¼ teaspoon pure vanilla extract

NOTE: *Most grocery stores carry Biscoff spread (look for it in the peanut butter aisle), or you can order it online.*

I travel a lot, but I don't mind getting on the plane if I know I'm going to get a Biscoff cookie—those perfectly crispy-yet-buttery, caramel-y cookies that I get on Delta flights. I decided to create the ultimate homemade version: a sandwich cookie complete with a filling of Biscoff-flavored buttercream. Because two cookies are always better than one!

1 Make the cookies: Preheat the oven to 350°F. Line a large baking sheet with a silicone baking mat or parchment paper and set aside.

2 In a medium bowl, whisk together the oats, flour, baking soda, cinnamon, and salt. Set aside.

3 In the bowl of a stand mixer fitted with the paddle attachment, combine the butter, Biscoff spread, granulated sugar, and brown sugar and beat on medium speed until smooth and creamy, 2 minutes. Add the egg and vanilla and beat until smooth.

4 Reduce the mixer speed to low and add the oat-flour mixture, beating just until blended into a dough.

5 Drop the dough by the rounded tablespoon onto the prepared baking sheet, about 2 inches apart. Not all the cookies will fit on the sheet for one batch. Bake for 10 minutes, until the cookies are golden and just firm around the edges. Let the cookies

cool on the baking sheet for 5 minutes before transferring to a cooling rack to cool completely. Once the baking sheet has cooled completely, repeat with the remaining dough.

6 Make the buttercream: In the bowl of a stand mixer fitted with the paddle attachment, beat together the butter and Biscoff spread until creamy. Add the confectioners' sugar and beat until smooth. Scrape down the sides of the bowl with a spatula. Add the milk and vanilla and again beat until smooth.

7 To assemble the cookies, scoop the Biscoff buttercream into a pastry bag fitted with a coupler, and pipe about 1 tablespoon filling onto the flat side of half the cookies. Alternatively, you can spread the filling onto the cookies with a butter knife. Place the remaining cookies on top, and gently press on each to squeeze the filling to the edges.

8 Store the cookies in an airtight container at room temperature for up to 2 days.

toffee–chocolate chunk skillet cookie

prep: **15 MINUTES** | bake: **20 TO 24 MINUTES** | total: **40 MINUTES** | serves **8 TO 10**

¾ cup (12 tablespoons) unsalted butter, cut into tablespoon-sized pieces

1 cup packed light brown sugar

½ cup granulated sugar

2 large eggs, at room temperature

2 teaspoons pure vanilla extract

2 cups all-purpose flour

1 teaspoon cornstarch

¾ teaspoon baking soda

½ teaspoon sea salt, plus more for sprinkling

1 cup chocolate chunks (or chips, if that's all you can find)

1 cup Heath toffee bits (see Note)

Vanilla ice cream, for serving (optional)

NOTE: *If you can't find Heath toffee bits, buy four regular-sized Heath or Skor candy bars and chop them up.*

Skillet cookies are a home baker's secret weapon. Whenever I don't feel like scooping out three dozen cookies and dealing with a bunch of dirty baking sheets, I just press the dough into a skillet! It makes for a really impressive presentation, which you could just put right on the table with a few scoops of vanilla ice cream. The ice cream will melt into the warm cookie, making pretty much the most delicious sauce you can imagine. Pass out spoons and go to town—no extra dishes required!

This skillet cookie in particular is a family favorite because of the combination of slightly salty toffee and sweet chocolate chunks, along with rich brown butter. I'm always sure to underbake the cookie just a touch so you get a deliciously gooey center.

1   Preheat the oven to 350°F.

2   In a 10-inch cast-iron skillet, melt the butter over medium heat, swirling it in the pan occasionally as it melts. The butter will foam and pop, so be careful. Once the butter starts to brown and smell nutty, remove the pan from the heat. There should be small brown bits on the bottom and the butter will have an amber color. Pour the butter into a large bowl, making sure to get all the brown bits, and cool to room temperature. Do not wipe out the pan.

3   Once the brown butter has cooled, add the brown sugar and granulated sugar and whisk until smooth. Add the eggs and vanilla and mix until combined.

4   In a medium bowl, whisk together the flour, cornstarch, baking soda, and salt until combined. Add the flour mixture to the wet ingredients and mix just until the flour disappears. Stir in the chocolate chunks and toffee bits.

5   Spread out the dough in the still-buttered cast-iron skillet, pressing down gently with your hands or a spatula to even out the dough. Sprinkle the top with a little sea salt. Bake for 20 to 24 minutes, until golden brown. Don't overbake; you want the cookie to be slightly gooey in the center.

6   Let the cookie cool for 10 to 15 minutes before serving warm, with ice cream if desired.

DESSERT

● ●

If this book's entire chapter devoted to cookies didn't tip you off, let me tell you once again what a serious sweet tooth I have. I *always* save room for dessert. Actually, maybe that's why I eat so many veggies—it's a great excuse to finish off a meal with a slice of cake or pie, a warm-from-the-oven brownie or blondie, or a heaping bowl of ice cream. With a side of cookies, of course. If a waiter asks if I want to see a dessert menu, the answer is always "yes," unless it's "one of each, please." That said, while I'm lucky enough to travel and eat in fancy restaurants, I can't tell you how many times I've been disappointed by desserts that are mucked up with too-fancy exotic glazes, strange flavor combinations, or skimpy portions. Desserts shouldn't have to have anything to prove— they just need to be *good!* That's why my favorite recipes are the ones for classic treats, where you don't have to be a pastry chef to make them. That's exactly what you'll find in this chapter: my favorite, tried-and-true desserts that always have people asking for the recipe. These desserts are simple enough that you can reach for one on a weeknight if someone gets an A on their science test, or when you're having people over for a birthday or a holiday, or to bring to someone's home. And don't forget that dessert can be a meal on its own! We love having people over for "just desserts." No one minds grabbing a bite of dinner before coming over if you're offering up a spread of cake, brownies, and ice cream.

peach cobbler with buttermilk biscuit topping

prep: **20 MINUTES** | bake: **45 TO 50 MINUTES** | total: **1 HOUR 10 MINUTES** | serves **10 TO 12**

• •

PEACH FILLING

8 peaches, pitted, peeled, and sliced (6 cups)

⅓ cup granulated sugar

Grated zest of 1 large lemon

2 tablespoons packed light brown sugar

1 tablespoon cornstarch

1 teaspoon ground cinnamon

BUTTERMILK BISCUIT TOPPING

2 cups all-purpose flour

⅓ cup granulated sugar

2 teaspoons baking powder

½ teaspoon kosher salt

½ cup (8 tablespoons) unsalted butter, cold, cut into pieces

1 cup buttermilk, cold

1 teaspoon pure vanilla extract

Heavy cream or whole milk, for brushing

Turbinado sugar, for sprinkling

Vanilla ice cream, for serving (optional)

I make this cobbler every summer when Utah peaches are in season. Utah has the *best* peaches (sorry, Georgia!) so, without fail, we come home from the farmers market with waaaaay too many. It's a pretty familiar story for us—Josh is a little too good at loading up on fruit. At least it's not Cheetos or doughnuts, but we still need to figure out how to put all that fresh produce to good use. Enter the cobbler. It pops up a lot in our kitchen because you basically just dump the fruit in a pan (pretty much any fruit will work), top with an easy biscuit-like topping, and bake. Serve warm with a scoop of ice cream for dessert, and then break it out again for breakfast. It's totally acceptable. The cobbler can also be refrigerated, covered, for up to 2 days if you want to make it ahead. Just reheat in the oven or microwave.

1 Make the filling: Place the sliced peaches in a large bowl. In a small bowl, combine the granulated sugar and lemon zest and rub together with your fingers until fragrant. Add the lemon sugar to the peaches along with the brown sugar, cornstarch, and cinnamon. Gently stir until the peaches are well coated. Let the mixture sit while you prepare the topping.

2 Make the biscuit topping: In a medium bowl, whisk together the flour, granulated sugar, baking powder, and salt. Cut the cold butter into the flour mixture with a pastry blender or two forks, or by using clean hands and pinching the butter between your forefinger and thumb. Mix until the butter pieces are pea-sized.

3 In a medium bowl, whisk together the cold buttermilk and vanilla. Pour the mixture into the dry ingredients and stir with a spatula until the dough just comes together. It will be sticky; don't overmix.

4 Preheat the oven to 375°F.

5 Assemble the cobbler: Pour the peach mixture into a 9 × 13-inch pan. Drop pieces of the biscuit topping on top of the peaches—it is fine if there is space between the dollops. Lightly brush the topping with the cream and sprinkle with the turbinado sugar.

6 Bake for 45 to 50 minutes, until the topping is golden brown and the peaches are bubbling. Let cool on a wire rack for 15 minutes before serving with vanilla ice cream, if desired.

lemon–poppy seed bundt cake

prep: **20 MINUTES** | bake: **55 TO 65 MINUTES** | total: **1 HOUR 25 MINUTES, PLUS COOLING** | serves **12 TO 16**

● ●

CAKE

Nonstick cooking spray or softened butter

3 cups all-purpose flour, plus more for dusting

2 teaspoons baking powder

1 teaspoon kosher salt

2 cups granulated sugar

Grated zest of 2 large lemons

½ cup (8 tablespoons) unsalted butter, at room temperature

½ cup vegetable oil or canola oil

1 tablespoon fresh lemon juice

4 large eggs, at room temperature

1 teaspoon pure vanilla extract

1 cup plain, full-fat Greek yogurt or sour cream

¼ cup poppy seeds

LEMON SYRUP

¼ cup fresh lemon juice (2 to 3 lemons)

¼ cup granulated sugar

LEMON ICING

1½ cups confectioners' sugar

3 tablespoons fresh lemon juice (2 lemons)

You can't go wrong with a classic, and this cake is no exception. It's bursting with fresh lemon flavor thanks to an extra drizzle of lemon-infused syrup, and the Greek yogurt in the batter makes it perfectly moist. I love making this simple-but-lovely confection for bridal or baby showers, or when having the ladies over for a light lunch or tea on the porch.

1 Make the cake: Preheat the oven to 350°F. Generously grease a 10- to 12-cup Bundt pan with nonstick cooking spray or softened butter, lightly dust with flour, and set aside.

2 In a medium bowl, whisk together the flour, baking powder, and salt. Set aside.

3 Combine the granulated sugar and lemon zest in a small bowl and rub together with your fingers until fragrant. In the bowl of a stand mixer fitted with the paddle attachment, beat together the lemon sugar and butter until creamy and smooth, about 2 minutes. Scrape down the sides of the bowl with a spatula. Add the oil and lemon juice and mix until combined. Beat in the eggs one at a time, mixing well after each addition. Add the vanilla and yogurt and mix until smooth.

4 With the machine running on low, slowly add the flour mixture and mix until just combined. Don't overmix. Fold in the poppy seeds with a spoon or spatula.

5 Pour the cake batter evenly into the prepared Bundt pan. Bake for 55 to 65 minutes, until the cake is golden brown and a toothpick inserted in the center comes out clean. Let the cake cool on a cooling rack in the pan for 20 minutes.

6 Run a butter knife around the edges of the cake to loosen it. Turn the pan upside down on the rack and remove the cake from the pan.

7 Make the syrup: In a small saucepan, combine the lemon juice and granulated sugar. Heat over medium heat, stirring until the sugar dissolves.

8 While the cake is still warm, use a long wooden skewer or a knife to gently poke holes in the cake. Slowly spoon the lemon syrup over the cake, making sure the glaze seeps into the entire cake. You might have a little extra syrup, and that is fine.

9 Make the icing: In a medium bowl, combine the confectioners' sugar and lemon juice and whisk until smooth. Once the cake has cooled, drizzle with the icing, slice, and serve. Or cover with plastic wrap and save at room temperature for up to 3 days.

peanut butter–fudge ice cream pie
with chocolate cookie crust

prep: 25 MINUTES | bake: 10 MINUTES | total: 35 MINUTES, PLUS 3 HOURS FREEZING | serves 12

CHOCOLATE COOKIE CRUST

Nonstick cooking spray

1 (9-ounce) package chocolate wafer cookies, finely crushed

2 tablespoons granulated sugar

½ cup (8 tablespoons) unsalted butter, melted

PEANUT BUTTER HOT FUDGE

¾ cup heavy cream

½ cup light corn syrup or golden syrup

¼ cup packed brown sugar

¼ cup cocoa powder

2 tablespoons unsalted butter

¼ teaspoon fine sea salt

1 cup (6 ounces) semisweet chocolate chips

3 tablespoons creamy peanut butter

1 teaspoon pure vanilla extract

ICE CREAM FILLING

3 cups softened vanilla ice cream

1 cup chopped peanut butter cups

¼ cup creamy peanut butter

TO ASSEMBLE

1 cup chopped peanut butter cups

Whipped cream, for decorating (optional)

There are certain matches made in heaven when it comes to dessert: ice cream and pie, chocolate and peanut butter...so why not put them all together?! Add a chocolate cookie crust, and you pretty much have the *ultimate* dessert. With a filling of vanilla ice cream dotted with peanut butter cups and peanut butter hot fudge, and topped with fresh whipped cream, this dessert gets a big ol' "Whoa!" every time we serve it.

1 Make the crust: Preheat the oven to 350°F. Grease a 9-inch pie pan with nonstick cooking spray.

2 In a medium bowl, stir together the crushed cookies, granulated sugar, and melted butter. Press the cookie mixture into the bottom and up the sides of the prepared pie pan. Bake for 10 minutes. Let cool completely.

3 Make the hot fudge: In a medium saucepan, combine the cream, corn syrup, brown sugar, cocoa, butter, and salt. Bring to a simmer over medium heat, then reduce to low. Cook, stirring, until all of the ingredients are combined and melted, about 1 minute. Remove the pot from the heat and stir in the chocolate chips until they are melted. Add the peanut butter and vanilla and stir until smooth. Pour ½ cup of the hot fudge into the bottom of the cooled crust. Reserve the remaining fudge at room temperature to use in the filling and to top the pie.

4 Make the filling: In a large bowl, stir together the ice cream, peanut butter cups, and peanut butter. Fold in ¼ cup of the reserved peanut butter hot fudge.

5 Assemble the pie: Pour the filling into the cooled piecrust and smooth the top with a spatula. Sprinkle with the peanut butter cups and drizzle with the remaining peanut butter hot fudge, reheating it first to loosen, if necessary.

6 Carefully cover the pie with plastic wrap or aluminum foil. Place in the freezer until the filling is firm, at least 3 hours. Fill a pastry bag with the whipped cream (if using) and pipe it in any decorative way you like. (If you don't have a pastry bag you can fill a zip-top bag with the whipped cream and cut a hole in one of the corners of the bag.) Use a sharp knife to cut the pie into slices and serve immediately.

chocolate celebration cake

prep: **1½ HOURS** | bake: **24 TO 28 MINUTES** | total: **2 HOURS, PLUS COOLING** | serves **12 TO 16**

• •

CHOCOLATE CAKE

Nonstick cooking spray

1 cup buttermilk, at room
    temperature

½ cup vegetable or canola oil

1 tablespoon pure vanilla extract

1¾ cups all-purpose flour

2 cups granulated sugar

¾ cup Dutch-process cocoa
    powder, sifted

2 teaspoons baking soda

1 teaspoon baking powder

1 teaspoon kosher salt

2 large eggs, at room temperature

1 cup hot water

CHOCOLATE BUTTERCREAM

2 cups (1 pound) unsalted butter,
    at room temperature

7 cups (2 pounds) confectioners'
    sugar, sifted

1 cup Dutch-process cocoa
    powder, sifted

¼ cup plus 2 tablespoons whole
    chocolate milk (or regular
    milk or heavy cream), at room
    temperature

2 teaspoons pure vanilla extract

⅛ teaspoon kosher salt

⅔ cup semisweet chocolate chips,
    melted and slightly cooled

For decorating (optional):
    chocolate shavings, sprinkles, or
    mini chocolate chips

Everybody likes chocolate cake! If you don't, then I don't know if we can be friendsr…just kidding! I will still be your friend—so I can eat your piece of cake. This ultimate chocolate cake is our household favorite for any celebration—because every celebration needs a cake, right? It's three layers of moist, chocolaty cake frosted with a chocolate buttercream that includes cocoa, semisweet chocolate, *and* a secret ingredient: chocolate milk. Make sure to enjoy the cake with a glass of milk or a scoop of vanilla ice cream close by.

1 Make the cake: Preheat the oven to 350°F. Grease three 8-inch round cake pans generously with nonstick cooking spray. Line the pans with parchment paper, then spray the paper. Set aside.

2 In a medium bowl, whisk together the buttermilk, oil, and vanilla.

3 In the bowl of a stand mixer fitted with the paddle attachment, mix together the flour, granulated sugar, cocoa powder, baking soda, baking powder, and salt. With the mixer on low speed, add the buttermilk mixture. Add the eggs, one at a time, and mix until well combined. Slowly add the hot water and stir just to combine, stopping to scrape down the sides of the bowl with a spatula before mixing briefly again.

4 Divide the batter evenly among the prepared pans and bake for 24 to 28 minutes, until a cake tester comes out clean when inserted into the centers of the cakes.

5 Set the cakes on wire cooling racks to cool in the pans for 30 minutes. Turn out the cakes onto the racks to cool completely. You can refrigerate or freeze the cakes at this time (see Note, page 274).

6 Make the buttercream: In the bowl of a stand mixer fitted with the paddle attachment, beat the butter until creamy and lighter in color, about 3 minutes, scraping down the bowl halfway through. Add the confectioners' sugar, 2 cups at a time, and then the cocoa. Pour in the chocolate milk, vanilla, and salt. With the mixer on low speed, add the melted chocolate. Mix for an additional 2 to 3 minutes, until the buttercream is light and fluffy.

recipe continues

7 Assemble: If the cake layers are slightly domed on top, carefully level them off with a sharp serrated knife. To build the cake, place the first layer bottom side up on a flat plate or cake pedestal. Using a knife or offset spatula, spread the top of the cake evenly with buttercream. Place the second layer on top, top side up, and spread more buttercream evenly over the top. Repeat with the third layer and frost the top and sides of the cake. Decorate with chocolate shavings, sprinkles, or chocolate chips, if desired. Slice and serve.

NOTE: *Since this is a bigger undertaking than other desserts, you can break up the project by making the cakes in advance. I like to do this so the cake has time to chill, which makes it easier to frost. Carefully wrap the cooled cake layers in plastic wrap and store them in the fridge for up to 2 days. You could also freeze them wrapped in plastic wrap for up to 1 month. Just defrost before frosting and assembling.*

janette's key lime bars

prep: **30 MINUTES** | bake: **ABOUT 1 HOUR** | total: **1½ HOURS PLUS 3 HOURS COOLING AND CHILLING** | serves **12**

●●

GRAHAM CRACKER CRUST

1½ cups graham cracker crumbs
(about 9 full sheets; see Notes)

¼ cup sugar

6 tablespoons unsalted butter, melted

¼ teaspoon kosher salt

KEY LIME FILLING

2 (14-ounce) cans sweetened condensed milk

1 tablespoon grated lime zest

½ cup key lime juice (fresh or bottled, see Notes)

½ cup plain Greek yogurt

1 large egg yolk

WHIPPED CREAM

⅔ cup heavy cream

2 tablespoons sugar

1 teaspoon pure vanilla extract

Limes, thinly sliced, for garnish, if desired

NOTES: *If you don't have a food processor to make graham cracker crumbs, just add graham crackers to a large zip-top bag and crush them with a rolling pin. Instead of taking the time to juice fresh key limes, I recommend buying the juice bottled. It's good enough for Janette, so it's good enough for me! Or you can use the juice of 6 to 8 regular limes.*

Josh *loves* key lime—he would take a key lime dessert over chocolate any day, and the more tart, the better. So our good friend Janette makes these bars for Josh's birthday every year, and they're always the highlight of the celebration. They have a cool, creamy filling atop a sweet graham cracker crust, and are finished off with a dollop of whipped cream and a slice of lime—though you could serve yours with strawberries, raspberries, or even toasted coconut. The bars *do* need to be made in advance because they need some time to cool and then chill in the fridge, but then all you need to do is add whipped cream and garnishes for them to be party-ready.

1 Make the crust: Preheat the oven to 350°F. Line an 8-inch square baking dish with aluminum foil in both directions, making a plus sign. Press the foil into the pan and fold the edges over the sides.

2 In a medium bowl, combine the graham cracker crumbs, sugar, melted butter, and salt and stir until the crumbs are moist. Spread the mixture firmly in the bottom of the prepared pan. Use a measuring cup or other flat tool to press the crust down until it is smooth and even. Bake for 10 to 14 minutes, until golden brown. Allow the crust to cool completely.

3 Make the filling: Reduce the oven to 325°F.

4 In a large bowl, combine the condensed milk, lime zest and juice, yogurt, and egg yolk and stir well. Pour the filling over the cooled crust.

5 Place the pan with the bars inside a larger baking dish and add enough boiling water to reach halfway up the sides of the smaller pan. Bake for 45 minutes, until the bars are set.

6 Carefully remove the pan from the water bath and let the bars cool to room temperature, about 2 hours. Cover the pan with plastic wrap and chill the bars in the refrigerator for at least 1 hour, preferably overnight.

7 When ready to serve, whip the cream: In the bowl of a stand mixer fitted with the whisk attachment, beat together the cream, sugar, and vanilla until stiff peaks form, about 1 minute.

8 Use the foil to help lift the bars from the pan. Carefully transfer the bars to a cutting board and slice into squares. Top each with a dollop of whipped cream and garnish with a lime slice, if desired. You can store the bars in an airtight container in the refrigerator for up to 3 days.

peanut butter caramelitas

prep: **15 MINUTES** | bake: **ABOUT 40 MINUTES** | total: **55 MINUTES, PLUS 3 HOURS COOLING** | serves **12 TO 18**

Nonstick cooking spray

2 cups all-purpose flour

2 cups old-fashioned rolled oats

1 teaspoon baking soda

½ teaspoon sea salt

1½ cups packed brown sugar

½ cup granulated sugar

1 cup (½ pound) unsalted butter, at room temperature

1 cup creamy peanut butter

2 large eggs

2 teaspoons pure vanilla extract

1½ cups (9 ounces) chocolate chips (semisweet or milk—go with your favorite)

1 cup Salted Caramel Sauce (page 70) or store-bought caramel sauce

NOTE: *These are great to make ahead because the caramel needs at least 3 hours to cool and set before you can slice the bars.*

My friend Rachel, my sweet-tooth sister, helped me dream up these decadent bars. She loves the classic caramelita—an oatmeal cookie stuffed with gooey caramel and melty chocolate—but decided she wanted to take it to the next level of insane deliciousness. So we invited peanut butter to the party! After testing them three times in one week (we had to be sure we'd gotten the recipe right…), we considered our work complete. One secret was using my salted caramel sauce, though you could cheat and use store-bought instead. We also debated over what kind of chocolate chips to use, and while I'm normally a semisweet gal all the way, milk chocolate was the clear winner. That said, you can't go wrong with either, so I just suggest using your favorite.

1 Preheat the oven to 350°F. Generously grease a 9 × 13-inch pan with nonstick cooking spray.

2 In a large bowl, whisk together the flour, oats, baking soda, and salt. Set aside.

3 In the bowl of a stand mixer fitted with the paddle attachment, cream together both sugars with the butter and peanut butter until smooth, about 2 minutes, scraping down the sides of the bowl with a spatula if necessary. Add the eggs and vanilla and mix until combined.

4 Add the dry ingredients and mix until just combined. Press half of the dough into the prepared pan and bake for 12 minutes.

5 Remove the pan from the oven and sprinkle the chocolate chips evenly over the cookie crust, then drizzle the caramel sauce evenly over the chocolate chips. Top with the remaining dough, gently pressing it into an even layer on top of the chocolate and caramel. (It helps to lightly spray your hands with nonstick cooking spray.)

6 Return the pan to the oven and bake for 24 to 30 minutes, until the bars are golden brown. Let the bars cool for at least 3 hours before cutting, so the caramel has time to set up. Slice the caramelitas into squares and serve. You could also cover the pan with plastic wrap or store the squares in an airtight container at room temperature for up to 3 days.

berry galette with vanilla-mascarpone whipped cream

prep: **1 HOUR** | bake: **45 TO 50 MINUTES**
total: **1¾ HOURS, PLUS CHILLING THE DOUGH AND COOLING THE GALETTE** | serves **8**

● ●

If there's one dessert you choose to master, a galette should definitely be it. It's basically a rustic pie that doesn't require any fancy dough work, and yet you get the same deep flavors from baked fruit sitting within a flaky, buttery crust. Even though you can put just about anything in a galette—sweet *or* savory—my favorite is this berry version. To make it extra-special, I top the cooled galette with a rich vanilla-mascarpone whipped cream that balances out the tartness of the berries and keeps the flavors feeling light and fresh.

GALETTE DOUGH

1¾ cups all-purpose flour

⅓ cup granulated sugar

¼ cup coarse cornmeal

¼ teaspoon kosher salt

½ cup (8 tablespoons) unsalted butter, cold, cut into small pieces

⅓ cup buttermilk

TO ASSEMBLE THE GALETTE

1 heaping cup blueberries

1 heaping cup raspberries

1 heaping cup blackberries

1 large egg

2 tablespoons turbinado sugar

VANILLA-MASCARPONE WHIPPED CREAM

8 ounces mascarpone cheese

1 cup heavy cream

⅓ cup confectioners' sugar

1 teaspoon pure vanilla extract

1   Make the dough: **In a food processor, combine the flour, granulated sugar, cornmeal, and salt and pulse two or three times. Add the butter and pulse four or five times, until the mixture resembles a coarse meal. With the processor running, slowing pour the buttermilk through the chute, processing until the dough forms a ball.**

2   Turn out the dough onto a piece of plastic wrap or parchment paper. Wrap up the dough and refrigerate for at least 45 minutes before rolling out.

3   Preheat the oven to 350°F.

4   To assemble the galette: **Remove the dough from the refrigerator, unwrap, and place on a clean sheet of parchment paper. Starting at the center of the dough, use a rolling pin to roll outwards, forming a 14-inch circle. Transfer the dough with the parchment paper to a baking sheet.**

5   Arrange the berries over the dough, leaving a 2-inch border. Fold the 2-inch dough edge gently over the berries, pressing gently to adhere the folds. It will not look perfect, and that's okay!

6   In a small bowl, beat the egg with 1 tablespoon water. Lightly brush the outer edge of the dough with the egg mixture and sprinkle the turbinado sugar over the dough.

recipe continues

7 Bake the galette for 45 to 50 minutes, until the crust is golden brown. Transfer the baking sheet to a wire rack and let the galette cool to room temperature before slicing.

8 While the galette is cooling, make the whipped cream: In the bowl of a stand mixer fitted with the whisk attachment, whip the mascarpone, cream, confectioners' sugar, and vanilla on high speed until thickened to medium peaks, about 1 minute.

9 Cut the galette into 8 slices and serve each with a dollop of whipped cream! You can store this for up to 3 days at room temperature, but it's best the day it's made.

NOTE: *I highly recommend keeping a batch of galette dough ready in the fridge or freezer for when the mood strikes; it will last for up to 3 days in the fridge or 1 month in the freezer (just defrost before rolling it out).*

brown butter banana cake
with brown butter–cream cheese frosting

prep: **15 MINUTES** | bake: **30 TO 35 MINUTES** | total: **50 MINUTES, PLUS COOLING** | serves **16**

●●

CAKE

Nonstick cooking spray

½ cup (8 tablespoons) unsalted butter, cut into tablespoon-sized pieces

2 cups all-purpose flour

1 teaspoon baking soda

½ teaspoon kosher salt

½ teaspoon ground cinnamon

1½ cups granulated sugar

2 large eggs, at room temperature

2 teaspoons pure vanilla extract

3 to 4 medium brown bananas, mashed (about 1 cup)

1 cup plain Greek yogurt or sour cream, at room temperature

BROWN BUTTER-CREAM CHEESE FROSTING

½ cup (8 tablespoons) unsalted butter, cut into tablespoon-sized pieces

8 ounces plain cream cheese, at room temperature

4 cups (1 pound) confectioners' sugar, sifted

1 teaspoon pure vanilla extract

Pinch of kosher salt

This cake is basically dressed-up banana bread, complete with that classic rich, moist flavor and texture. The secret is adding Greek yogurt to the batter (or sour cream, if that's what you have), then slathering the cake with a brown butter–infused cream cheese frosting. Not bad for putting your brown bananas to work! If anyone asks if I can contribute a dessert to a party or potluck, this is usually what I bring because I can make it ahead (I actually think it's better the second day), it travels well in the pan, and I never have to worry about bringing home leftovers.

1   Make the cake: Preheat the oven to 350°F. Grease a 9 × 13-inch baking pan with nonstick cooking spray and set aside.

2   Melt the butter in a medium skillet over medium heat, swirling the pan occasionally or stirring with a spatula. The butter will start to foam and pop. When the butter starts to turn amber in color and has a nutty aroma, remove the pan from the heat. Pour the butter into a small bowl, making sure you get all of the brown bits from the bottom of the pan. Put the bowl in the refrigerator to cool while you prepare the cake.

3   In a medium bowl, whisk together the flour, baking soda, salt, and cinnamon.

4   In a stand mixer fitted with the paddle attachment or in a large mixing bowl with a hand mixer or spoon, beat together the brown butter and granulated sugar until well combined. Beat in the eggs and vanilla, then mix in the mashed bananas and yogurt. Slowly add the dry ingredients and mix until the flour is fully incorporated. Take care not to overmix.

5   Spread the cake batter evenly in the prepared pan. Bake for 30 to 35 minutes, until a toothpick inserted into the center comes out clean and the cake is a light golden brown. Allow the cake to cool completely in the pan.

recipe continues

6 Make the frosting: While the cake is baking, melt the butter in a medium skillet over medium heat, swirling the pan occasionally or stirring with a spatula. The butter will start to foam and pop. When the butter starts to turn amber in color and has a nutty aroma, remove the pan from the heat. Pour the browned butter into a small bowl, making sure you get all of the brown bits from the bottom of the pan. Put the bowl in the refrigerator to cool for about 30 minutes.

7 In the bowl of a stand mixer fitted with the paddle attachment or in a large mixing bowl with a hand mixer, beat the cooled brown butter and cream cheese on high until smooth. Slowly add the confectioners' sugar, 1 cup at a time. Beat on high until the sugar is fully incorporated. Mix in the vanilla and salt, then beat until the frosting is smooth.

8 Once the cake has cooled completely, use a knife or offset spatula to spread the frosting over the cake. At this point you can cut the cake into squares and serve, or store the cake, covered, in the refrigerator or at room temperature for up to 4 days. I actually love eating this cake cold!

NOTE: *For an extra-decadent version, sometimes I add chocolate chips. If you want your chocolate fix, stir 1 cup chips into the cake batter after you mix in the bananas and yogurt.*

apple crisp with oatmeal cookie crumble

prep: **30 MINUTES** | bake: **45 MINUTES** | total: **1¼ HOURS** | serves **12**

• •

Nonstick cooking spray

OATMEAL COOKIE CRUMBLE

1 cup all-purpose flour

1 cup old-fashioned rolled oats

¾ cup packed light brown sugar

¼ cup granulated sugar

2 teaspoons ground cinnamon

1 teaspoon kosher salt

¾ cup (12 tablespoons) unsalted butter, cold, cut into tablespoon-sized pieces

APPLE FILLING

10 cups sliced peeled cored Granny Smith apples (see Note), about 10 medium apples

1 tablespoon fresh lemon juice

¾ cup granulated sugar

1 teaspoon ground cinnamon

1 teaspoon cornstarch

1 teaspoon pure vanilla extract

Vanilla ice cream, for serving (optional)

When the leaves start to turn and the air takes on a chill, I get super excited because that means two things: 1) It's finally cozy sweater weather and 2) It's time to make apple crisp. We always kick off our fall festivities with a trip to the apple orchard and—of course—end up bringing home more apples than we could ever eat. We'll share them with friends and neighbors, but we're sure to keep some extras so we can bake them into this quintessential fall dessert. I prefer a crisp to apple pie because you get that same warm, gooey baked-apple filling but without the fuss of crust. Because it feeds about 12 people, I love bringing a big pan to a fall gathering so everyone can just tuck right in. It's great at room temperature, but served warm with some vanilla ice cream on top so the ice cream melts and creates a sauce? Pure heaven.

1   Preheat the oven to 350°F. Grease a 9 × 13-inch baking pan with nonstick cooking spray and set aside.

2   Make the cookie crumble: In a medium bowl, combine the flour, oats, brown sugar, granulated sugar, cinnamon, and salt. Mix in the cold butter pieces with your fingers or a pastry cutter until the mixture comes together and large clumps form. Set aside; or, if it is warm in your house, refrigerate while you prepare the filling.

3   Make the filling: In a large bowl, combine the apple slices, lemon juice, granulated sugar, cinnamon, cornstarch, and vanilla. Stir until the apples are well coated.

4   Pour the apple mixture evenly into the prepared pan. Sprinkle the topping over the apples. Bake for 45 minutes, until the topping is golden brown and the apples are soft and bubbling around the edges. Let the crisp cool for 10 minutes. Serve warm with vanilla ice cream, if desired.

NOTE: *We like to use Granny Smith apples for this recipe because their crisp texture and tart flavor are perfect for baking. Other good options are Honeycrisp and Fuji, or you could use a mix of apples.*

EASY ENTERTAINING

● ●

We love company and we love food, so entertaining is a big part of our life and something we do year-round. There's our annual Christmas white elephant party, a holiday cookie exchange, the Super Bowl/my birthday celebration (go Pats!), the Golden Globes and the Oscars, March Madness (a *big* deal in our house), Cinco de Mayo, NBA playoffs (go Golden State Warriors!), the neighborhood Fourth of July breakfast, the boys' birthdays, National Ice Cream Day (ice cream sundae bar!), anything involving the University of Utah (go Utes!) or college football, and pretty much any other reason to get people together.

Our ultimate goal is to create memories—as well as to show people that they can absolutely do it themselves. When our friends see how easy and seamless hosting a big gathering can be, they think, *I could do that!* We want you to feel the same! My advice is that you stick to things that you know will feed a lot of people and are easy to pull together yet still taste good. We also always make sure to have something for everyone to eat—because I know firsthand what it's like to be stuck not having anything to eat—whether it's because of eating vegetarian, gluten-free, dairy-free, or other dietary reasons.

These recipes are particularly great for when you've invited over a crowd and are pulling out all the stops—like big trays of DIY nachos, a make-your-own pasta bar, or a mix-and-match ice cream sandwich party. But whether we're feeding 10 or 100, the philosophy stays the same: We want everyone to come in, relax, have a good time, and feel comfortable enough to help themselves to seconds.

Entertaining Tips for Low-Stress, High-Fun Gatherings

There's rarely a weekend that goes by that Josh and I don't have extra people in the house, and we're no strangers to get-togethers with guest lists in the double digits. So out of necessity, we've made a point of keeping our entertaining style super laid-back and stress-free—that way we get to actually enjoy ourselves, and our guests end up having an even better time too. Here are some of the lessons we've learned over the years for throwing parties that are pressure- and hassle-free.

- **Just do it.** Some people get in their heads about how a party "should" look—whether they have enough space, a nice enough table, or a big enough guest list—so they end up never hosting. But entertaining doesn't have to be a big production! Start small with an appetizer or two, or organize a potluck. Or make a batch of cookies and call your neighbors to say, "Hey, we just baked; want to help us eat?" I guarantee no one will turn down an offer of fresh-out-of-the-oven cookies. Use paper plates and napkins and whatever timesaving shortcuts you have to—just set a date and make it happen! I promise that it will get easier every time.

- **Relax and have fun.** If you're stressed, your guests won't be able to relax. Focus on the things that you enjoy and your guests will follow suit.

- **Forget perfection.** It's okay if the house isn't perfectly spotless or if you didn't have time to get flowers for the table. Be real; there's no need to put on a show! Just make your guests feel welcome and at home—even if that home has toys scattered on the floor.

- **Be mindful of your guests.** When planning your menu, consider who's coming. Ask your guests if they have any allergies, dietary restrictions, or simply dislikes. That way you won't serve a big, cheesy lasagna to someone who's lactose intolerant, or a big bowlful of mushroom risotto to the person who can't stand fungi. If there'll be kids, make sure at least one thing will be appealing to little ones. If you're not sure what that entails, ask the parents—they'll definitely know what their kids will and won't eat!

- **Prep and plan.** Decide what you're going to be serving and make a plan. Choose a time to go grocery shopping and double-check that you have all the ingredients. Consider prepping a majority of the food in advance so you aren't rushing before guests come over. I also recommend coming up with a strategy for where all the food will be served—on the dining room table? Living room coffee table? Kitchen island? Map it out and make sure there's enough space. I also recommend setting the table in advance, or if you're doing the meal buffet-style, have all the silverware, plates, and napkins set out. Anything you do ahead of time will be less you have to scramble to do as your guests are arriving. And *always* give yourself more time than you think you will need, just in case. If you're done early, sit down and relax before everyone arrives.

- **Remember that more is more.** We always plan for a little extra food. We would rather have too much than not enough. You can always have leftovers another night that week or send your guests home with some food!

- **Start with appetizers.** We always like to have something ready for people to nibble on when they arrive so they can start relaxing and we can finish up any last-minute touches on the meal. This is also helpful for hungry (and not-so-patient) kids! Check out the appetizer chapter, page 67, for some of our favorite starters.

- **Stick with the standbys.** We love creating and testing new recipes, but when we have people over, we go with our tried-and-true dishes. We want to feel confident in the meal we have planned and don't want *any* surprises.

- **Don't be afraid to ask for help.** One of the biggest mistakes people make is thinking that just because they're hosting, that means they need to do every last thing. That's just not true! Guests feel more involved when they're asked to pitch in, whether it's bringing an appetizer, side dish, or dessert; picking up toppings for a nacho bar or ice cream sundae party; or lending a hand with setting the table or rolling out pizza dough.

- **Turn on the tunes.** Or the big game—this will help your guests relax and prevent awkward silences.

- **DIY decorating.** On the rare occasion I have a tablescape scheme, I keep it simple with fresh flowers in a vase or mason jars, or seasonal fruit in a pretty bowl. It's never formal, but a few small touches elevate the vibe of the party. I also light some candles around the house. One finishing touch that goes a long way is making sure the areas of the house where your guests will be—entryway, living room, kitchen, powder room—are clean. Maybe not tidy, if your boys are like mine, but clean.

- **Keep it in the kitchen.** Not every party needs to be in a formal dining room, or even the living room. Our guests always end up in the kitchen to keep us company while we finish up the cooking, and sometimes we just stay in there, gathered around the island, eating standing up. Let the party happen naturally!

- **Clean up later.** Sure, you can clear the table, but don't worry about washing and putting away every last dish while your guests are still over. Enjoy your time with them; you can clean up the house after they leave. That said, if you have offers to help wash or dry, bring the party into the kitchen and make tidying up a group activity.

weekend waffle bar

• •

Waffles are a weekend tradition at our house, and we love a party first thing in the morning, so when we wanted to come up with an idea for getting the community together for the Fourth of July, it came to us pretty easily: Waffle Party! Now we have an annual breakfast on the Fourth where we cook up waffles for over 200 people. We get a bunch of waffle irons going, set out a spread of toppings, and let everyone come up with their own creations.

You can either borrow waffle irons from friends and neighbors, or make the waffles in advance and reheat them the day of your party. Then just set them out stacked high on a tray along with toppings that range from the diet-friendly (Greek yogurt, granola, berries) to the downright decadent (whipped cream, ice cream, sprinkles). And feel free to add sides of bacon, sausage, and eggs to round out the meal.

WAFFLE BAR

Belgian Waffles (recipe follows)

Butter

Maple syrup

Vanilla-Mascarpone Whipped Cream (page 278)

Fruit (sliced bananas, strawberries, blueberries, raspberries, blackberries, peaches)

Nut butter (peanut butter, almond butter, Nutella)

Honey

Assorted jams

Greek yogurt

Chopped nuts

Granola

Ice cream (if you want to go all out!)

Sprinkles

OUR FAVORITE WAFFLE COMBOS

- Whipped cream + strawberries
- Whipped cream + peaches
- Nutella + raspberries
- Nutella + banana slices
- Peanut butter + banana slices + honey
- Peanut butter + jam + berries + chopped peanuts
- Almond butter + berries + granola
- Ice cream + sprinkles
- Greek yogurt + berries + granola

recipe continues

Belgian Waffles

prep: **10 MINUTES**
cook: **15 MINUTES**
total: **25 MINUTES**
serves **6 TO 8**

Welcome to your perfect waffle recipe! Don't be fooled by its simplicity—this recipe makes the *best* waffles. Some of our secrets include mixing all-purpose and whole-wheat flours to create hearty waffles that are still light and fluffy; using buttermilk, which keeps the waffles soft on the inside; and adding brown sugar, which helps the waffles get nice and crispy while adding a slightly sweet, caramel-y flavor. Make sure that the buttermilk, melted butter, and eggs are at room temperature before mixing them together—you don't want the butter to clump up. And don't overmix the batter or you'll end up with a tough waffle. We also highly recommend using a good waffle maker and making sure it's nice and hot before adding the batter.

NOTE: *You can make the waffles the day before your party. Just let them cool completely, then store them in a zip-top bag or container at room temperature. In the morning, preheat the oven to 200°F. Place the waffles on a large baking sheet and reheat for 10 to 15 minutes to crisp them up. You could also freeze the cooled waffles for up to 2 months. To reheat, place in the toaster or oven until warmed through.*

1 cup all-purpose flour

1 cup white or regular whole-wheat flour

3 tablespoons packed light brown sugar

1 teaspoon baking powder

½ teaspoon baking soda

1 teaspoon kosher salt

3 large eggs, at room temperature

4 tablespoons unsalted butter, melted and cooled slightly

2 cups buttermilk, at room temperature

1 teaspoon pure vanilla extract

Nonstick cooking spray

1   Preheat your waffle iron according to the manufacturer's directions.

2   In a large bowl, whisk together the all-purpose flour, whole-wheat flour, brown sugar, baking powder, baking soda, and salt. If there are any brown sugar clumps, use your clean hands to break them up and whisk again.

3   In a medium bowl, beat together the eggs and melted butter. Stir in the buttermilk and vanilla.

4   Add the wet ingredients to the dry ingredients and stir until just combined. Don't overmix.

5   For each waffle, spray the waffle iron with nonstick cooking spray. Pour the recommended amount of waffle batter onto the hot waffle iron. Close the iron and cook until the waffle is golden on both sides and easily releases from the iron. Serve immediately, keep warm in a 200°F oven until ready to serve, or cool completely and store at room temperature or freeze.

He Said, She Said: Party Favorites

HE SAID

Food: Nothing beats homemade pizza with *all the cheese*. I can't think of a single person who doesn't love making their own pie with all their favorite toppings.

Drinks: I'm a San Pellegrino kinda guy (lemon-flavored is my favorite)—plus Maria thinks the cans look pretty.

Music: Tom Petty, Bruce Springsteen, anything '80s—something you can blast and sing along to…then Maria usually changes the music…

Vibe: *Loud, fun,* and the more the merrier! I love a spur-of-the-moment party that just happens to pop up one afternoon.

Theme: We love throwing parties for any and all sporting events. If there is a game on, we are having a party!

Decor: We have to decorate?! Maybe we'll throw in some balloons for the kids' birthdays…but it's honestly all about the food and the friends.

SHE SAID

Food: Anything Mexican so we can eat guacamole. And cookies for dessert, obviously!

Drinks: Sparkling water, regular or flavored—I love how festive it is and you can pair it with tons of creative garnishes like slices of citrus, pomegranate arils, or flavored simple syrups

Music: Upbeat pop music is good for getting people in the party mood.

Vibe: Planned! Josh is the spontaneous one—he'll see people at the grocery store and the next thing I know there's going to be company for dinner in 30 minutes. But whether or not it's scheduled in advance, I always keep the vibe relaxed. Nothing fussy, nothing complicated, and *always* with good food.

Theme: I love letting the food do the talking—dinner parties, dessert parties, brunch parties, barbecues in the summer, and cookie-making parties in the winter.

Decor: Simple. I'll sometimes decorate with some fresh flowers, seasonal produce, and fun napkins, but usually it's just my all-white plates (which make the food look even more delicious) and a giant, colorful spread.

loaded nachos bar

•••

NACHO BASE

Tortilla chips

Shredded cheddar cheese

Shredded pepper Jack cheese

Sliced steak (see Grilled Steak Tacos with Chimichurri, page 210)

Shredded rotisserie chicken meat

Canned black beans, drained and rinsed

Canned pinto beans, drained and rinsed

TOPPINGS

Chopped tomatoes

Chopped avocados

Chopped fresh cilantro

Sliced scallions

Sliced radishes

Sliced jalapeños

Crumbled queso fresco

Sour cream or plain Greek yogurt

Easy Blender Salsa (page 93)

Go-To Guacamole (page 92)

Nachos are—not surprisingly—the perfect party food. You can prep the ingredients and toppings in advance and leave a stack of baking sheets or disposable aluminum pans at one of the spead, so when your guests arrive all they need to do is go down the line making their own nacho creations. In the summer, we love including charred corn—just shuck a couple ears and place them directly on a hot grill, turning occasionally until the kernels have a nice char, about 10 minutes. And definitely make a quick batch of our guacamole and blender salsa.

1   Preheat the oven to 375°F.

2   On your kitchen counter or island, or a large table, set out all of the ingredients and toppings along with a stack of baking sheets. Have people start with the chips and add their choice of cheese, steak, chicken, and beans. Place the sheet pan in the oven until the cheese is melted, 5 to 7 minutes. Let your guests finish off their nachos with the toppings of their choice and enjoy them warm.

NOTE: *This "recipe" can easily be made on a smaller scale for a family night or amped way up if you're having a bigger crowd! And for even easier entertaining: Ask guests to bring their favorite toppings.*

diy pizza party

· ·

On Friday nights we invite over friends and family to celebrate the end of the week with some major TGIF spirit and lots and lots of pizza. We put out a wide assortment of toppings and sauces and let everyone do up their own pie, whether they want to keep it simple with just tomato sauce and cheese or go all out and throw together some fun new combinations. Sometimes we ask people to bring their favorite toppings, so we end up with an even wider selection—and some unexpected additions! Don't be afraid of some mess—a little flour or sauce splatter never hurt anyone!—just embrace that everyone's in the kitchen, spending time together. So serve up a big Everyday Butter Lettuce Salad (page 98), sit back while everyone makes their creations, and start enjoying the weekend.

CRUSTS

Josh's Pizza Dough (page 201), Whole-Wheat Pizza Dough (page 173), or store-bought dough

French bread sandwich rolls, halved

Flatbreads

SAUCES

Classic Marinara Sauce (page 180)

Spinach-Basil Pesto (page 186) or store-bought pesto

Store-bought barbecue sauce

TOPPINGS

Sliced pepperoni

Crumbled Italian sausage

Shredded chicken

Sliced prosciutto

Cooked bacon pieces

Sliced mushrooms

Sliced red onion

Artichoke hearts

Sliced roasted red peppers

Greens (spinach, arugula, kale)

Fresh basil

Sliced tomatoes

Sun-dried tomatoes

Chopped or sliced olives

Sliced jalapeño

Diced pineapple

Crushed red pepper flakes

Balsamic glaze

Shredded mozzarella cheese or sliced fresh mozzarella

Ricotta cheese

Shredded cheddar cheese

Crumbled goat cheese

Grated Parmesan cheese

NOTE: *You can make your own pizza dough from scratch (our favorite recipes will get you there every time!), but you certainly don't have to. Store-bought dough, or even store-bought flatbreads or French bread, is perfectly acceptable and completely delicious.*

1   If making the dough from scratch, make it the day before and store in the fridge in large zip-top bags. Remove the dough from the fridge 30 minutes before you'll want to start making pizzas.

2   Decide if you want everyone to create their own individual-sized pizzas or if you want to put people on teams to work together on larger pizzas. We try to make sure there's a variety so everyone can sample and share.

3 Before your guests arrive, designate one area of the kitchen for pizza assembly, like an island or kitchen table. Have one station where people can be rolling out the dough (if applicable) and one station for adding the toppings. Set out all your ingredients in advance so the pizza-making can start as soon as people arrive. You could also do this outside if you plan to grill your pizzas, which is what we do in the summer so we're not heating up the house!

4 Preheat the oven to 450 to 550°F—as high as it will go. Using a rolling pin, roll out the pizza dough to a ½-inch thickness; it should be roughly the same size as the baking sheets you've selected. Place the dough on lightly greased baking sheets, pushing the dough into the corners and rolling the edges around the lip of the pan to create a nice crust all the way around. Once the pizzas are assembled, bake them for 10 to 15 minutes, until the crust is golden and the cheese is melted. If using French bread or flatbread, cook just long enough to melt the cheese and toast the bread to light golden brown.

5 Slice and share!

the perfect party board

• •

I'm pretty sure that a cheese board is the essential party food for any event or occasion—even for the occasional family dinner, if I'm being honest! It can be an appetizer for people to graze on, or it can be the main event. You can make your board mini for a small group or epically sized for bigger crowds. You can mix and match flavors and textures, making sure there's always something for everyone, and even tailor them to your event with a theme. (I particularly love making kid-friendly boards, which I've outlined on page 302.) And the best part? It takes barely any time to make something that seriously impresses. Actually, maybe the best part is actually getting to enjoy your spread while you mingle with friends and family! Here are my basic rules of thumb for assembling the ultimate cheese board.

THE CHEESE

- Try to include a variety of textures and flavor: soft, semi-firm, and aged/hard cheeses.

- Also serve different types of cheese: cow's milk, sheep milk, and goat.

- Serve at least one familiar cheese, such as pepper Jack, Muenster, or plain cheddar.

- Allow for 3 to 4 ounces of cheese per person.

THE ACCOMPANIMENTS

Serve lots of extras to go with the cheese. These items are what makes a board shine! Make sure you are varying the textures, sizes, and colors, along with sweet and salty. Here are some of my favorites:

- Assorted crackers, breadsticks, and baguette slices

- Cured meats, such as prosciutto and salami

- Assorted nuts

- Dried fruits, such as apricots and cranberries

- Fresh fruits, such as grapes, figs, and pomegranate arils

- Baby pickles and pickled vegetables

- Assorted olives

- Marinated artichoke hearts

- Roasted red peppers

- Jam, honey, or hot and sweet pepper jelly

- Coarse mustard

- Fresh herbs for garnish, such as rosemary, sage, basil, and thyme

recipe continues

SERVING TIPS

- You can assemble a cheese board using a platter, bread board, cutting board, or plate—or a combination of a few, depending on how big a spread you're putting out.

- Display the cheese in different shapes and sizes—wedges, spears, cubes, cut into slices, etc. Label each cheese so people know what their options are. Include spreaders with softer cheeses and knives with cheese wedges.

- Arrange the different cheeses around the edges of the board, as well as one or two in the middle. If you have a really strong cheese, you can put it off to the side, so it doesn't overpower the board.

- Let the cheese sit out for 30 to 60 minutes before serving.

- Use small bowls, ramekins, and dishes for some of the accompaniments and mound the rest of the items around and between the cheeses. Don't be skimpy and don't be too organized—it is okay if you have big piles of nuts, crackers, etc. It will encourage people to dig in!

KID-FRIENDLY CHEESE BOARD

If we're having a lot of kids coming over, whether for a play date, birthday party, or friends-and-family gathering, I like to make a special board just for them that's loaded up with (both healthy and indulgent) crowd-pleasing treats. That includes:

Cheese sticks, cut in half

Cheddar cheese, cut into shapes

Babybel cheese rounds

Goldfish crackers

Ritz crackers

Triscuits

Pretzels

Ranch dressing

Hummus

Baby carrots

Snap peas

Baby pickles

Pitted black olives

Pepperoni

Cucumber slices

Grape tomatoes

Grapes

Berries

Raisins or dried cranberries

Chocolate-covered sunflower seeds

pasta party

• •

When the weather turns chilly and we start craving extra carbs, we know it's time to throw one of our epic pasta parties. We put on a pot of sauce (or defrost what we have in the freezer), whip up a batch of pesto, and set out tons of toppings. When it's almost time to eat, we boil up a selection of pastas, including stuffed varieties like tortellini and ravioli. And we might even make some mac and cheese for the kids. (Rest assured, the adults dig into it too!) All that's left to do is toss together a salad or two (or ask guests to bring one), make a batch of Caprese Garlic Bread (page 74), and throw on some stretchy pants. Because this is one party where seconds (and thirds and fourths) are strongly encouraged.

PASTA

Cooked pasta in various shapes (spaghetti, farfalle, penne, fettuccine, orecchiette, etc.)

Cooked filled pasta (tortellini, ravioli)

Shells with Cheese and Trees (page 187), Pesto-Havarti Mac and Cheese (page 185), or store-bought mac and cheese

SAUCES

Classic Marinara Sauce (page 180), Roasted Tomato Sauce (page 213), or store-bought marinara sauce

Spinach-Basil Pesto (page 186) or store-bought pesto

Store-bought Alfredo sauce

TOPPINGS

Slow Cooker Meatballs (page 226)

Shredded or cubed cooked chicken

Cooked ground beef or Italian sausage

Sun-dried tomatoes

Roasted broccoli

Sautéed or roasted mushrooms

Sautéed zucchini

Sautéed greens (spinach or kale)

Artichoke hearts

Roasted red peppers

Fresh arugula

Crispy garlic

Balsamic glaze

Grated Parmesan cheese

Shredded mozzarella cheese

1 Aim to have at least two or three different types of pasta. I like to do a long noodle (spaghetti or fettuccine); a smaller pasta (farfalle, penne, or orecchiette); and a filled pasta (tortellini or ravioli). If you have gluten-free guests coming, be sure to include gluten-free pasta, zucchini noodles, or spaghetti squash for them to enjoy.

2 Just before guests arrive, put several large pots of salted water on to boil. Cook the pasta to al dente and drain. Transfer each to a large serving bowl, drizzle with olive oil, and toss so the pasta doesn't stick. Serve immediately or cover the bowls with aluminum foil to keep the pasta warm.

3 Arrange the toppings so guests can help themselves. I like to keep the sauces on the stove so they'll stay warm, and we put out the meatballs in the slow cooker to keep those warm too.

ice cream sandwich party

•●

Every July we have an ice cream sandwich party to celebrate National Ice Cream Month. Why ice cream sandwiches instead of just plain ol' ice cream? Because you know I can't miss an opportunity to make cookies! And cookies plus ice cream is pretty much the best dessert ever. An ice cream sandwich party is the ultimate crowd-pleaser, and it's such an easy way to entertain a group because you can bake the cookies in advance and then serve them with your favorite store-bought ice creams for everyone to make their own sandwiches. I also like putting out a selection of toppings to roll the sandwiches in, such as chopped nuts, mini chocolate chips, and even crushed pretzels. It's perfect for birthdays, Memorial Day, Fourth of July, Labor Day, and any other warm-weather occasion that could use a few extra sprinkles. Just remember to have wet wipes available for the inevitable sticky faces and hands.

COOKIE AND ICE CREAM PAIRING IDEAS

Our Favorite Chocolate Chip Cookies (page 241) with vanilla, chocolate, Neapolitan, chocolate chip, mint chocolate chip, salted caramel, coffee, or chocolate chip cookie dough ice cream

Toasted Coconut, White Chocolate, and Macadamia Cookies (page 245) with vanilla or coconut ice cream

Triple-Chip Chocolate Cookies (page 259) with vanilla, chocolate, chocolate chip, rocky road, cookies 'n' cream, mint chocolate chip, or strawberry ice cream

Biscoff Oatmeal Sandwich Cookies (page 260, without the filling) with vanilla, coffee, toffee, pecan praline, or cinnamon ice cream

Chocolate cookie-cakes (without the filling) from Chocolate-Mint Whoopie Pies (page 248) with mint chocolate chip, raspberry, strawberry, vanilla, chocolate, pistachio, or peanut butter ice cream

TOPPINGS

Sprinkles

Chopped nuts

Mini chocolate chips

Toffee bits

Crushed pretzels

Toasted coconut

Chopped candy (Butterfingers, Snickers, M&M's, Kit Kats, etc.)

Granola

Crumbled Oreos

1 Choose at least two or three different cookies along with several ice cream flavors. If you have a big crowd or want to save yourself some work, ask guests to bring their favorite type of cookie and/or ice cream. Have the cookies baked and cooled before the party starts.

2 Keep the ice cream in the freezer until ready to serve. Prepare buckets full of ice for keeping the ice cream cold during the party. I also recommend choosing a shady location for the party, or putting the spread indoors. Remember the ice cream scoops!

3 Make an assembly line: Put cookies first, then ice cream, and toppings last. Arrange the toppings in shallow dishes and bowls so people can easily roll their sandwiches in them.

4 To assemble the sandwiches: While you want to encourage everyone to make their own, feel free to do a demonstration! Place a scoop of ice cream on the inside of one cookie. Top with another cookie (it doesn't necessarily have to match the first cookie!) and gently press together. Roll the ice cream edge of the sandwich in the toppings, carefully pressing the toppings into the ice cream so they stick.

5 To make ice cream sandwiches in advance: If you want to simply hand out pre-made treats, assemble the sandwiches as described above, tightly wrap in plastic wrap, and store in the freezer until party time. Make different flavor and cookie combinations so your guests can sample them all—and definitely don't forget to hide a few extras in the back of the fridge for a late-night treat…

Acknowledgments

To Josh, who has been my partner at every turn in this adventure. Who could have imagined that a wedding day centered on family and a love of food would have taken us on this amazing journey together? Thank you for always supporting me and for being my everything in and out of the kitchen. Most of all thank you for being the best dad to our little peas and for being the glue that holds this family together. I love you!

To Caleb and Maxwell, my official taste testers. Thank you for giving me your honest feedback on all of the recipes in this book. I didn't quit until I got two thumbs up from my favorite food critics. Thank you for always reminding me to laugh and enjoy every second of life. I love you so much!

A special thanks to my dad for teaching me how to cook and for helping me find my happy place, the kitchen. I have so many special memories of our time together in the kitchen, especially learning how to make cinnamon rolls (Parry Rolls). They are the best! Thank you for always believing in me and for teaching me the meaning of being magnanimous. I am lucky to have you as my dad and my confidant. Love you lots.

To Rachel Holtzman, my writer, I don't have the proper words to thank you because you know words aren't my strength, but thank you for turning my kitchen vocabulary and random ramblings into a wonderful cookbook. I could not have accomplished this task without your constant direction and support.

This project would not have moved forward without the vision and grounding direction of my original editor, Karen Murgolo, a true professional in every sense of the word. I am most thankful that you took a complete novice under your wing and allowed my opinions to be trusted and respected. Thank you for believing in my dream.

To Morgan Hedden, thank you for continuing to encourage and guide me. This process felt so much more comfortable with you by my side.

To Amanda Pritzker and Andy Dodd, thank you for helping to get this book in as many kitchens as possible.

Thank you to the entire Grand Central team—it was a pleasure working with all of you. Thank you for making this book a reality.

To Janis Donnaud, my fabulous agent, thank you for the gentle nudge that I needed to pursue this cookbook and for making sure it is everything I had dreamed of and more.

To Colin Price, my photographer, and Marian Cooper Cairns, my food stylist—you guys are the ultimate dream team! Thank you for making my recipes look beyond beautiful and for being so much fun to work with.

To Laura Palese for designing a book that I absolutely love!

To Whitney, thank you for letting me bounce endless recipe ideas off of you and for testing hundreds of recipes with us. You are welcome to cook with us anytime!

To Lacy, you are my lifesaver. Thank you for everything you do for me and our family. We love you!

To all of our friends, family, and neighbors who tested recipes, tasted recipes, and encouraged us during the cookbook process. I promise the next time you come over for dinner we won't ask you twenty questions about the taste, texture, presentation, etc. You can just eat and enjoy!

To my blogging friends, it's crazy how blogging has introduced me to so many dear friends who live all over the world. Thank you for always being so generous with your knowledge and for being so supportive over the years.

To our blog readers, you have been asking for a cookbook for years, and I am thrilled to finally share this book with you. This book would not have been possible without you. Thank you for following along our journey and for all of your comments, emails, and messages over the years. You are part of our family and we are so grateful for your never-ending support.

Index

About the Author

Maria Lichty's blog *Two Peas & Their Pod* began after friends and family asked for the recipes she and her husband used to cater their own wedding, and Maria and Josh have been blogging ever since, sharing stories of their culinary and lifestyle adventures.

When Maria isn't in the kitchen, she enjoys watching sports (football, baseball, basketball—you name it!), traveling, reading, watching movies, working out (to balance out all those cookies!), and going to the park with her special taste testers, sons Maxwell and Caleb. Maria and her family live in Salt Lake City, Utah.